Mid-Year Economic Analysis 2012-2013

Outcome of the review of the trends in receipts and expenditure in relation to the budget at the end of the second quarter of the financial year 2012-2013

and

Statement explaining deviations in meeting the obligations of the Government under the Fiscal Responsibility and Budget Management Act, 2003

(vide Section 7(1) and 7(3)(b) of the said Act)

Ministry of Finance
Department of Economic Affairs
Economic Division

OXFORD
UNIVERSITY PRESS

OXFORD
UNIVERSITY PRESS

Oxford University Press is a department of the University of Oxford.
It furthers the University's objective of excellence in research, scholarship,
and education by publishing worldwide. Oxford is a registered trademark of
Oxford University Press in the UK and in certain other countries

Published in India by
Oxford University Press
YMCA Library Building, 1 Jai Singh Road, New Delhi 110 001, India

First Edition published in 2013

ISBN-13: 978-0-19-809240-7
ISBN-10: 0-19-809240-7

Printed in India by Rakmo Press, New Delhi 110 020

The priced edition of *Mid-Year Economic Analysis 2012–13* corresponds to the web version of the document placed at http://indiabudget.nic.in/. It is corrected for errata in the non-priced edition of the document printed by the Government of India Press. Ministry of Finance is not responsible for any subsequent errors and omissions in the priced edition of the document.

MID-YEAR ECONOMIC ANALYSIS

CONTENTS

CHAPTER I

OVERVIEW OF THE ECONOMY

GROWTH AND INVESTMENT

The Indian economy after reporting fairly robust growth of over 9 per cent during 2005-08, moderated to a growth of 6.7 per cent in 2008-09 because of the global financial crisis. Because there was fiscal and monetary space, timely stimulus allowed the economy to recover fairly quickly to a growth of 8.4 per cent in 2009-10 and 2010-11. Since then, however, the fragile global economic recovery and a number of domestic factors have led to a slowdown once again.

1.2 The slowdown in the Indian economy that began in the second quarter of 2011-12, when the growth rate declined to 6.7 per cent from a level of 8.0 per cent in the first quarter, continued in subsequent quarters. Growth has been in the range of 5.3-5.5 per cent in the last three quarters (Q4 of 2011-12 to Q2 of 2012-13). The slowdown is not just confined to India.There has been a general slowdown in the global economy which has been passing through a rather prolonged phase of uncertainty. The recovery from the global crisis of 2008-09 in the advanced economies has been uneven, with a decisive resolution yet to emerge to the sovereign debt problem in the Euro zone. Having achieved a GDP growth of 5.1 per cent in 2010, the rate of growth in the global economy declined to 3.8 per cent in 2011 and is expected to decline further to 3.3 per cent in 2012, as per the World Economic Outlook released by the IMF in October 2012. The rate of growth of advanced economies declined from 3.0 per cent in 2010 to 1.6 per cent in 2011 and is expected to decline further to 1.3 per cent in 2012. Even the emerging economies have slowed down during this period, partly as a result of the slowdown in their export markets. China's growth declined from 10.4 per cent in 2010 to 9.2 per cent in 2011 and is expected to be 7.8 per cent in 2012. Brazil's growth dipped from 7.5 per cent in 2010 to 2.7 per cent in 2011 and is expected to be 1.5 per cent in 2012.

1.3 The growth rate of the Indian economy (measured in terms of GDP at factor cost at 2004-05 prices) was 5.4 per cent in the first half (H1) of year 2012-13 as against 7.3 per cent in the corresponding time period of the previous year. The growth for the full year of 2011-12 was 6.5 per cent vis-à-vis the growth rate of 8.4 per cent achieved in each of the previous two years i.e. 2009-10 and 2010-11. The slowdown has been all pervasive and almost all the sectors have been affected. The growth rate has been 2.1 per cent for agriculture and allied sectors, 3.2 per cent for industry sector and 7.0 per cent for the services sector in the first half of 2012-13. The growth rates were 3.4 per cent, 4.7 per cent and 9.5 per cent, for agriculture, industry and services, respectively in H1 of 2011-12. The growth of GDP in the first and second quarters of 2012-13 was 5.5 per cent and 5.3 per cent respectively (Table 1.1).

Table 1.1 : Quarterly Growth in GDP (per cent)

		2011-12				2012-13		2011-12	2012-13
		Q1	Q2	Q3	Q4	Q1	Q2	H1	H1
1	**Agriculture, forestry & fishing**	**3.7**	**3.1**	**2.8**	**1.7**	**2.9**	**1.2**	3.4	2.1
2	**Industry**	**5.6**	**3.7**	**2.5**	**1.9**	**3.6**	**2.8**	4.7	3.2
a	Mining & quarrying	-0.2	-5.4	-2.8	4.3	0.1	1.9	-2.8	0.9
b	Manufacturing	7.3	2.9	0.6	-0.3	0.2	0.8	5.1	0.5
c	Electricity, gas & water supply	8.0	9.8	9	4.9	6.3	3.4	8.9	4.8
d	Construction	3.5	6.3	6.6	4.8	10.9	6.7	4.9	8.8
3	**Services**	**10.2**	**8.8**	**8.9**	**7.9**	**6.9**	**7.2**	9.5	7.0
a	Trade, hotels, transport & communication	13.8	9.5	10	7	4	5.5	11.6	4.7
b	Financing, insurance, real estate & business services	9.4	9.9	9.1	10	10.8	9.4	9.6	10.1
c	Community, social & personal services	3.2	6.1	6.4	7.1	7.9	7.5	4.7	7.7
	GDP at Factor Cost	**8.0**	**6.7**	**6.1**	**5.3**	**5.5**	**5.3**	7.3	5.4

Source: CSO.

1.4 The slowing growth rate in India during the first half of 2012-13 can be explained in terms of both global factors and domestic factors. The slowdown in growth in advanced economies and near recessionary conditions prevailing in Europe resulted not only in lower growth of international trade but also lower capital flows. The growth rate of India's exports declined. At the same time, however, the international price of crude oil remained high. India's trade and current account deficits widened. Turning to domestic factors, rainfall in the monsoon season of 2012-13 has been below normal, particularly in the key months of June and July. This affected sowing and resulted in a lower growth rate of agriculture and allied sectors. The Reserve Bank of India continued to follow a relatively tight monetary policy to control inflation, although there has been some relaxation in the recent months in the Statutory Liquidity Ratio (SLR) as well as Cash Reserve Requirement (CRR). The cost of borrowing remains at elevated levels and this has had an impact on investment and growth in the economy, particularly that of the industry sector. Finally, bottlenecks in project implementation have made financing more difficult and investors more cautious.

1.5 The reduction in the growth rate of the services sector in the first half of current year vis-à-vis the first half of 2011-12 was primarily due to a reduction in the growth rate of 'Trade, hotels, transport and communications' sector from 11.6 per cent in H1 of 2011-12 to 4.7 per cent in H1 of 2012-13. Within the services sector, this sub sector is the most crucial and accounts for nearly 45 to 50 per cent of the value added of services sector. Growth in activities like trade, hotels and transport, etc. are linked with the growth of agriculture and industry sectors and a slowdown in these activities has had an adverse impact on the growth of the trade and transport sectors. In contrast, the growth of financial, business and community and social services in the first half of the current year was in fact, higher than the growth rate for these sectors in the corresponding period of 2011-12.

Table 1.2 : Sectoral Contribution of GDP at factor cost (per cent)									
		2011-12				2012-13		2011-12	2012-13
		Q1	Q2	Q3	Q4	Q1	Q2	H1	H1
1	**Agriculture, forestry & fishing**	**13.5**	**11.1**	**17.2**	**13.9**	**13.2**	**10.7**	12.3	12.0
2	**Industry**	**27.7**	**27.5**	**26.1**	**26.7**	**27.2**	**26.9**	27.6	27.1
a	Mining & quarrying	2.1	2.0	2.0	2.2	2.0	1.9	2.0	2.0
b	Manufacturing	15.8	15.7	14.6	15.0	15.0	15.0	15.8	15.0
c	Electricity, gas & water supply	2.0	2.0	1.8	1.8	2.0	2.0	2.0	2.0
d	Construction	7.8	7.9	7.6	7.8	8.2	8.0	7.9	8.1
3	**Services**	**58.8**	**61.3**	**56.7**	**59.4**	**59.6**	**62.4**	60.0	61.0
a	Trade, hotels, transport & communication	28.9	28.5	27.1	28.1	28.5	28.6	28.7	28.5
b	Financing, insurance, real estate & business services	18.2	18.7	17.4	17.4	19.1	19.4	18.4	19.3
c	Community, social & personal services	11.7	14.1	12.1	13.9	12.0	14.4	12.9	13.2

Source: CSO.

1.6 The sectoral composition of the GDP (in terms of its relative shares) undergoes a change depending on the relative performance of different sectors. The sectoral composition of GDP is shown in Table 1.2. The quarterly shares reflect seasonal aspects also and may not change significantly in the short run. However, the long-term trends clearly show that the share of agriculture sector has been declining. This is to be expected – agriculture declines as a share of GDP as countries grow. In India, however, the services sector became the dominant sector, without a significant increase in industrial sector. In fact, the share of the industrial sector in GDP has remained in the range of 25-29 per cent since the late 1960s. A decline in the share of the agricultural sector has been offset by an increase in services sector since then.

1.7 The contribution of services sector to incremental growth has been significantly increasing over time. Nearly 60 per cent of the increase in GDP is accounted for by the services sector in the last two decades. In fact, since 2008-09 the contribution of services sector in the increase in GDP has been 73 per cent (Fig 1.1).

1.8 The growth rate in terms of GDP at market prices fell even more sharply in the first half of 2012-13. The growth declined from 7.9 per cent in H1 of 2011-12 to 3.4 per cent in H1 of 2012-13.Almost all the major components of GDP at market prices viz. private final consumption expenditure, gross fixed capital formation, exports as well as imports declined significantly. The exception has been government final consumption expenditure that registered an increase. The sectoral composition of expenditure side of GDP is shown in Table 1.3.

1.9 The rate of growth of GDP at factor cost and at market prices have differed significantly over recent quarters. In 2008-09 and in the first two quarters of 2009-10, growth of GDP at market prices was

Fig 1.1: Point contribution of three sectors to GDP Growth

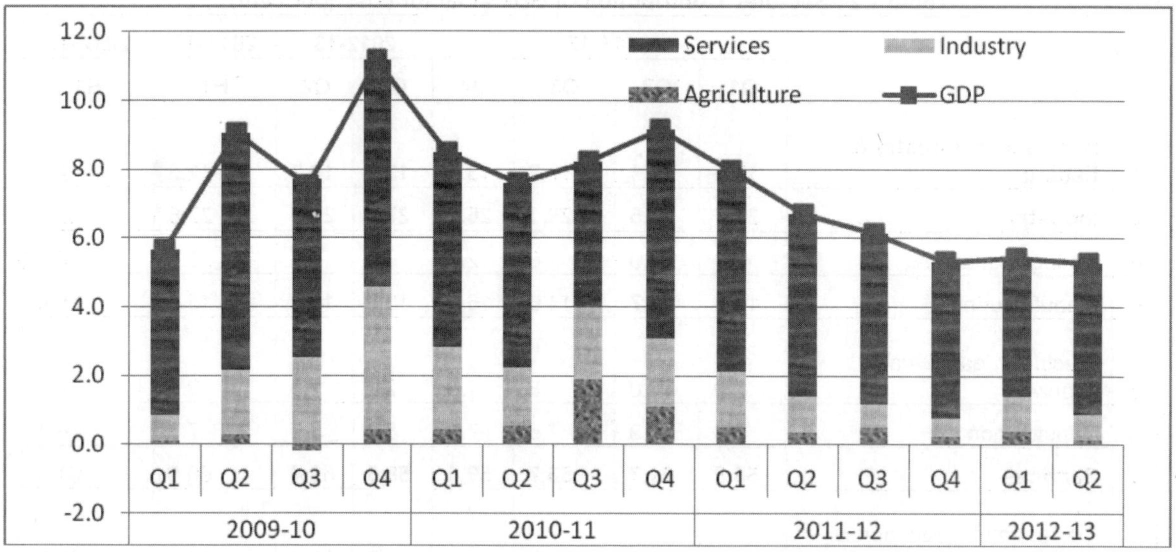

Table 1.3 : Sectoral Composition of GDP at Current Market Prices								
	2011-12				2012-13		2011-12	2012-13
Items	Q1	Q2	Q3	Q4	Q1	Q2	H1	H1
1. Total final consumption expenditure	**66.7**	**68.8**	**71.3**	**64.3**	**67.6**	**70.1**	67.8	68.8
1.1 Private final consumption expenditure	55.8	57.8	58.5	52.5	56.0	58.3	56.8	57.1
1.2 Government final consumption expenditure	11.0	11.0	12.8	11.8	11.7	11.8	11.0	11.7
2. Gross capital formation	**37.9**	**37.6**	**33.6**	**33.7**	**34.8**	**36.5**	37.7	35.7
2.1 Gross fixed capital formation	31.2	30.9	27.8	28.6	29.9	30.6	31.0	30.3
2.2 Changes in stocks	3.4	3.3	3.0	3.1	3.2	3.3	3.4	3.2
2.3 Valuables	3.3	3.4	2.7	1.9	1.7	2.6	3.4	2.2
3. Exports	23.0	24.2	23.1	27.8	24.4	24.5	23.6	24.5
4. *Less* Imports	29.5	32.9	31.8	25.8	30.8	34.3	31.2	32.5
GDP at 2004-05 market prices	**100**	**100**	**100**	**100**	**100**	**100**	100	100
Source: Compiled from CSO data.								
Totals may not add up to hundred due to discrepancies.								

lower than the growth of GDP at factor cost. This was largely due to the stimulus package and a decline in the ratio of taxes to GDP (indirect taxes are subtracted from GDP at market prices and subsidies are added to obtain GDP at factor cost). In the next seven quarters, the growth of GDP at market prices exceeded the growth of GDP at factor cost. In last two quarters (Q1 and Q2 of 2012-13) the growth of GDP at market prices has been lower than the growth of GDP at factor costs largely because of the increase insubsidies

(Fig 1.2). Higher growth of GDP at market prices relative to the growth of GDP at factor cost has occurred in the quarters which had a positive growth of net indirect taxes and vice versa.

1.10 The share of private final consumption expenditure has generally been in the range of 55 to 60 per cent. The share of gross fixed capital formation has been lower in the first half of 2012-13 as compared to its share in 2011-12.A detailed examination of the contribution of various components of GDP to growth (Fig 1.3) suggests a decline in the contribution of investment (gross fixed capital formation, inventories and valuables) beginning with Q2 of 2011-12.

Fig 1.2 : Rate of growth of GDP at factor cost and at market prices

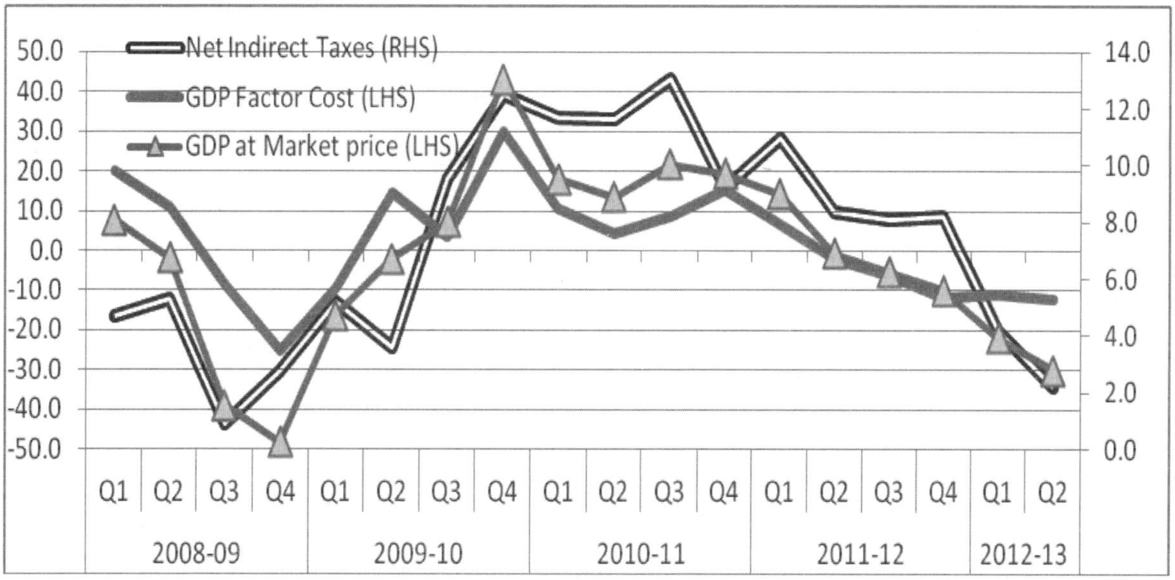

Fig 1.3: Point Contribution of GDP at market prices

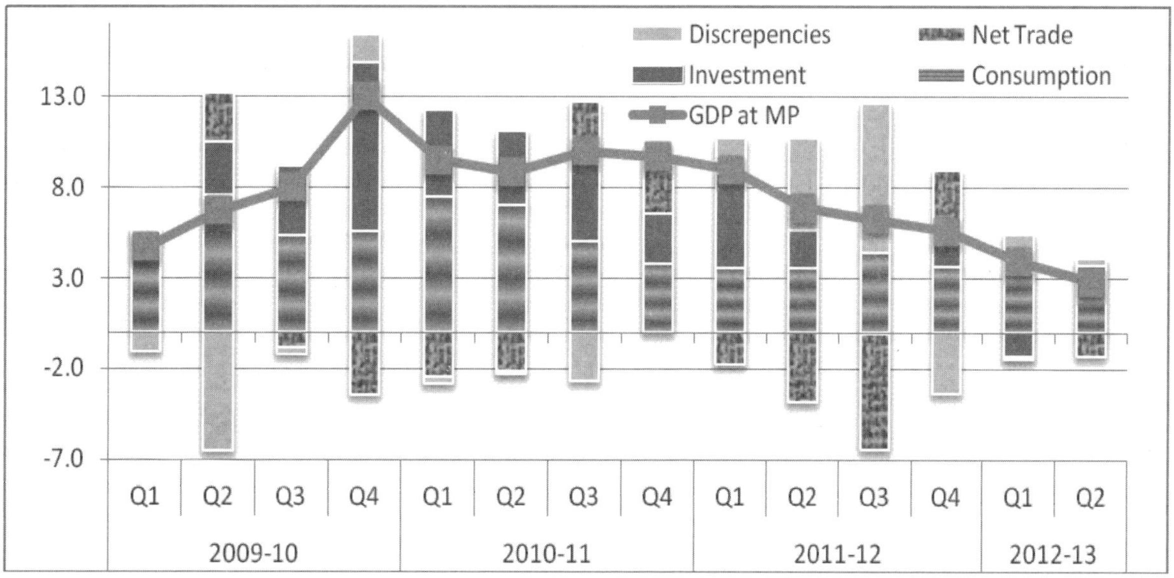

AGRICULTURE

1.11 Rainfall during the South West Monsoon (01st June – 30th September) in 2012 has been both erratic and uneven. It was deficient by 28 per cent in June, 2012 and 13 per cent in July, 2012 as compared to the respective monthly Long Period Averages (LPA). With better rainfall in August and September, the deficiency declined. During the monsoon season, the country as a whole received 819.8 mm of rainfall against a normal rainfall of 887.5 mm which represents a deviation of 8 per cent from the LPA. (Table 1.4). At the meteorological sub-division level, 23 out of 36 met sub-divisions received excess or normal rainfall and 13 met sub-divisions received deficient rainfall. Out of 628 districts for which rainfall data were available, 62 districts (10 per cent) received excess rainfall, 303 (48 per cent) received normal rainfall, 235 (37 per cent) received deficient rainfall and 28 districts (5 per cent) received scanty rainfall.

Agricultural Growth

1.12 As per the National Accounts Statistics, the agriculture and allied sector registered a growth of 2.1 per cent during the first half of 2012-13 which is lower than the growth rate of 3.4 per cent in the first half of 2011-12.

Kharif Sowing

1.13 Due to erratic and deficient rainfall, area coverage under kharif crops has declined as compared to last year (Table 1.5). Coarse

Table 1.4: Rainfall Pattern in Monsoon(June to September) 2012

Regions	Actual Rainfall(mm)	LPA (mm)	Percentage deviation from LPA
Central India	935.5	975.5	4
Northwest India	569.3	615.0	7
South Peninsula	643.9	715.5	10
North East India	1275.3	1438.3	11
All India	819.8	887.5	8

Source: 2012 South West Monsoon End of Season Report.

Table 1.5: Crop wise area sown during kharif 2012 (Lakh hectares)

Crops	Area Sown(Kharif)		Increase/ decrease over last year(+/-)
Major cereals crops	**2012**	**2011**	
Paddy	391.62	400.68	-9.06
Coarse Cereals	178.17	206.73	-28.56
Jowar	24.12	25.96	-1.84
Bajra	65.11	86.95	-21.84
Maize	71.92	73.88	-1.96
Pulses	95.24	113.45	-18.21
Arhar	36.86	40.4	-3.54
Urad	22.86	24.15	-1.29
Moong	19.63	26.78	-7.15
Total Foodgrains	665.03	720.86	-55.83
Oilseeds	175.09	184.91	-9.82
Groundnut	37.81	42.97	-5.16
Soyabean	105.88	101.79	4.09
Sesamum	17.12	19.17	-2.05
Other crops			
Cotton	116.14	121.78	-5.64
Sugarcane	51.00	50.87	0.13
Jute	7.76	8.09	-0.33

Source: Department of Agriculture & Cooperation

cereals and pulses, grown mostly in rainfed conditions, have suffered a major decline in their area under cultivation. These accounted for nearly 83 per cent of the total decline in area under food crops. Sugarcane, largely because it is an irrigated crop, and soyabean, however, witnessed an increase in acreage.

Agriculture Production

1.14 In 2011-12 food grain production was a record 257.4 million tonnes (4th Advance Estimates) primarily due to a good monsoon and supportive government policies. This level of production was higher by 12.7 million tonnes as compared to the previous record food grain production of 244.8 million tonnes (Final Estimates) achieved during 2010-11. It comprised 129.9 million tonnes of kharif foodgrains and 127.5 million tonnes of rabi food grains. Production of oilseeds was estimated at 30.0 million tonnes, sugarcane at 357.7 million tonnes, which is an all-time record. Production of cotton at 35.2 million bales of 170 kg each in 2011-12. In fact, the record production of rice and wheat at 104.3 million tonnes and 93.9 million tonnes, respectively largely contributed to the record production in 2011-12. First advance estimates (which cover the kharif crops) indicate a decline in production across all major crop groups (Table 1.6).

1.15 Given the limited possibility of increasing area, improvements in productivity of major agricultural crops is the only long term solution to bridge the gap between demand and supply. In fact, the country achieved significant improvements in the yield levels of major agricultural crops (Table 1.7). Notwithstanding the increase in yield levels in food crops, there still exists considerable gap between potential and actual yields even in high productivity irrigated areas with the current technology (Table 1.8). For these areas, balanced use of fertilizers and micro nutrients, and water and soil saving technology may need to be considered. In case of wheat, at national level actual average yield (2.79 t/ha) is significantly lower than the yields demonstrated on farmers' fields (3.32 t/ha) and yields under research conditions (4.2 t/ha). Much larger gaps exist in case of Bihar and Madhya Pradesh. Major yield gaps are reported to be due to deficiencies in crop management practices.

Table 1.6 : Kharif production in 2011-12 and 2012-13 (Million tonnes)

Crop	2011-12 (4th advance estimate)	2012-13 (1st advance estimate)	Absolute difference (col3-2)	Percentage
Foodgrains	129.94	117.18	-12.76	-9.82
Oilseeds	20.79	18.78	-2.01	-9.67
Sugarcane	357.67	335.33	-22.34	-6.25
Cotton@	35.20	33.40	-1.80	-5.11

@Production in million bales of 170 kg each.

Source: Department of Agriculture & Cooperation

Table 1.7: Area, Production and Yield of major Crops

Crops	Area (lakh hectare)			Production (million Tonnes)			Yield (kg/hectare)		
	2009-10	2010-11	2011-12*	2009-10	2010-11	2011-12*	2009-10	2010-11	2011-12*
Foodgrains	1213.3	1267.7	1250.3	218.1	244.8	257.4	1798	1931	2059
Oilseeds	259.6	272.2	264.4	24.9	32.5	30.0	958	1193	1135
Sugarcane	41.8	48.9	50.9	292.3	342.4	357.7	70020	70091	70317
Cotton@	101.3	112.4	121.8	24.0	33.0	35.2	403	499	491

*4th advance estimates @production in million bales of 170 kg each.

Source: Department of Agriculture & Cooperation

Table 1.8: Yield gaps in cereal crops in major States						
State	Cereal Crops	Stimulated Potential Yield(t/ha)	Max attainable Experienced yield(t/ha)	Average Yield(t/ha)	Total Yield Gap I (%)	Management Yield Gap II (%)
		A	B	C	{100(AC)/A}	{100(B-C)/B}
Punjab	Rice	8.8	7.0	4.0	54.5	43.1
	Wheat	6.5	5.2	4.3	33.8	17.3
Haryana	Rice	8.7	7.0	2.8	67.8	59.9
	Wheat	5.6	4.5	3.8	32.1	14.2
UP	Rice	7.2	5.2	3.8	47.2	26.9
	Wheat	5.4	4.6	2.4	55.6	47.4
Bihar	Rice	8.7	7.0	2.1	75.9	70.5
	Wheat	5.5	4.4	2.3	58.2	47.7
Tamil Nadu	Rice	8.4	6.7	2.1	75.0	69.0
Source- Twelfth Five Year Plan						

Rabi prospects

1.16 Though kharif output in 2012-13 is estimated to be lower for major agricultural crops, it is expected that this would partly be made up by higher rabi production through additional coverage under rabi crops, greater soil moisture, as well as through adequate and timely supply of inputs (fertilizers and seeds) and better extension services. Average annual growth of foodgrain production in rabi season during 2000-01 to 2011-12 at 2.7 per cent has also been significantly higher than the growth of production during kharif season, which has averaged 1.2 per cent only (Fig 1.4). This has been due to the dominance of irrigated wheat and rice in Rabi crops and a smaller share of area under coarse cereals.

Price Policy of Agricultural Produce

1.17 Agricultural production in the country is greatly influenced by policies such as pricing, procurement, storage, etc. The Minimum Support Prices (MSPs) for major crops have been raised substantially by the Government in 2012, in line with the objective of ensuring remunerative prices to farmers for their produce and with a view to encouraging higher investment and production in the sector (Table 1.9). This policy also resulted in higher procurement of foodgrains by Food Corporation of India (FCI) and the State agencies. The procured foodgrains are being made available to the consumers under the targeted public distribution system (TPDS) at central issue prices(CIPs) that are much less than the economic costs to the procuring agencies. Needless to say, this policy puts

Fig 1.4: Production of foodgrains during Kharif and Rabi seasons (Million tonnes)

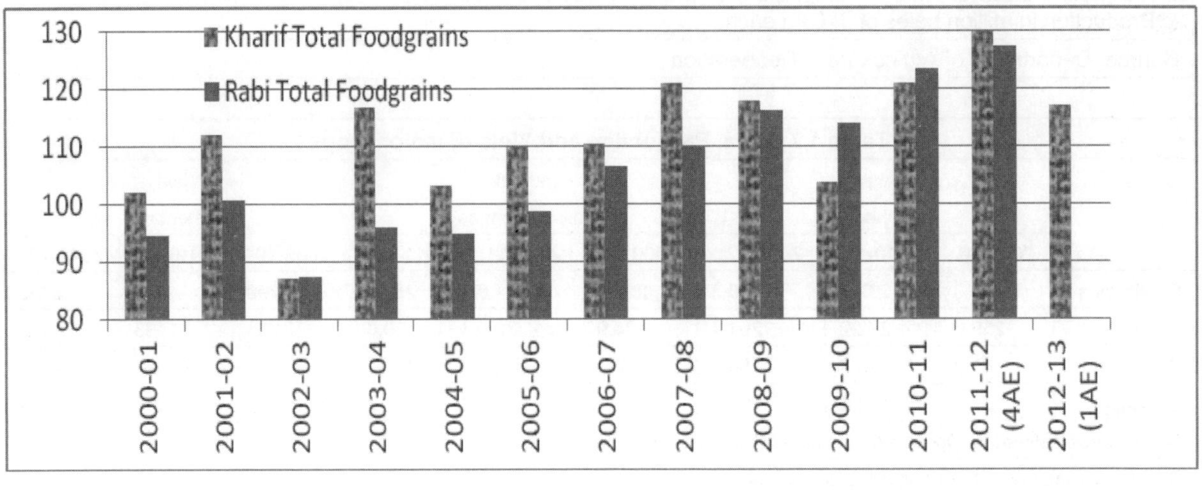

Table 1.9: Minimum Support Prices (Per quintal and increase in per cent)							
Kharif Crops	2008-09	2009-10	2010-11	2011-12	2012-13	Average Annual Increase 2012-13/2008-09	Increase in 2012-13/2011-12
Paddy (common)	900	1000	1000	1080	1250	8.6	15.7
Paddy (Gr.A)	930	1030	1030	1110	1280	8.3	15.3
Jowar (Hybrid)	840	840	880	980	1500	15.6	53.1
Jowar (Maldandi)	860	860	900	1000	1520	15.3	52.0
Bajra	840	840	880	980	1175	8.8	19.9
Maize	840	840	880	980	1175	8.8	19.9
Ragi	915	915	965	1050	1500	13.2	42.9
Arhar (Tur)	2000	2300	3500	3700	3850	17.8	4.1
Moong	2520	2760	3670	4000	4400	15.0	10.0
Urad	2520	2520	3400	3800	4300	14.3	13.2
Groundnut in shell	2100	2100	2300	2700	3700	15.2	37.0
Sunflower	2215	2215	2350	2800	3700	13.7	32.1
Soyabean (black)	1350	1350	1400	1650	2200	13.0	33.3
Soyabean (yellow)	1390	1390	1440	1690	2240	12.7	32.5
Sesamum	2750	2850	2900	3400	4200	11.2	23.5
Nigerseed	2405	2405	2450	2900	3500	9.8	20.7
Cotton (medium staple)	2500	2500	2500	2800	3600	9.5	28.6

Note: Inclusive of bonus wherever applicable.

substantial claims on the exchequer in the form of food subsidy provided to procuring agencies.

Procurement, Storage and Distribution

1.18 A significant proportion of marketable surplus of foodgrains is procured at the Minimum Support Price (MSP) fixed by the Government. Higher procurement prices have resulted in large build-up of stocks of rice and wheat and raise the concerns for its safe storage. The Scheme of Decentralised Procurement of foodgrains was introduced by the government in 1997-98 with a view to effecting savings in the outgo of food subsidy, enhancing the efficiency of procurement and distribution and encouraging local procurement thereby extending the benefits of MSP to local farmers. The State Governments presently undertaking decentralised procurement are West Bengal, Madhya Pradesh, Chhattisgarh, Uttarakhand, Andaman & Nicobar Islands, Odisha, Tamil Nadu, Gujarat, Karnataka and Kerala. Andhra Pradesh has agreed to adopt the DCP scheme with effect from Kharif marketing season 2012-13. Procurement of rice and wheat in different states is indicated in Table 1.10 and 1.11.

Table 1.10: State-wise Procurement of Rice for Central Pool (Kharif Marketing Season: October-September) (Lakh tonnes)					
State	2008-09	2009-10	2010-11	2011-12	2012-13
Andhra Pradesh	90.58	75.55	96.09	75.40	0.40
Chhattisgarh	28.48	33.57	37.46	41.15	0.49
Haryana	14.25	18.19	16.87	20.07	24.99
Odisha	28.01	24.96	24.65	28.64	0.00
Punjab	85.54	92.75	86.34	77.31	80.54
Tamil Nadu	12.01	12.41	15.43	15.96	0.01
Uttar Pradesh	40.07	29.01	25.54	33.55	0.21
West Bengal	17.44	12.40	13.10	20.36	0.00
Others	24.66	21.50	26.50	37.87	0.20
All India Total	341.04	320.34	341.98	350.31*	106.84*

* Procurement figure as on 14.11.2012

Source: Department of Food & Public Distribution

Table 1.11: State-wise Procurement of wheat for Central Pool (lakh tonnes)					
State	**2008-09**	**2009-10**	**2010-11**	**2011-12**	**2012-13**
Haryana	52.37	69.24	63.47	69.28	86.65
MP	24.10	19.68	35.39	49.65	84.93
Punjab	99.40	107.25	102.09	109.58	128.34
Rajasthan	9.35	11.52	4.76	13.03	19.64
U.P.	31.37	38.82	16.45	34.61	50.63
Others	10.30	7.31	2.98	7.20	11.29
All India	**226.89**	**253.82**	**225.14**	**283.35**	**381.48**
Source: Department of Food and Public Distribution					

1.19 Wheat and rice are issued from the central pool to state governments/UTs at Central Issue Prices(CIPs) for distribution under the TPDS. The CIPs of foodgrains issued under the TPDS are fixed much below their economic cost. The Central government bears subsidy burden on this account, especially for making available foodgrains at highly subsidized rates for households in the Below Poverty line (BPL) and Antodaya Anna Yojana (AAY) category (Table 1.12). The CIPs have not been revised since the year 2002, even though there have been corresponding large increases in MSP and economic cost.

1.20 Besides meeting the requirements of distribution of foodgrains under TPDS and welfare schemes, the Central Pool of food stocks is required to have sufficient quantities of rice and wheat in order to meet emergencies like drought/failure of crop and to enable open market intervention in case of sharp price increases. The minimum buffer norms for the Central Pool have been fixed by taking into consideration the seasonality in the arrival of the grains and distribution requirements. Food stocks have remained significantly higher than the buffer norms (Table 1.13). Keeping in view the comfortable stock position a liberalized approach has been adopted towards allocation of additional foodgrains under different schemes and exports.

Table1.12: Economic Cost and Issue Price of Wheat and Rice								
Year	Rice ($)	Wheat	Rice			Wheat		
	Economic Cost		APL	BPL	AAY	APL	BPL	AAY
			830	565	300	610	415	200
			Issue Price as per cent to Economic Cost of FCI					
2010-11 (Prov.)	2002.4	1526.4	41.5	28.2	15.0	40.0	27.2	13.1
2011-12 (RE)	2184.2	1651.9	38.0	25.9	13.7	36.9	25.1	12.1
2012-13 (BE)	2418.7	1822.5	34.3	23.4	12.4	33.5	22.8	11.0
($)- Weighted average of common and Grade A Rice taken together								

Table 1.13: Details of Buffer norms and actual stock position

(in lakh tonnes)

Date	Rice		Wheat		Total		Actual Stock as per cent to Buffer Norms
	Actual Stock	Buffer norms	Actual Stock	Buffer norms	Actual Stock	Buffer norms	
1.01.2010	243.5	138.0	230.9	112.0	474.5	250.0	189.8
1.04.2010	267.1	142.0	161.3	70.0	428.4	212.0	202.1
1.07.2010	243.0	118.0	335.8	201.0	578.5	319.0	181.3
1.10.2010	184.4	72.0	277.8	140.0	462.2	212.0	218.0
1.01.2011	255.8	138.0	215.4	112.0	471.2	250.0	188.5
1.04.2011	288.2	142.0	153.6	70.0	441.8	212.0	208.4
1.07.2011	268.6	118.0	371.5	201.0	640.1	319.0	200.6
1.10.2011	203.6	72.0	314.3	140.0	517.9	212.0	244.3
1.01.2012	297.2	138.0	256.8	112.0	553.9	250.0	221.6
1.04.2012	333.5	142.0	199.5	70.0	533.0	212.0	251.4
1.07.2012	307.1	118.0	498.1	201.0	805.2	319.0	252.4
1.10.2012	233.7	72.0	431.5	140.0	665.3	212.0	313.8

Source: Department of Food and Public Distribution

Agriculture Credit - Enabling farmers to deliver higher output

1.21 It has been the endeavour of the government to ensure timely and adequate availability of agricultural credit at affordable cost to farmers. Agriculture credit flow at the end of July, 2012 stood at ₹ 1,86,243 crore achieving 32 per cent of the target at ₹ 5,75,000 crore for 2012-13. The achievement during the year 2011-12 amounts to ₹ 5,11,029 crore (108 per cent) against the target of ₹ 4,75,000 crore (Table 1.14).

1.22 The Kisan Credit Card (KCC) Scheme introduced in August 1998 has since stabilized, with a major share of crop loans being routed through it. By the end of June 2012, the number of live KCCs issued by commercial banks, cooperative banks, and regional rural banks reached 9.08 crore, while total loans outstanding amounted to ₹ 444,421 crore in March 2012.

Table 1.14:Target and Achievement of Credit Flow to Agriculture Sector during 2011-12 and 2012-13(up to July 2012)

(₹ Crore)

Agency	2011-12			2012-13		
	Target	Achievement (Provisional)	Per cent Achieved	Target	Achievement (Provisional)	per cent Achieved
Commercial Banks	3,55,000	3,68,616	103.84	4,20,000	1,11,543	26.56
Cooperative Banks	69,500	87,963	126.57	84,000	52,630	62.65
Regional Rural Banks	50,500	54,450	107.82	71,000	22,070	31.08
Total	4,75,000	5,11,029	107.59	5,75,000	1,86,243	32.39

Source: Commercial Banks' data from IBA; Cooperative & RRBs data from NABARD ROs

INDUSTRY AND INFRASTRUCTURE

Industrial Output - Prolonged Stagnation

1.23 The deceleration in the industrial sector was sharper during the first half of the current financial year in comparison to that in the same period of the previous year. The combination of factors that affected industrial production during 2011-12, continued to be a drag on industrial output even during the current financial year. However, a major cause of manufacturing sluggishness in this financial year has been the drop in investment as reflected in the slower rate of growth in disbursement of bank credit and lower investment in new projects. The cycle of adverse business sentiment leading to lower investment and aggregate demand slowdown has delayed the industrial recovery. Corporate sector capacity utilization and sales growth have also continued to be low. Further, infrastructure bottlenecks also impinged on the performance of the mining and electricity sectors. During April-September 2012-13, IIP growth was 0.1 per cent as compared to 5.1 per cent in April-September 2011-12 (Table 1.15).

1.24 IIP based comparative growth rates of broad industrial groups are given in Table 1.15. IIP followed a declining trend since the third quarter of 2010-11 till the first quarter of 2012-13. A reversal in this trend is observed only in the second quarter. Keeping in line with the overall IIP, the growth in the manufacturing sector also exhibited a similar trend. In the last 15 months, growth has averaged less than 1 per cent. In the first six months of the current financial year, growth in the manufacturing sector has been (-)0.4 per cent as compared to the 5.5 per cent growth during the same period of the previous year. Mining sector performance was dragged down by the sharp reduction in natural gas output and the near stagnant production of crude oil. Electricity generation growth during the current financial year slowed down to 4.6 per cent as compared to a robust 9.4 per cent increase recorded in the first half of previous year. Shortage of coal led to capacity underutilization in the thermal based power generation during the first half.

1.25 As per the use based classification of sectoral growth, the slowdown was pervasive (Fig 1.5). Basic goods, intermediate goods and consumer goods sectors had comparatively lower growth during the first half of the current financial year. Higher borrowing costs and the dip in investment impacted the capital goods sector the most.

1.26 Output of the capital goods sector had declined by 4 per cent in 2011-12. This trend continued during 2012-13 with the output growth of this sector further declining by 20.1 per cent and 6.9 per cent in the first and second quarters respectively of the current financial year (FY). Overall, there was a decline of 13.7 per cent in the capital goods sector during April-Sept. of the current FY as compared to 4.6 per cent growth during the corresponding period of 2011-12. During the first half of the current financial year, the dip in production had

Table 1.15: Growth in broad industrial groups based on IIP (Base 2004-05 =100)

(per cent)

		Mining	Manufacturing	Electricity	General
	Weight	141.57	755.27	103.16	1000
	Q1	8.0	10.4	5.4	9.6
	Q2	6.3	7.4	2.1	6.8
	Q3	6.3	9.2	6.5	8.6
2010-11	Q4	1.1	8.9	8.1	7.9
	Q1	0.7	7.7	8.3	7.0
	Q2	-4.1	3.4	10.5	3.2
	Q3	-4.2	1.1	9.6	1.2
2011-12	Q4	-0.4	0.3	4.5	0.6
	Q1	-1.5	-0.8	6.4	-0.3
2012-13	Q2	1.8	0.2	2.8	0.5
April-September					
2011-12		-1.6	5.5	9.4	5.1
2012-13		0	-0.4	4.6	0.1

Source: Central Statistics Office

Figure 1.5:Industrial growth: use based industrial classification (per cent)

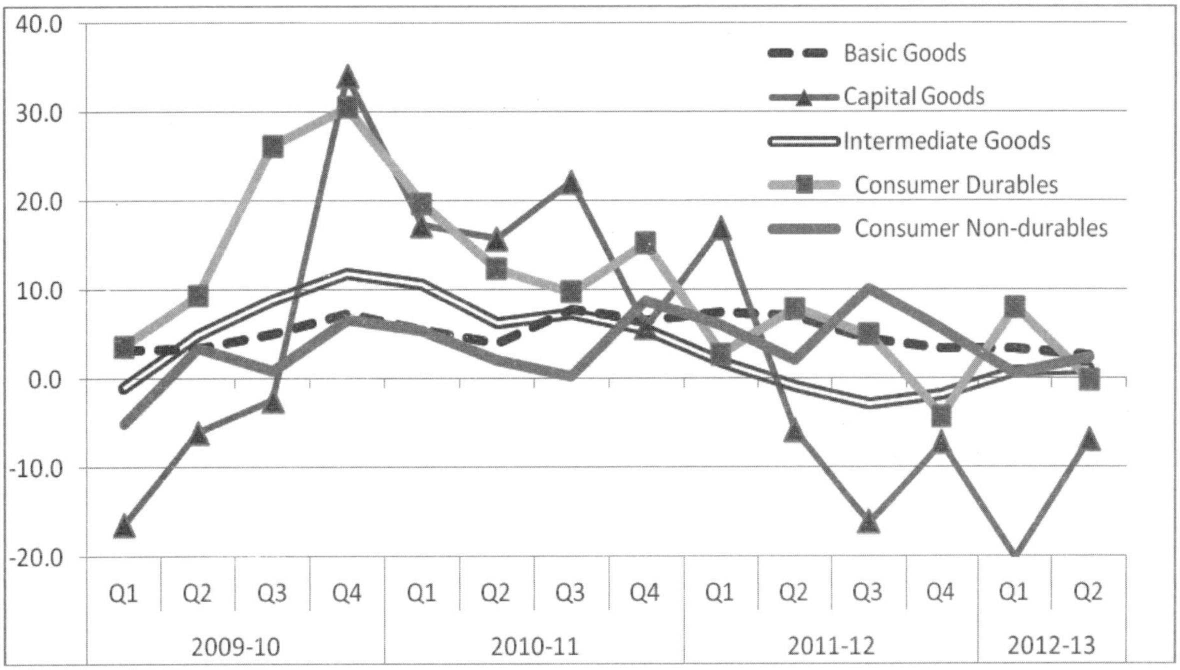

been under the categories "machinery and equipment", "electrical machinery" and "transport". The dip in the transport segment was mainly due to the decline in output of commercial vehicles and three wheelers. Production of major individual products falling under the capital goods sector namely computers, UPS, transformers, insulated cables, turbines and construction machinery declined. While imports of capital goods increased significantly during 2010-11 and 2011-12, the trend reversed during the first two quarters of the current financial year as imports contracted in line with the overall performance of the manufacturing and capital goods sector. There appears to be complementarity at times between the growth of production of capital goods and the growth of imports of these goods, as can be seen from Figure 1.6 in the period before Q1 2011-2012, perhaps because investment drives them both. More recently, though, there seems to be more substitution, though some caution is necessary in extrapolating recent trends.

Fig 1.6: Growth of imported and domestically produced capital goods

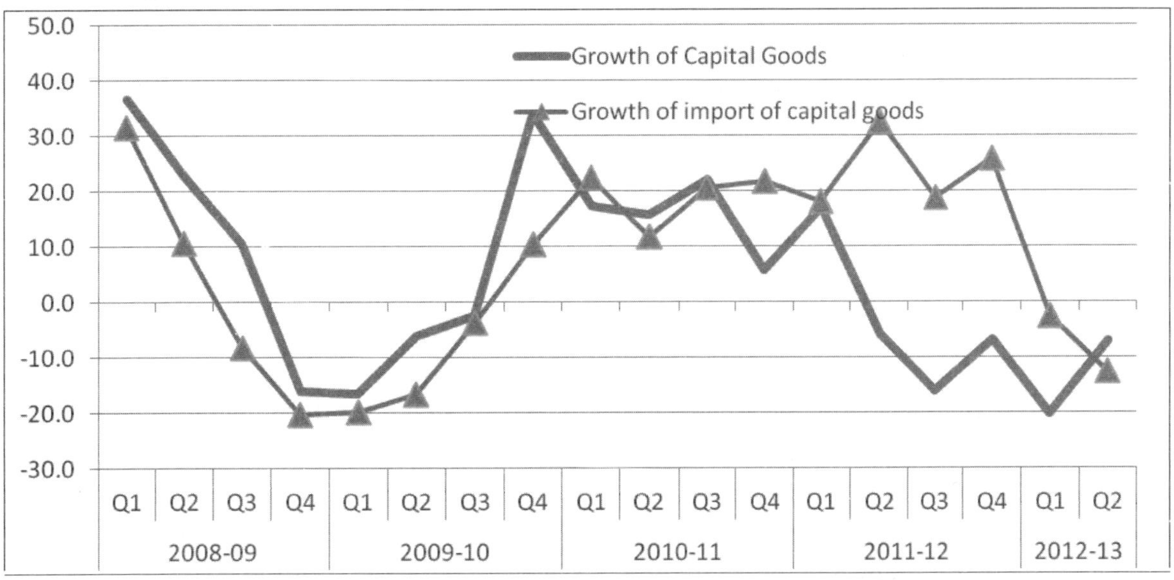

1.27 At the 2-digit level, out of the 22 sub-sectors under manufacturing activities, 12 sub-sectors witnessed negative growth during the second quarter of 2012-13 as compared to 8 sub-sectors during the first quarter of the year. On a cumulative basis, 8 sub-sectors witnessed a negative growth during April-September, 2012-13. There had been, however, an improvement in the performance of some segments during Q2. The food sub-group exhibited a growth of 1.7 per cent in the second quarter vis-à-vis a decline of 0.9 per cent during the first quarter of 2011-12. The textile sub-group also registered a turnaround. Overall, this sub-group exhibited a cumulative growth of 6.8 per cent during April-September, 2012-13 as compared to the contraction of 1.2 per cent during the corresponding period of 2011-12. Wearing apparel (mainly ready-made garments) segment has bounced back during the Q2 as it exhibited a growth of 5.7 per cent during the second quarter as compared to a contraction of 6.4 per cent during the first quarter of 2012-13. There has also been recovery in case of chemicals and chemical products segment during Q2. This sub-group exhibited a growth of 5.8 per cent during the second quarter as compared to contraction of 1.2 per cent during the first quarter of 2012-13. Overall this sub-group exhibited a cumulative growth of 2.3 per cent during April-September 2012-13 as compared to 0.7 per cent rise during the corresponding period of 2011-12.

Reasons for industrial sector slowdown

1.28 The prevailing slowdown in industrial production is due to combination of domestic and external factors. While the global economic slowdown had affected the export dependent sectors, depressed sentiments, high interest rates, moderation in credit growth and a deceleration in growth of investment also contributed to the reduction in growth. Monetary tightening and higher cost of borrowing have dented overall investment flow into industry and infrastructure during the current financial year. Poor business sentiment, the decline in gross fixed capital formation, the dip in the launch of new projects and lower exports continue to put demand side constraints on industrial growth. The supply side constraints mainly on account of infrastructure bottlenecks have resulted in moderation in the output of many sub-sectors. Mining sector growth has also been affected by delays in regulatory and environment clearances.Non-food credit off-take had been lower during the current financial year as compared to the corresponding period of the last year. Year on year growth rate of gross credit deployed to industry as a whole is about 10 per cent lower during the current financial year.

Major infrastructure sectors and universal intermediaries

1.29 The eight core infrastructure supportive industries, with an overall weight of 37.9 per cent in IIP, registered a growth of 3.6 per cent and 2.8 per cent in the first and second quarters of 2012-13 respectively. The year on year growth during April-September of the current financial year was 3.2 per cent as against growth of 5 per cent during the corresponding period of the previous year (Table 1.16). Coal, refinery products and cement sectors achieved comparatively higher growth in the current financial year. Growth rates of the steel sector and electricity generation were comparatively lower. Production of crude oil, natural gas and fertiliser contracted during the first half of current financial year vis-à-vis the production in the first half of 2011-12. The slowdown has impacted revenue earning on account of reduced cargo, freight handling by railways, civil aviation and ports sectors.

Table 1.16: Trends in Growth of Infrastructure and Universal Intermediaries (per cent)					
Industry	2009-10	2010-11	2011-12	April-September	
				2011-12	2012-13
i Electricity	6.2	5.5	8.1	**9.3**	**4.7**
ii Coal	8.1	-0.3	1.2	**-4.8**	**8.3**
iii Steel	6.0	8.9	7.0	**9.5**	**2.6**
iv Crude oil	0.5	11.9	1.0	**5.1**	**-0.8**
v Refinery products	-0.4	3.0	3.2	**4.6**	**5.4**
vi Cement	10.5	4.5	6.7	**3.8**	**7.4**
vii. Natural Gas	44.6	10.0	-8.9	**-8.5**	**-12.5**
Viii Fertilizers	12.7	0.0	0.4	**0.6**	**-5.6**
Overall Index	**6.6**	**5.7**	**4.4**	**5.0**	**3.2**
Source: O/O The Economic Adviser, DIPP					

Corporate sector performance

1.30 Based on the abridged results of non-government non-financial listed companies, the deceleration in sales growth (Y-o-Y) which started in Q4 of 2011-12 continued in the first half of 2012-13 as shown in Table 1.17. Sales growth decelerated to a 11-quarter low of 11.6 per cent in Q2 of 2012-13. Further, due to a higher rate of growth of expenditure as compared to sales, net profits declined for four consecutive quarters up to Q1 of 2012-13. However there has been a marked improvement in the growth of net profits during Q2 of 2012-13 due to lower growth in interest expenses and higher growth in 'other income'

Table 1.17: Performance of Non-Government Non-Financial Listed Companies						
	Growth Rates[1] (in Per cent)					
	2011-12				2012-13	
Item	**Q1**	**Q2**	**Q3**	**Q4**	**Q1**	**Q2(P)**
No. of Companies	2,615	2,627	2,637	2,597	2,790	1,435
Sales	22.5	19.0	19.2	15.0	13.4	11.6
Expenditure, of which	23.0	22.4	24.7	16.1	15.8	11.9
Raw Material	27.6	23.1	25.1	16.4	13.4	11.6
Staff Cost	19.6	17.6	18.9	14.2	17.3	16.0
Operating Profits (EBITDA)	12.1	-1.0	-5.9	-1.8	-3.7	13.8
Other Income*	39.4	25.8	66.1	47.2	29.5	54.8
Depreciation	9.5	9.7	10.5	11.1	10.3	8.6
Gross Profits (EBIT)	15.7	-0.3	-2.8	2.1	-2.5	23.8
Interest	21.6	47.1	42.6	34.8	37.9	7.4
Tax Provision	21.0	3.3	-2.4	1.9	-3.6	19.8
Net Profits	5.7	-14.8	-31.3	-7.2	-10.7	31.2
Net Profits to Sales	7.4	6.1	4.8	6.8	5.9	8.4

**: Other income excludes extraordinary income/expenditure if reported explicitly*

1.Growth rates are per centage changes in the level for the period under reference over the corresponding period of the previous year for common set of companies.

Source : RBI.

Industry and infrastructure financing

1.31 The sectoral deployment of credit by the scheduled commercial banks indicates a moderation in credit growth for the manufacturing and infrastructure sector (telecommunication & other infrastructure sectors) in the current year (Table 1.18). Within the manufacturing sector, food processing and textiles witnessed a reduction in the credit growth.

PRICES

Inflation is moderating

1.32 Inflation as measured by the Wholesale Price Index (WPI), which averaged 9.6 per cent in 2010-11, moderated to 8.9 per cent for 2011-12 and further decelerated to 7.7 per cent in 1st half (April-September) of 2012-13. WPI inflation was 7.81 per cent in September 2012, which was a decline from 8.01 per cent in August 2012. It has fallen further to 7.45 per cent in October 2012. The recent decline in inflation was mainly because of the decline in inflation of manufactured products (non-metallic mineral products, leather, basic metals, chemical and chemical products), primary articles (spices, fruits & vegetables) and fuel & power (bitumen, petrol and electricity). Inflation, however, increased in crude petroleum, non-food articles, cereals, protein foods, mineral oils, edible oils, beverages, tobacco & tobacco products.

1.33 Inflation as measured by the consumer price indices,which averaged 10.0 per cent to 10.5 per cent in 2010-11, moderated to 8.2 per cent to 8.4 per cent in 2011-2012. However, it has again gone up and is in the range of 8.5 per cent to 10.0 per cent during 1st half of 2012-2013 (Table 1.19).

Table 1.18: Growth of Credit by Scheduled Commercial Banks (per cent)

	2009-10		2010-11		2011-12		2012-13
	Apr-Sep	Oct-Mar	Apr-Sep	Oct-Mar	Apr-Sep	Oct-Mar	Apr-Sep
Industries	19.7	18.3	26.3	26.6	23.7	20.7	17.8
Manufacturing	12.3	10.0	18.2	20.5	21.4	20.8	19.2
Mining	19.6	14.8	28.7	27.2	41.9	43.0	34.7
Electricity	45.1	51.7	51.5	45.5	37.6	25.1	16.7
Construction	28.0	10.1	16.8	15.8	12.8	17.9	17.5
Other Infrastructure	39.0	38.3	44.4	38.4	19.6	14.4	11.8
Manufacturing sub sectors							
Food Processing	6.1	11.5	26.3	32.4	26.3	20.8	18.2
Textiles	7.9	10.8	16.9	19.5	19.3	13.1	8.0
Petroleum & Nuclear Fuels	11.0	-11.3	3.9	-11.5	-1.6	3.7	7.9
Chemicals & Chemical Products	6.5	5.0	15.1	16.8	11.7	12.4	19.9
Cement & Cement Products	43.8	20.1	29.0	33.8	14.9	18.5	20.0
Basic Metal & Metal Product	23.1	20.7	24.6	27.4	29.9	25.0	19.6
All Engineering	15.1	6.3	20.0	29.8	25.8	20.9	25.2
Transport Equipment	7.1	3.9	11.4	14.2	23.3	21.3	22.5
Other Industries	9.8	14.1	17.3	20.9	23.7	29.2	24.7

Source : RBI

Table 1.19: Food and non-food inflation for WPI and CPI (IW, AL, RL and New Series)

	2010-11			2011-12			2012-13 (Apr-Sep)		
	General	Food	Non-Food	General	Food	Non-Food	General	Food	Non-Food
WPI	9.6	11.1	9.0	8.9	7.2	9.6	7.7	9.0	7.1
CPI-IW	10.5	9.9	11.3	8.4	6.3	11.6	10.0	11.0	8.9
CPI-AL	10.0	9.4	11.4	8.2	5.2	15.1	8.5	7.0	11.8
CPI-RL	10.0	9.6	11.0	8.4	5.3	14.9	8.8	7.2	12.0
CPI-NS	-	-	-	-	-	-	10.0	11.1	9.0

Food and Non-food inflation

1.34 Non-food inflation in terms of consumer price indices which averaged 11.0 per cent to 11.4 per cent in 2010-11 accelerated in the range of 11.6 per cent to 15.1 per cent in 2011-2012 and, it has decelerated in the range of 8.9 per cent to 12.0 per cent during 1st half of 2012-2013.

1.35 Inflation in food items has been a major source of high headline CPI inflation. Food inflation based on CPIs (weight 46.20 per cent to 69.15 per cent), which averaged 15.2-15.7 per cent in 2009-10 due to supply shocks,moderated to 9.4 - 9.9 per cent in 2010-11 and further to 5.2-6.3 per cent in 2011-12. CPI food inflation during April-September of the current year varied from 7.0 per cent to 11.1 per cent (Table 1.19).

1.36 In case of WPI and CPI-IW and CPI new series, the primary sources of inflation have switched to food from April 2012. Persistent supply constraints in many protein food products have generated price pressures in these commodities. However, in case of CPI-AL and CPI-RL, the sources of inflation have continued to be non-food commodities from August 2010.

Contribution to inflation of major groups

1.37 The year-on-year headline WPI inflation in August 2012 was 8.0 per cent, little higher from previous level of 8 months. It declined somewhat in September and in October 2012. During the current financial year, weighted contribution of primary articles and fuel to headline inflation was relatively higher than their respective weights, while the weighted contribution of manufactured products has been relatively lower than its weight. The movement of point contribution to headline inflation of major groups for last three years is presented in Fig 1.7.

1.38 The reasons behind persistent inflation are (a) higher international prices of crude, precious metals, edible oil etc. (b) change in dietary pattern leading to structural demand supply mismatch for protein rich items (c) revision in MSP prices for some of the essential commodities (d) revision in petroleum prices in September 2012 among others. Inflation has been a major cause of concern for both the Government and Reserve Bank of India who are taking a number of measures to contain it as indicated in Box 1.1. Ultimately, though, short term measures will only have short term effects, and not always in the desired direction. Periodic bans of exports, institution and removal of tariffs, and repeated closure of futures markets tend to make it hard for producers to plan, distorts their incentives, and inhibits the production increases that are needed to bring prices under more sustained control.

Fig 1.7: Weighted point contribution of major group to headline WPI inflation

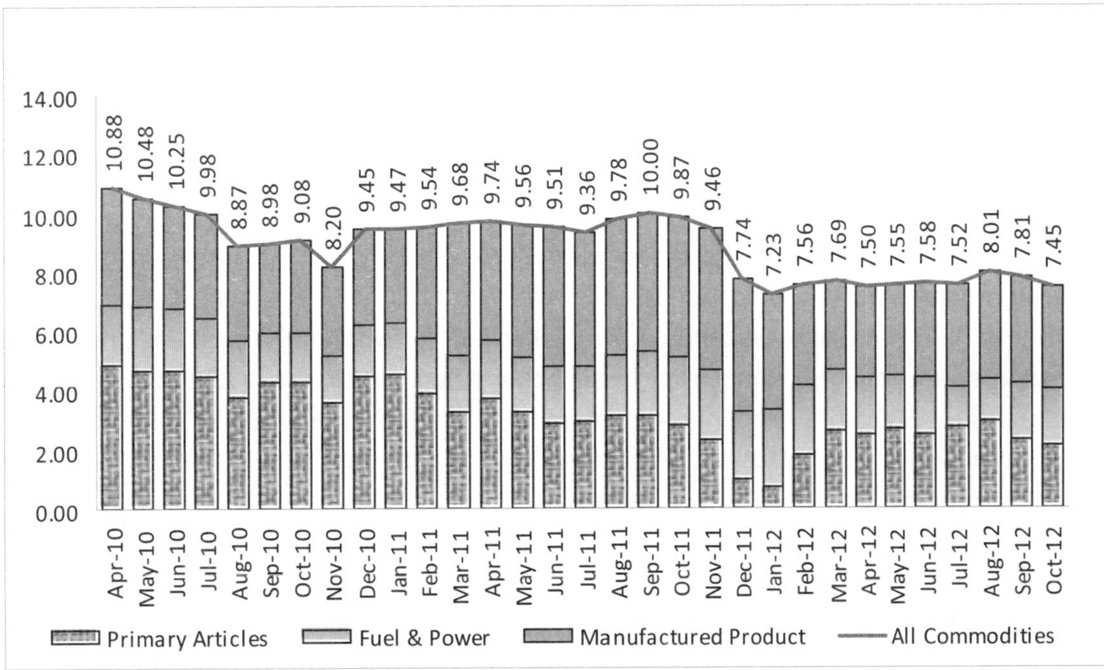

Box 1.1Measures taken and proposed by the Government to contain price rise

1. Fiscal & Administrative measures

- Reduced import duties to zero - for wheat, onion, pulses, crude palmolein and to 7.5 per cent for refined & hydrogenated oils & vegetable oils.
- Duty-free import of white and raw sugar was extended up to 30.6.2012; however, import duty of 10 per cent was instituted in June 2012.
- Banned export of edible oils (except coconut oil and forest based oil) and edible oils in blended consumer packs upto 5 kg with a capacity of 20,000 tons per annum and pulses (except Kabuli chana and organic pulses and lentils up to a maximum of 10000 tonnes per annum).
- Imposed stock limits from time to time in the case of select essential commodities such as pulses, edible oil, and edible oilseeds and in the case of paddy and rice for specific seven states upto 30.11.2012.
- Ban on export of onion was imposed for short period of time whenever required. Exports of Onion were calibrated through the mechanism of Minimum Export Prices (MEP).
- Maintained the Central Issue Price (CIP) for rice (at Rs 5.65 per kg for BPL and Rs 3 per kg for AAY) and wheat (at Rs 4.15 per kg for BPL and Rs 2 per kg for AAY) since 2002.
- Suspended Futures trading in rice, urad, tur, guar gum and guar seed.
- To ensure adequate availability of sugar for the households covered under TPDS, the levy obligation on sugar factories was restored to 10 per cent for sugar season 2011-12.
- Government allocated rice and wheat under Open Market Sales Scheme.
- Resumed the scheme for subsidized imported pulses through PDS in a varied form with the nomenclature " Scheme for Supply of Imported Pulses at Subsidized rates to States/UTs for Distribution under PDS to BPL card holders" with a subsidy element of ₹ 20/- per kg to be paid to the designated importing agencies upto a maximum number of BPL card holders for the residual part of the current year and extended the scheme for subsidized imported edible oils w.e.f. 1.10.2012 to 30.9.2013 with subsidy of ₹ 15/- per kg for import of upto 10 Lakh tonnes of edible oils for this period.

2. Budgetary and other measures

A number of measures were announced in Union Budget 2012-13 to augment supply and improve storage and warehousing facilities. Government launched a National Mission for Protein supplements in 2011-12 with allocation of Rs 300 crore. To broaden the scope of production of fish to coastal aquaculture, apart from fresh water aquaculture, the outlay in 2012-13 was stepped up to Rs 500 crore. Recently, Government permitted Foreign Direct Investment (FDI) in multi-brand retail trading. This will help consumers and farmers as it will improve the selling and purchasing facilities.

3. Monetary measures

The Reserve Bank of India (RBI) had also taken suitable steps to contain inflation with 13 consecutive increases by 375 bps in policy rates from March 2010 to October 2011.

MONEY AND BANKING

Monetary Policy stance

1.39 Mounting inflationary pressures during the period January 2010-October 2011 required adoption of a tight monetary policy by the Reserve Bank of India (RBI). An increase in policy rates by 375 basis points (repo rate was increased from 4.75 per cent to 8.5 per cent) during this period, helped in moderation of inflation from a peak of 10.9 per cent in April, 2010 to an average of 7.7 per cent during April-September 2012. However, the economy may have slowed down more than what was anticipated earlier. Since April, 2012, monetary policy has attempted to balance the growth-inflation dynamics though a calibrated softening of policy rates. The repo rate was reduced by 50 basis points to 8 per cent in April, 2012. There was a reduction in the Cash Reserve Ratio (CRR) from 6 per cent in October 2011 to 4.25 per cent in October 2012 and a reduction in Statutory Liquidity Ratio (SLR) from 24 per cent since May 2012 to 23 per cent in August, 2012. Movements of key policy rates have been as indicated below (Table 1.20):

1.40 Global economic and financial conditions continued to deteriorate during this period and with a sharper moderation in domestic growth, the growth-inflation trade-off needs a revisit. In the assessment of the Reserve Bank of India, keeping in view the inflation in the country, further reduction in policy rates at this juncture, could accentuate inflationary pressures rather than supporting growth. Further, since the risk to inflation was also emanating from the high fiscal deficit, uncertainty in international prices of crude oil and structural imbalances in demand-supply of food (particularly protein foods), a cautious monetary policy stand was preferable. However, the actions taken by the Government since September, particularly with regard to the increase in the administered prices of diesel, announcement of a fiscal road map with clear medium term fiscal deficit targets and initiatives to improve investor perception have created a favourable environment and have signalled a shift towards investment and capacity addition. As it anticipates some of the inflationary pressures from excess demand will be alleviated, the RBI should have room for more accommodative monetary policy.

1.41 The slow-down of economic activity was also getting reflected through a moderation in money supply and bank credit growth. While liquidity conditions continue to remain manageable, a widening of the gap between deposit and credit growth combined

Table 1.20: Revision in Policy Rates

Effective date	Bank Rate	Repo	Reverse Repo	CRR	SLR
01.01.2011	6.00	6.25	5.25	6.00	24.00
25.01.2011		6.50	5.50		
17.03.2011		6.75	5.75		
03.05.2011		7.25	6.25		
16.6.2011		7.50	6.50		
26.7.2011		8.00	7.00		
16.09.2011		8.25	7.25		
25.10.2011		8.50	7.50		
28.01.2012				5.50	
13.02.2012	9.50				
10.03.2012				4.75	
17.4.2012	9.00	8.00	7.00		
11.08.2012					23.00
22.9.2012				4.50	
03.11.2012				4.25	

* Prevailing rates as on 1st January 2011

with a seasonal pick up in credit demand are likely to keep up the pressure on liquidity. Policy actions in terms of reduction in CRR and SLR, in the recent months have been supportive and have tended to pre-empt a prospective tightening of liquidity conditions and reinforce the growth stimulus.

Macro parameters and targeted money and credit growth

1.42 The monetary policy of RBI was based on its indicative projection of macroeconomic parameters for 2012-13. In its policy review on April, 17, 2012, RBI expected GDP growth at 7.3 per cent and inflation to slow to 6.5 per cent by March, 2013. Consistent with this growth and inflation it had set an indicative target of M3 growth and non-food credit growth of 15 per cent and 17 per cent respectively (Table 1.21).

1.43 However, based on its latest assessment of economic situation, it reduced the projection for GDP growth to 5.8 per cent with inflation expected to average 7.5 per cent. Consistent with macro parameters, the targets of money supply and credit growth were also reduced (Table 1.21).Actual M3 growth at 13.6 per cent in Q2 of 2012-13 appears to be converging to the indicative target of 14 per cent set by RBI. Non-food credit growth has also been hovering around 16 to 17 per cent in the last 3 quarters and is only slightly higher than the indicative targets. The ratio of M3 to GDP is currently slightly higher than its medium term average of 3.1, largely on account of a moderation in the growth itself (Fig 1.8).

Liquidity Conditions

1.44 During 2011-12, liquidity conditions had remained benign to mid-November, but pressures intensified in the subsequent part of the year, with average net borrowing under theliquidity adjustment facility (LAF) reaching as high as ₹ 1,570 billion in March 2012, with an all-time high of ₹ 2,028 billion on March 30,

Table 1.21: Indicative Projections of Macro Parameters by RBI for 2012-13

	Indicative projections for growth rates (per cent)		
	Annual Policy 2012-13 (April 17, 2012)	First Quarter Review (July 31, 2012)	Second Quarter Review (Oct 30, 2012)
GDP growth	7.3	6.5	5.8
WPI inflation	6.5	7.0	7.5
Money supply growth (M_3)	15.0	15.0	14.0
Non-food credit	17.0	17.0	16.0

Fig 1.8: Growth of Non-food credit, M3, GDP and M3/GDP

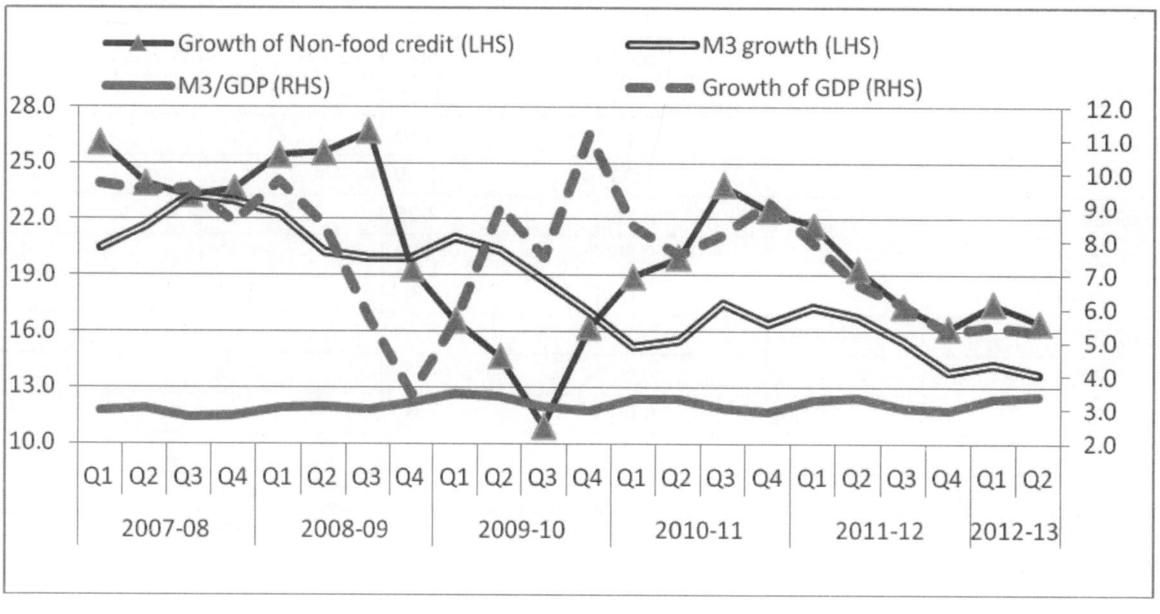

2012. Both structural and frictional factors - such as foreign exchange market interventions by the RBI, divergence between credit and deposit growth, build-up of government cash balances with RBI and the increase in currency in circulation - contributed to the liquidity pressures. Responding to the tight liquidity conditions, the RBI had conducted open market operations (OMOs) aggregating ₹ 1.3 trillion between November 2011 and March 2012, besides sequentially reducing CRR, injecting thereby primary liquidity of around ₹ 0.8 trillion into the banking system.

1.45 Liquidity conditions eased gradually during the first half of 2012-13. The turnaround in liquidity conditions was due to a decline in government's cash balances, injection of liquidity of about ₹ 860 billion by way of OMOs purchases of securities and increased use of the export credit refinance facility by banks. Reduction in SLR by one percentage point also improved the access of banks to potential liquidity. In September and October 2012 liquidity conditions tightened, taking the average net LAF borrowing to ₹ 904 billion since October 15, 2012, which was well above the (+/-) one per cent of net demand and time liabilities (NDTL) comfort level for liquidity. A CRR cut by 25 basis points (from 4.5 per cent to 4.25 per cent) by RBI on October 30, 2012, injected primary liquidity of ₹ 0.20 trillion into the banking system (Fig 1.9).

Deployment of Credit

1.46 The disaggregated data on sectoral deployment of gross bank credit available upto September, 2012 indicate that except for agriculture, there has been a reduction in the rate of growth of credit flow to other sectors. The sectoral shares of the non-food credit indicate that for the personal loans and priority sector lending, there has been a decline in the share in the last three years (Fig 1.10 and Table 1.22).

Fig. 1.9: Net Injection/Absorption of Liquidity

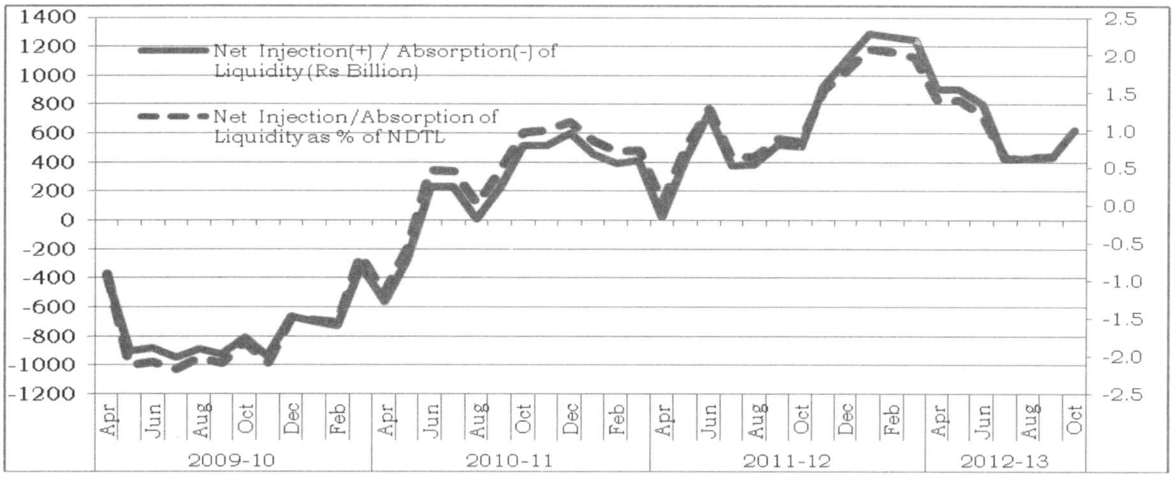

Figure 1.10: Sectoral Deployment of Non-food credit (April-September)

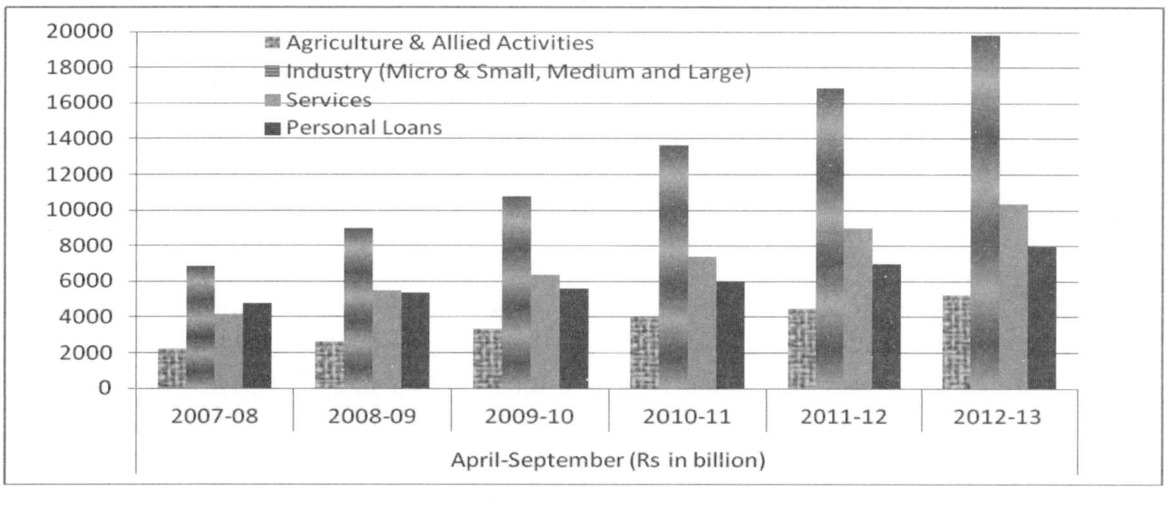

Table 1.22: Sectoral deployment of Bank credit (Rs. billion)

	2009-10		2010-11		2011-12		2012-13
	Apr-Sep	Oct-Mar	Apr-Sep	Oct-Mar	Apr-Sep	Oct-Mar	Apr-Sep
Non-food Credit	26,067	28,204	31,010	34,615	37,258	40,300	43,450
Agriculture	3,316	3,627	4,000	4,319	4,456	4,667	5,242
Industry)	10,774	12,092	13,610	15,311	16,831	18,479	19,831
Services	6,369	6,779	7,409	8,419	8,985	9,753	10,394
Personal Loans	5,608	5,706	5,992	6,566	6,986	7,401	7,984
Priority Sector	9,263	9,859	10,779	11,859	12,414	12,887	14,060
Sectoral Shares (per cent)							
Agriculture	12.7	12.9	12.9	12.5	12.0	11.6	12.1
Industry)	41.3	42.9	43.9	44.2	45.2	45.9	45.6
Services	24.4	24.0	23.9	24.3	24.1	24.2	23,9
Personal Loans	21.5	20.2	19.3	19.0	18.7	18.4	18.4
Priority Sector	35.5	35.0	34.8	34.3	33.3	32.0	32.4
Year on year rate of growth (per cent)							
Non-food Credit	15.6	13.3	19.0	22.7	20.1	16.4	16.6
Agriculture	25.1	22.0	20.6	19.1	11.4	8.1	17.6
Industry)	19.7	18.3	26.3	26.6	23.7	20.7	17.8
Services	15.7	11.5	16.3	24.2	21.3	15.8	15.7
Personal Loans	4.0	1.5	6.8	15.1	16.6	12.7	14.3
Priority Sector	18.7	16.0	16.4	20.3	15.2	8.7	13.3

1.47 Moderation in the growth in personal loans was sharp in first half of 2009-10 and 2010-11. Though credit growth significantly recovered in first half of 2011-12 and 2012-13, it continued to remain below the overall non-food credit growth. Within personal loans, loans for housing were affected more severely. Moderation in the growth of agricultural credit in second half of 2011-12 necessitated policy initiatives in this sector. Some of important initiatives for improving credit to agriculture sector were the following:

- The credit flow target for agriculture for the year 2012-13 was raised by to ₹ 575,000 crore from ₹ 475,000 crore in 2011-12. In the first half of the year, 42 per cent of the target was achieved and the banks have been asked to step up agriculture lending to achieve the target.
- The interest subvention for timely repayment of crop loans upto Rs 3 lakh was kept to 3 per cent for 2012-13, making the effective rate of interest for prompt payee farmers @ 4 per cent p.a.
- To strengthen NABARD's capital base in a phased manner, ₹ 2000 crore has been proposed for release in the financial year 2012-13.
- The Government of India has allocated ₹ 5000 crore for Rural Warehousing during the financial year 2012-13. Operational guidelines have been issued to NABARD.

1.48 Rural Infrastructure Development Fund (RIDF) was set up by the Government in 1995-96 for financing on-going rural infrastructure projects. The fund is maintained by NABARD. The contributions to the RIDF are made by those public and private sector banks who fail to meet the target for priority sector and/or agriculture lending. This fund is utilized to lend to State Governments to build rural infrastructure in the areas of roads, minor irrigation, soil conservation, drainage, forests, plantation etc. The total cumulative sanctions under RIDF (XVIII) as on 30th October, 2012 stood at ₹ 169,757 crore, while the disbursement was ₹ 1,18,828 crore. In addition, in past four years, ₹ 18,500 crore was sanctioned, and disbursed, to National Rural Road Development Agency (NRRDA) for rural roads under Bharat Nirman. During 2012-13, ₹ 20,000 crore has been allocated under RIDF, of which ₹ 5,000 crore has been allocated exclusive for Rural Warehousing.

Financial inclusion

1.49 Financial inclusion remained high on the list of priorities of the government and several steps were initiated to meet the target of extending banking outreach to all habitations having population of 1000 in North East and hilly states and to other habitations have crossed a population of more than 2000 as per Census 2011. Initiative taken for financial inclusion is given in Box 1.2.

Box: 1.2 - Financial inclusion

Opening of Bank Branches: In view of the continued need for opening of branches in rural areas for increasing banking penetration and financial inclusion, Government issued detailed guidelines on financial inclusion in October 2011, advising banks to open branches in all habitations of 5,000 or more population in under-banked districts and 10,000 or more population in other districts. As per reports received, out of 3,955 identified villages/habitation 2163 bank branches have been opened (including 1,437 Ultra Small Branches) by end of October, 2012.

"Swabhimaan" the Financial Inclusion Campaign : The Government had launched "Swabhimaan" - the Financial Inclusion Campaign in February 2011, under which over 74,000 habitations having a population of over 2000 have been provided with banking facilities through branches, business correspondent agents (BCAs), mobile vans etc. and about 3.16 crore Financial Inclusion accounts have been opened till March, 2012. Pursuant to the Finance Minister's Budget Speech 2012-13 the "Swabhimaan" campaign has been extended to habitations with population of more than 1000 in North Eastern and hilly States and to other habitations which have crossed population of 2,000 as per census 2011. Accordingly about 45,000 such habitations have been identified to be covered under the extended "Swabhimaan" campaign.

Direct Cash Transfer of Subsidies

Government has decided to introduce Direct Cash Transfers into the Bank account of the beneficiary under various programmes. In the first instance effective January, 2013, Direct Cash Transfer is being taken up in 51 districts in 18 States /UTs for various welfare schemes being implemented such as MGNREGA, Scholarship/Fellowship, JananiSurakshaYojna, IndraAwasYojana, National Rural Livelihood Mission etc. While the concerned Departments/ Agencies would provide details of the beneficiaries along with amounts to be credited, the banks have been advised -

(i) To be ready with the opening of bank account of the beneficiaries under various schemes.

(ii) To ensure that these can capture the Aadhaar numbers, since Aadhaar numbers would form the basis for transfer of benefits.

(iii) To provide adequate number of different access point (Branch, ATMs and others) to enable the beneficiary to withdraw the money as per his ease and convenience.

Opening of one Bank Account per family: In order to ensure electronic transfer of cash subsidies directly into the accounts of the beneficiaries under the various Schemes of Govt. of India and State Governments, it is important that the beneficiaries have an account in a bank having Core Banking Solutions (CBS). Accordingly, banks have been advised that the service area bank in rural areas and banks assigned the responsibility in specific wards in urban area ensure that every household has at least one bank account.

Interest Rates

1.50 Following the reduction in the policy (repo) rate by 50 bps in April 2012 coupled with the reduction in the CRR by 150 points during January -September 2012 and SLR by 100 bps in August 2012, there has been a moderation in both deposit and lending rates of scheduled commercial banks (SCBs) during 2012-13 (up to October). The modal deposit rate and base rate of SCBs witnessed moderation of seven basis points and 25 basis points, respectively, over this period (Table 1.23). With the reduction in CRR by 25 bps effective November 3, 2012, deposit and lending rates expected to moderate further.

Table 1.23: Deposit & Lending Rates of Scheduled Commercial Banks (SCBs)

(Per cent)

Items	Sept-11	Dec-11	Mar-12	Jun-12	Sep-12	Oct-12 (P)
(A) Domestic Deposit Rates						
(i) Public Sector Banks						
Up to 1Year	1.00-9.55	1.00-9.55	1.00-9.75	4.00-9.25	4.00-9.25	4.00-9.25
1 – 3 Years	8.55-9.75	8.55-9.75	9.00-9.75	8.75-9.50	8.50-9.30	8.50-9.25
Above 3 Years	8.00-9.50	8.00-9.50	8.50-9.50	8.00-9.50	8.50-9.30	8.50-9.25
(ii) Private Sector Banks						
Up to 1Year	3.00-9.40	3.00-9.25	3.00-9.50	3.00-9.25	3.00-9.25	3.00-9.00
1 – 3 Years	8.00-10.50	8.00-10.50	8.00-10.50	8.00-10.00	8.00-9.75	8.00-9.75
Above 3 Years	8.00-10.00	8.00-10.10	8.00-10.10	8.00-10.00	8.00-9.50	8.00-9.50
(iii) Foreign Banks						
Up to 1Year	3.00-10.00	3.50-10.00	3.50-11.80	3.50-9.25	2.43-9.25	2.43-9.25
1 – 3 Years	3.50-9.75	3.50-9.75	3.50-9.75	3.50-9.75	3.50-9.75	3.50-9.75
Above 3 Years	4.25-9.50	4.25-9.50	4.25-9.50	3.75-9.50	3.75-9.50	3.75-9.50
SCBs Modal Deposit Rate						
(All Tenors)	7.44	7.46	7.42	7.40	7.29	7.35
(B) Base Rate						
Public Sector Banks	10.00-10.75	10.00-10.75	10.00-10.75	10.00-10.50	9.75-10.50	9.75-10.50
Private Sector Banks	9.70-11.00	10.00-11.25	10.00-11.25	9.75-11.25	9.75-11.25	9.75-11.25
Foreign Banks	6.25-10.75	6.25-10.75	7.38-11.85	7.38-11.85	7.25-11.75	7.25-11.75
SCBs						
Modal Base Rate	10.75	10.75	10.75	10.50	10.50	10.50
(C) Median Lending Rate						
Public Sector Banks	10.50-15.25	10.25-15.25	10.60-15.35	10.50-15.50	**10.50-15.38**	-
Private Sector Banks	9.00-15.25	10.00-15.50	10.50-15.50	10.63-15.38	**10.20-15.63**	-
Foreign Banks	9.13-14.75	9.50-14.38	10.00-14.50	10.00-14.50	**9.83-14.50**	-

(Median range of interest rate on advances at which at least 60 per cent business has been contracted and figures for September, 2012 are provisional)

1.51 Rate of growth of deposits, not only was sticky, it continued to remain lower than the growth of non-food credit for most part of 2010-12. Persistently high inflation and increased preferences for gold partly reflected slower growth of deposits. The ratio of non-food credit to deposits, therefore, increased from around 67 per cent in June, 2009 to 73-75 per cent from February, 2012.

Government securities market

1.52 The Central Government completed a large part (74.1 per cent) of the budgeted gross market borrowing programme during April-November 2012 (up to November 08) as compared with 73.4 per cent in the corresponding period of the previous year. Most of the repayments during 2012-13 were scheduled in first half of the year necessitating the front loading of budgeted gross borrowings for the year. Interplay of factors influenced the yields on government securities during the year whereby policy rate cut by RBI in the beginning of the fiscal year, OMO purchases by RBI, slowdown in GDP growth rate and global economic outlook enabled a downward movement in yields while inflationary pressure, liquidity conditions and supply concerns exerted an upward pressure. The maturity of issuance during the year was elongated in view of the relatively flat yield curve and better appetite for longer term debt. The weighted average maturity of securities issued during 2012-13 (up to 08 November 2012) was 13.54 years as compared to 12.19 years in the corresponding period of the previous year. The weighted average yield during the same period was 8.43 per cent as compared to 8.48 per cent in the corresponding period of the previous year.

Treasury Bills

1.53 The cut off yields in case of 91-Day, 182-Day and 364-Day Treasury Bills (TBs) in 2012-13 eased vis-à-vis previous year due to reduction in repo and reverse repo rates by 50 bps in the beginning of the year. Moderation in yields was more pronounced at the longer end resulting in an inversion of the yield curve during the year, though the degree of inversion gradually corrected during the course of the year (Table 1.24).

Fig 1.11: Non-Food credit and Deposits' growth

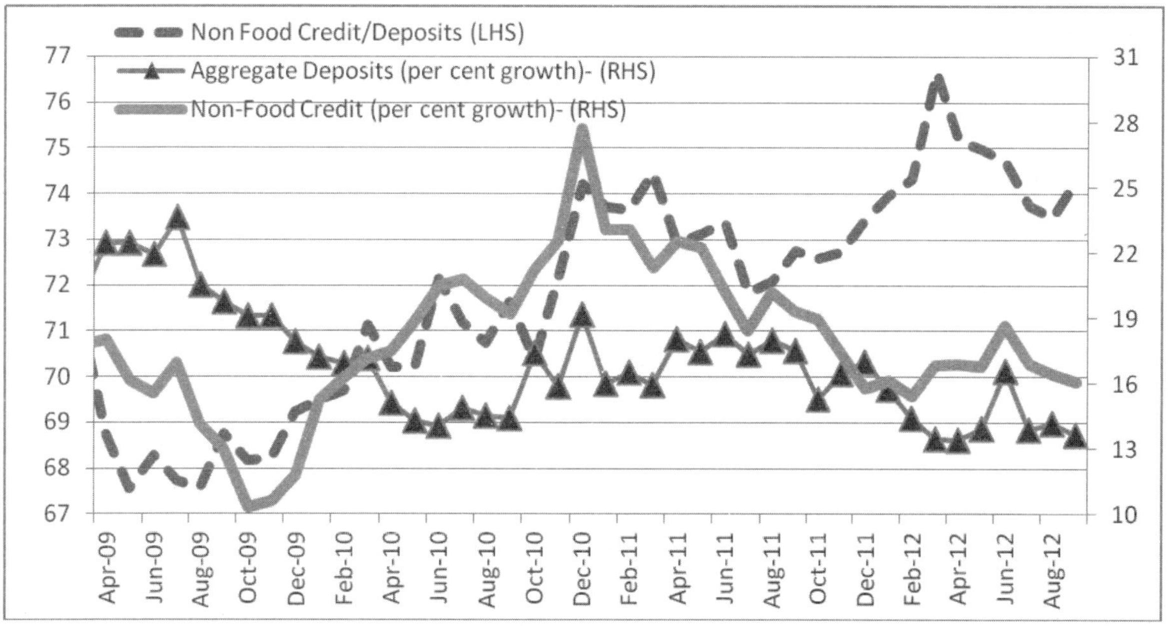

Table 1.24: Average Implicit Yield of Treasury Bills in the Primary Market

(per cent)

Month-end	91-Day	182-Day	364-Day
2010-11	6.14	6.47	6.66
2011-12	8.45	8.43	8.38
2012-13	**8.40**	**8.25**	**8.11**
Apr-12	8.55	8.48	8.25
May-12	8.41	8.42	8.30
Jun-12	8.28	8.24	8.07
Jul-12	8.20	8.19	8.02
Aug-12	8.24	8.25	8.09
Sep-12	8.13	8.14	8.07
Oct-12	8.09	8.08	7.98
Nov -12 (upto Nov 08)	8.14	8.16	8.11

CAPITAL MARKET

1.54 The development of an efficient and deep capital market is essential for sustained growth in an emerging market economy like India. The capital market fosters economic growth by channelling real savings to capital formation, and can help raise the productivity of investment by improving the allocation of investable funds. It also allocates risks to those who can best bear it. However, the quality of the market determines its effectiveness in meeting these objectives. Accordingly, to improve the quality of the market in terms of market efficiency, transparency, price discovery, preventing unfair trade practices, etc. and bringing it at par with international standards, a package of reforms comprising measures to liberalise, regulate and develop the Indian capital market have been implemented since the early 1990s. As a result of these initiatives, capital markets in India have emerged as an important source of funds for Indian companies and also as an avenue for the small and retail investors to productively channelising their savings.

1.55 Against this background and in the overall context of the evolving macro-economic situation, the Government in close collaboration with RBI and Securities and Exchange Board of India (SEBI) has taken several initiatives to meet the growing capital needs of the Indian economy. Some of the initiatives taken are as under:

Primary Market

1.56 **Comprehensive review of the extant Regulatory Framework :** In line with the announcement made in the Union Budget 2012-13, Securities and Exchange Board of India (SEBI) has undertaken a comprehensive review of the extant regulatory framework in the primary market and approved many progressive measures including:

- For distributing IPOs in electronic form, nationwide broker network to be made available at more than 1000 locations.
- To reduce the time from closure of issue to its listing and for enhancing the reach of Application Supported by Blocked Amount (ASBA) all ASBA banks are mandated to provide the facility in all their branches in a phased manner.
- Modifying the share allotment system to ensure that every retail applicant, irrespective of his application size, gets allotted a minimum bid lot subject to availability of shares in aggregates.
- Facilitating capital raising by issuers by reducing the requirement of average free float market capitalisation from ₹5,000 crore to ₹3,000 crore for follow on public offerings (FPOs) and rights issues through fast-track route.
- Allowing professionally and technically

qualified entrepreneurs to meet up to fifty per cent of 20 per cent promoters' contribution through SEBI registered Alternative Investment Funds, such as SME Funds, Infrastructure funds, PE funds, VCFs, etc.

- As required in terms of Securities Contracts (Regulation) Rules, listed companies and PSUs can achieve the minimum public shareholding of 25 per cent and 10 per cent, respectively by Rights and Bonus issues.
- For improving the quality of public offerings and investor protection, issuers with minimum average pre-tax operating profit of ₹15 crore only are allowed to access the market through the 'profitability route'; other issuers can continue to access capital markets either through SME platform or compulsory book building with increased Qualified Institutional Buyers (QIBs) participation of 75 per cent as against the existing 50 per cent;
- Putting in a place a framework for rejection of poor quality draft offer documents; disallowing any withdrawal or reduction of the size of bids for non-retail investors at any stage in the IPO process;
- Increasing transparency in capital raising by limiting 'General Corporate Purposes' as an object of the issue to 25 per cent of the issue size; restraining employee benefit schemes from acquiring their shares from the secondary market.

1.57 **Steps to Re-energise Mutual Fund Industry:**

- Increasing penetration of mutual fund products and energising distribution network by permitting a broader interpretation of the Total Expense Ratio (TER) which would enable Asset Management Companies (AMCs) to pay higher upfront commissions to distributors;
- Simplifying the distributors' registration process by introducing varied levels for certification and registration for different types of MF products; and reducing fees for registration / certification.
- AMCs have been permitted additional TER upto 30 basis points for improving the of MF products in smaller cities (beyond top 15 cities). Aligning the interest of investors, distributors and AMCs by setting apart a portion of the asset management fees annually for the investor education campaigns.
- Permitting direct investments with a lower expense ratio; ensuring single expense structure under a plan to eliminate discrimination between investors;
- Permitting investments in cash where PAN/ Bank accounts are not available.
- To enable the mutual fund industry to be in line with all other industries where service tax is borne by the end user, it is decided that the service tax payable on investment management fees should be charged to the scheme.
- Protecting the investor by curbing mis-selling and churning by creating a system of identification of agents and labeling of products and by requiring exit loads to be charged to the scheme while compensating the AMCs by allowing an additional TER to the extent of 20 basis points.
- Strengthening regulatory framework for mutual funds by streamlining disclosures on portfolios, performance and expenses and initiation of the process of setting up of a Self-Regulatory Organization (SRO) for regulation of MF distributors.

Secondary Market

1.58 **Market Developments**: The Indian stock market is one of the best performing markets in the world in 2012. Relative to its level on the last trading day in 2011, the Sensex gained 3050 points or 19.7 per cent and Nifty gained 995 points or 21.5 per cent as on 31 October, 2012. However, in the current financial year, Sensex gained 1101 points (or 6.3 per cent) whereas, Nifty gained 324 points (or 6.1 per cent). Market capitalisation is around 0.73 times the GDP of 2011-12.

1.59 The Indian market has been one of the better performing markets recently as evident from the returns in the Indian markets given in Table 1.25 below. Recent reform measures taken by the Indian government have had a positive impact on market sentiments.

FII Investment

1.60 The total net FII flows to India in 2009 stood at US$ 18.51 billion (Table 1.26). These flows grew remarkably in 2010 and India received net FII investment worth US$ 39.47 billion in 2010 which has been highest over the last decade. These flows were largely equity inflows. Similarly, about three-fourth of net FII inflow in 2012 is equity.

Table 1.25 : Comparative picture of Stock Exchanges – Level and growth

	31-Oct-11	30-Dec-11	30-Mar-12	31-Oct-12	Oct 2012 over March 2012	Oct 2012 over Oct 2011	Oct 2012 over Dec 2011
	Level				Per cent change		
BSE, India	17705.0	15454.9	17404.2	18505.4	6.33	4.5	19.7
NSE, India	5326.6	4624.3	5295.6	5619.7	6.12	5.5	21.5
S&P 500, US	1253.3	1257.6	1408.5	1412.2	0.26	12.7	12.3
DAX, Germany	6141.3	5898.4	6946.8	7260.6	4.52	18.2	23.1
FTSE 100, UK	5544.2	5572.3	5768.5	5782.7	0.25	4.3	3.8
NIKKEI 225, Japan	8988.4	8455.4	10083.6	8928.3	-11.46	-0.7	5.6
HANG SENG, Hong Kong	19864.9	18434.4	20555.6	21641.8	5.28	8.9	17.4
KOSPI, Korea	1909.0	1825.7	2014.0	1912.1	-5.06	0.2	4.7
DJIA, USA	11955.0	12217.6	13212.0	13096.5	-0.87	9.5	7.2
Straits Times, Singapore	2855.8	2646.4	3010.5	3038.4	0.93	6.4	14.8
TAIWAN TAIEX, Taiwan	7587.7	7072.1	7933.0	7166.1	-9.67	-5.6	1.3
SHANGHAI, China	2468.3	2199.4	2262.8	2068.9	-8.57	-16.2	-5.9
CAC 40, France	3242.8	3159.8	3423.8	3429.3	0.16	5.7	8.5

Source: Bloomberg

Table 1.26 : Net FII Investment in India during 2007-2012 in US $ Million)

Segments	2007	2008	2009	2010	2011	2012*
Equity	17655.8	-11974.3	17457.50	29361.83	-357.8	18034.2
Debt	2340.1	2636.4	1050.00	10112.16	8654.6	6270.5
Total	19995.9	-9337.9	18507.50	39473.99	8296.8	24304.7

**Investments up till October 31, 2012*
Source : SEBI

Initiatives taken to attract foreign investments and External Commercial Borrowings (ECB) Policy Reforms since March 2012

1.61 Initiatives to attract FII Investment :

- In June 2012, the FII limit for investment in G-Sec enhanced by US $ 5 billion raising the cap to US $ 20 billion with the following sub-limits;
  - USD 10 billion -Investment in G-Sec without any residual maturity criterion
  - USD 10 billion - Investment in G-Sec subject to residual maturity of at least three years.
- In order to make the scheme for FII investment in Long-term infra bonds attractive, the scheme has been rationalized as under:
  - US $10 billion investment in Infrastructure Debt Funds (IDF) -(a) Lock-in period of 1 Year (b) Residual maturity of at least 15 months.
  - US $ 12 Billion for FII investment in in long term infrastructure bonds - (a) Lock-in period of 1 Year (b) Residual maturity of at least 15 months.
  - USD 3 billion for Qualified Foreign Investors (QFIs) Investment in MF debt schemes which hold at least 25 per cent of their assets (either in debt or equity or in both) in the infrastructure sector.

At present the total limit prescribed for FII investment in various debt securities stands at US $ 65 billion.

1.62 Allowing qualified foreign investors (QFIs) to access Indian corporate bond market:

- Pursuant to the Budget Announcement 2012-13, Qualified Foreign Investors (QFIs) have been allowed to access Indian Corporate Bond market. QFI can invest in corporate debt securities (without any lock-in or residual maturity clause) and Mutual Fund debt schemes upto USD 1 billion.

1.63 Streamlining the QFIs Scheme

- Widening the Definition of QFI: The definition of QFI has been expanded to also include residents of the member countries of Gulf Co-operation Council (GCC) and European Commission as GCC and EC are the members of FATF.
- Allowing QFIs to open Individual bank accounts: QFIs have been allowed to open individual non-interest bearing Rupee Bank Accounts with Authorized Dealers banks in India for receiving funds and making payment for transactions in securities they are eligible to invest.

1.64 Liberalisation of ECB Policy During 2012-13

Five initiatives on External Commercial Borrowings were announced in the Budget 2012-13, with the focus to augment resources for infrastructure development. These include: (1) Enhancement in the limit for refinancing rupee loans from 25 per cent to 40 per cent for power sector (2) Allowing ECB for capital expenditure on the maintenance and operations of toll systems for roads and highways (3) Allowing ECBs for low cost/ affordable housing projects (4) Permitting ECB for working capital requirements of the airline industry (5) Reduction in the rate of withholding tax on interest payments on external commercial borrowings from 20 per cent to 5 per cent for three years (July 2012- June 2015).

1.65 A New Scheme under ECB

On 25th June, 2012, it was decided to add a new scheme for ECB. Indian companies in the manufacturing and infrastructure sector can now avail of ECBs for repayment of Rupee loan(s) availed of from the domestic banking system and/or for fresh Rupee capital expenditure, under the approval route upto a ceiling of USD 10 billion. The ECBs will be allowed to companies based on the foreign exchange earnings and its ability to service the ECB.

1.66 Decisions taken in the meeting of High Level Committee on ECB (HLCECB) held on August 22, 2012

- SIDBI has been permitted as an eligible borrower for accessing ECB for on-lending to MSME sector subject to certain conditions.
- National Housing Bank/ Housing finance companies have been permitted to avail ECBs for financing prospective owners of low cost / affordable housing units.
- Pursuant to the Budget Announcement 2012-13, ECBs have been permitted for low cost housing projects.
- Credit enhancement facility under the Structured Obligation Scheme has been extended to all companies with reduced minimum average maturity norms from 7 years to 3 years. FIIs have also been permitted to invest in these bonds upto the equivalent of US$5 billion within the overall corporate bond limit of US$45 billion.
- Re-financing of buyer's credit for import of capital goods in the infrastructure sector has been placed under automatic route subject to certain conditions. It has also been decided to increase the maturity of such buyer's credit to maximum five years.

1.67 Relaxation In ECB Policy for financing of 2G Spectrum Auction:

- On a review of the current ECB policy and keeping in view the large outlay of funds required to be paid directly to the Government within a limited period of time, the following relaxations are provided for the recently held 2G spectrum auction:-
  - The successful bidders in the 2G auction would be eligible to refinance their Rupee loans availed of from the domestic lenders for making the upfront payment with a long-term ECB, under the 'automatic route' subject to certain conditions.
  - Such bidders can also avail of short term foreign currency loan in the nature of bridge finance under the 'automatic route' for the purpose of making upfront payment towards 2G spectrum allocation and replace the same with a long term ECB under the 'automatic route' subject to certain terms and conditions.
  - Successful bidders will also be allowed to avail of ECB from their ultimate parent company without any maximum ECB liability-equity ratio under the 'automatic route' subject to certain conditions.

TRADE

1.68 India is the 19th largest merchandise exporter and 12th largest importer in the world with shares of 1.7 per cent and 2.5 per cent in world exports and imports respectively in 2011, as per the World Trade Organization (WTO). In commercial services, India is the 8th largest exporter and 7th largest importer in the world with shares of 3.3 per cent and 3.1 per cent in world exports and imports respectively.India's merchandise exports in US dollar terms increased by 21.3 per cent to reach US $ 304.6 billion while imports increased by 32.3 per cent to US $ 489.2 billion in 2011-12.The trade deficit increased to US$ 184.6 billion which was 55.6 per cent higher than US $ 118.6 billion in 2010-11. However, as a result of the global slowdown, the growth rate in exports became negative in first two quarters of 2012-13 (Fig 1.12).

Fig 1.12: Value of Exports (US $ Billion) and rate of growth (per cent)

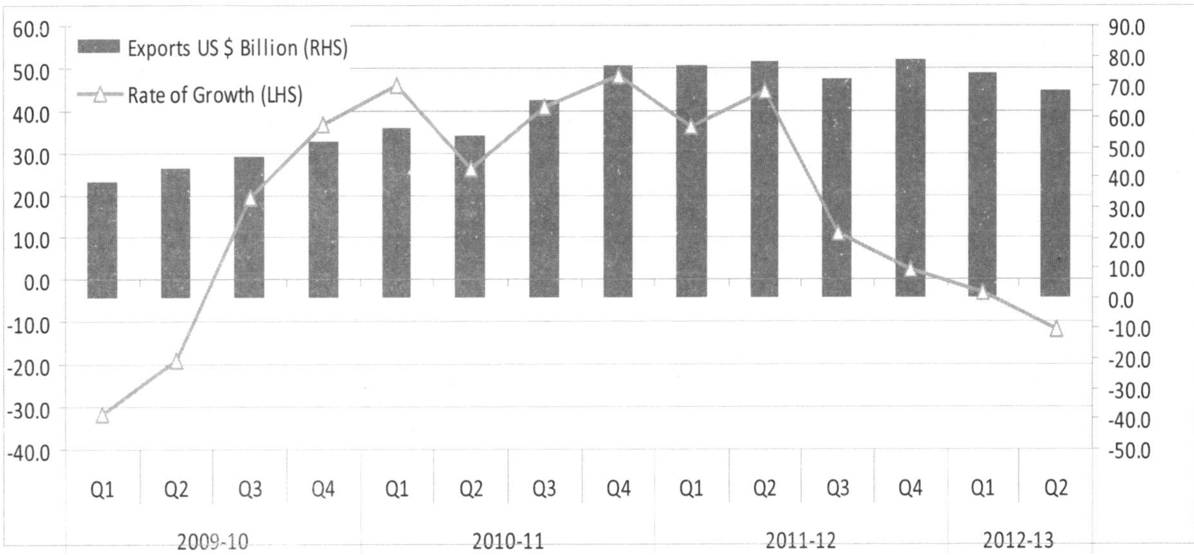

1.69 In 2011-12, high export growth was observed in petroleum products (34.1 per cent), chemicals and related products (28 per cent), agriculture and allied products (57.8 per cent), marine products (31.3 per cent) and leather and manufactures (22.7 per cent). Moderate growth was registered by engineering goods (16.9 per cent), gems & jewellery (15.9 per cent), textiles (17.1 per cent) and electronic goods (8.8 per cent). Rising crude oil prices, along with increase in gold and silver prices contributed significantly to the import bill in 2011-12. Petroleum, Oil and Lubricants (POL) imports accounted for about 32 per cent of India's total imports. The value of imports of gold and silver increased from US$ 29.8 billion in 2009-10 to US 61.5 billion in 2011-12. The share of gold and silver in total imports increased from 7.6 per cent in 2005-06 to 12.6 in 2011-12.

Global scenario

1.70 As per IMF's World Economic Outlook (WEO) update of October 2012, World Trade Volume (goods & services) is projected to grow by 3.2 per cent in 2012 as compared to 12.6 per cent in 2010 and 5.8 per cent in 2011. Imports of advanced economies are projected to grow at 1.7 per cent in 2012 as compared to the 4.4 per cent growth in 2011. Imports of emerging & developing economies are expected to grow by 7.0 per cent in 2012 as compared to the 8.8 per cent in 2011. Exports are projected to grow at 2.2 per cent in 2012 as compared to 5.3 per cent growth in 2011 for advanced economies, while the projected growth for emerging and developing economies is 4.0 per cent for 2012 as compared to 6.5 per cent growth in 2011.

Trade Performance during 2012-13 (April-October):

1.71 During 2012-13 (April-October), exports at US$ 167 billion registered a negative growth of 6.2 per cent over the corresponding period of the previous year. Imports at US$ 277.1 billion also registered a negative growth of 2.7 per cent. POL imports at US$ 95.6 billion were 10 per cent higher than the corresponding previous period. Non-POL imports at US$ 181.6 billion in April-October 2012 declined by 8.2 per cent over the corresponding period of the previous year. The trade deficit during April-October 2012 was US $ 110 billion.

1.72 In the first half of 2012-13 (April-September), agriculture and allied exports and chemicals and related products exports registered a growth of 47.9 per cent and 5.9 per cent respectively. The sectors that witnessed decline in growth in exports include, petroleum & oil products (-14.8 per cent), engineering goods (-9.2 per cent), gems & jewellery (-9.1 per cent), textiles (-8.9 per cent), electronic goods (-7.0 per cent) and leather and manufactures, (-4.3 per cent). Among imports, there was a deceleration in the growth of POL imports to 6.1 per cent. A notable feature on the import side was the declining trend in gold and silver imports with a negative growth of 32.5 per cent. Import growth of pearls, precious & semi-precious stones was also negative at 39.8 per cent. Some other major items which registered negative growth include machinery (-7.6 per cent), coal, coke and briquette (-9.7 per cent) and electronic goods (-8.8 per cent).

1.73 Quarter wise growth performance of exports and imports (Table 1.27) shows that the growth of total exports, POL and non POL exports started decelerating from Q3 of 2011-12 and became negative in Q1 and Q2 of 2012-13. Growth in POL import has shown swings on both sides with deceleration from 52.5 per cent in Q1 of 2011-12 to (-) 0.1 per cent in Q1 of 2012-13 and then growth of 12.7 per cent in Q2 of 2012-13. Non POL import growth which was at 35.7 per cent in Q2 of 2011-12, started decelerating and registered growth of (-) 9.2 per cent and (-) 6.7 per cent in Q1 and Q2 of 2012-13 respectively.

1.74 Growth of non-POL, non-gold and silver imports (which reflect the import of capital goods and inputs needed for exports and industrial activity) started decelerating from Q1 of 2011-12, and became negative at (-) 47.3 per cent in Q1 of 2012-13. Negative growth continued in Q2 of 2012-13 at (-) 12.5 per cent. Capital goods imports (including machine tools, machinery both electrical and non-electrical, transport equipment, project goods and manufacture of metals), which had registered a growth of 30.4 per cent in 2011-12, declined to (-) 11 per cent in Q2 of 2012-13.

Composition and direction of exports

1.75 The destination-wise exports of major items of the major trading partners from 2009-10 to the first half of 2012-13 show significant changes in the composition of exports to USA and China. In the case of India's exports to USA, the share of exports of primary products increased from 6.8 per cent in 2009-10 to 23.8 per cent in 2012-13 (April-September). The share of manufactured goods in India's exports to USA declined from 89.1 per cent to 71.4 per cent during the same period. This decline was mainly due to fall in growth rate of exports of textiles and gems & jewellery. In the case of India's exports to China, the share of primary products declined from 65.7 per cent to 41.0 per cent due to the fall in growth rate of ores & minerals. Share of manufactures in India's exports to China increased from 32.2 per cent to 55.8 per cent during this period, mainly due to the rise in share of engineering goods, textiles and chemicals and related products and rise in growth rates of textiles. In the case of India's exports to European Union (EU), there is a marginal rise in the share of primary products and manufactured goods and a fall in the share of petroleum products which have moved from a high growth rate to negative growth rate (Table 1.28).

Table 1.27 : Year on Year growth of exports and imports

	2010-11				2011-12				2012-13	
	Q1	Q2	Q3	Q4	Q1	Q2	Q3	Q4	Q1	Q2
Exports	46.1	26.2	40.6	48.1	36.4	44.7	10.8	2.7	-4.3	-11.7
POL exports	95.6	42.0	21.5	52.1	76.2	53.5	21.5	3.2	-20.4	-8.7
Non POL exports	39.6	23.4	45.1	47.3	29.1	42.9	8.8	2.5	-0.3	-12.3
Imports	44.3	31.3	17.2	24.1	36.3	40.0	29.5	24.7	-6.2	-0.9
POL imports	55.3	15.1	4.9	20.7	52.5	51.1	39.3	42.8	-0.1	12.7
Non POL imports	40.3	38.9	22.6	25.7	29.7	35.7	25.8	16.8	-9.2	-6.7
Non POL and Non-gold and silver imports	36.0	77.5	49.4	23.9	123.1	34.2	26.1	19.4	-47.3	-12.5
Net POL imports	40.9	33.3	18.3	26.1	16.2	35.9	25.8	16.2	1.5	-5.6

Computed from Directorate General of Commercial Intelligence &Statistics (DGCI&S) data

Table 1.28: Composition of exports by major markets

		Per centage share				Growth rate			
		2009-10	2010-11	2011-12	2012-13	2009-10	2010-11	2011-12	2012-13
		April-March			(Apr-Sept.)	April-March			(Apr-Sept.)
I	**Primary Products**								
	World	14.9	13.2	15.2	16.4	3.8	23.9	39.8	24.4
	USA	6.8	8.0	14.6	23.8	-13.5	52.8	149.4	147.1
	EU	8.6	8.2	9.7	10.0	-5.7	22.2	33.8	-3.4
	China	65.7	51.5	55.7	41.0	26.9	4.7	24.8	-23.6
	Others	13.1	11.7	13.1	14.7	-1.7	31.7	35.7	24.2
II	**Manufactured goods**								
	World	67.2	69.0	66.1	65.1	-5.9	44.2	16.1	-12.1
	USA	89.1	87.4	82.3	71.4	-8.7	27.0	27.9	-1.9
	EU	73.2	72.1	74.9	75.6	-15.4	25.8	18.6	-14.7
	China	32.2	42.3	39.5	55.8	29.5	75.4	7.8	0.0
	Others	65.1	67.8	63.3	61.8	-2.5	53.4	13.6	-14.2
III	**Petroleum, crude & products**								
	World	16.1	16.8	18.7	17.8	4.6	46.8	34.9	-15.5
	USA	2.3	3.7	3.6	3.8	180.3	110.9	30.1	-24.5
	EU	16.9	18.8	15.0	13.9	45.4	42.7	-9.4	-7.2
	China	0.8	5.3	6.3	3.0	-8.4	745.2	38.1	-80.3
	Others	19.9	19.4	23.4	22.7	-3.9	43.6	47.0	-13.6
	Total Exports								
	World	100	100	100	100	-3.5	40.5	21.3	-8.0
	USA	100	100	100	100	-7.6	29.5	35.8	14.2
	EU	100	100	100	100	-8.4	27.9	14.1	-12.7
	China	100	100	100	100	24.2	33.6	15.3	-19.7
	Others	100	100	100	100	-3.4	47.2	21.6	-9.6

Computed from Directorate General of Commercial Intelligence &Statistics (DGCI&S) data

Foreign Trade Policy (FTP) 2009-14:

1.76 To enhance the competitiveness of India's exports by supporting upgradation in technologies and diversification of the export markets, the Government announced the annual supplement to Foreign Trade Policy (FTP) on 05.06.2012. Special attention has also been given to the labour intensive sectors. Some important FTP measures are given in Box 1.3.

Box 1.3 :Annual Supplement to Foreign Trade Policy (2009-14): Some important Measures

- Two per cent Interest Subvention Scheme available to Handlooms, Handicrafts, Carpets and SMEs extended till 31st March 2013 and also extended to labour intensive sectors, namely, Toys, Sports Goods, Processed Agricultural Products and Ready-Made Garments.
- Zero Duty Export Promotion Capital Goods (EPCG) Scheme extended up to 31st March 2013 and its scope has been enlarged by making it available even if the benefit of Technology Upgradation Fund Scheme (TUFS) has been availedfor another line of business by the same applicant.
- Introduction of a new Post-Export EPCG Scheme with reduced transaction cost coupled with comparatively reduced export obligation.Exporters if they choose so may import Capital Goods on payment of duty in cash and subsequently receive duty credit scrip on completion of export obligation.
- Under the EPCG Scheme, non-applicability of the condition of maintenance of average level of exports has been extended toCarpet, Coir and Jute.
- To promote manufacturing activity and employment in the North Eastern Region of the country, export obligation under the EPCG Scheme has been fixed at 25 per cent of the normal export obligation.
- Export of specified products through notified Land Customs Stations of North Eastern Region shall be provided additional incentive to the extent of 1 per centof FOB value of exports. This benefit shall be in addition to any other benefit that may be available under Foreign Trade Policy in respect of these exports.
- To promote exports of 16 identified green technology products, export obligation for manufacturing of these products, under the EPCG Scheme, reduced to 75 per cent of the normal export obligation.
- Status holders exporting products under ITC (HS) Chapter 1 to Chapter 24 (both inclusive) are provided Duty Credit Scrip equivalent to 10 per cent of FOB value of agricultural products so exported. These scrips are issued for import of Capital Goods and equipment for Cold Storage Units, Pack-houses etc. These scrips will be eligible for import of 14 specified equipment for setting up of Pack-houses.
- Status holders are issued Status Holders Incentive Scrip (SHIS) to import Capital Goods for promoting investment in up-gradation of technology of some specified labour intensive sectors. Up to 10 per cent of the value of these scrips will be allowed to be utilized to import components and spares of capital goods imported earlier.
- Scrips under different schemes of Chapter 3 of Foreign Trade Policy are now allowed for payment of Excise Duty for domestic procurement.
- Algeria, Aruba, Austria, Cambodia, Myanmar, Netherland Antilles, and Ukraine have been added to Focus Market Scheme (FMS). The scheme now covers a total of 119 markets. Belize, Chile, El Salvador, Guatemala, Honduras, Morocco, and Uruguay were added to Special Focus Market Scheme (Special FMS).
- 46 new items are being added to Market Linked Focus Product Scheme (MLFPS). This would have the effect of including 12 new markets for the first time. MLFPS is being extended till 31st March 2013 for export to USA and EU in respect of items falling in Chapter 61 and Chapter 62 (textiles and clothing).
- 100 new items added to the Focus Product Scheme (FPS) list.

The Doha Round of Trade Negotiations in the WTO

1.77 The Doha Round effectively made little progress after 2008. At present, apart from Trade Facilitation, negotiations in other committees are not moving at all. On Trade Facilitation, developed countries are pressing for early conclusion in time for the Ninth Ministerial Conference of the WTO scheduled to be held in Bali, Indonesia in December 2013. Though Trade Facilitation includes export facilitation, which is of special interest to developing countries, most of the proposals under negotiation today in the area of trade facilitation are about import facilitation. Since most developing countries are not in a position to undertake major reforms (especially relating to exports infrastructure) because of resource constraints, they do not anticipate significant benefits.Benefits through effective additional market access, primarily provided by the developing countries, will accrue mainly to the developed countries and a few strong exporting developing countries and aggravate the already adverse balance of trade of many developing countries. Other areas being pushed by the developed countries are a plurilateral agreement in Services and a second Information Technology Agreement. They are also pushing for new "21st Century" issues to be brought onto the WTO agenda, namely, Investment, Competition, Government Procurement, Food Security, Energy Security, Environment, etc. India is working with other like-minded members towards a more balanced package for the Ninth Ministerial Conference of the WTO so that the development agenda of the Doha Round is not jeopardised.

Special Economic Zones (SEZs)

1.78 In a span of about six years since SEZs Act and Rules were notified in February, 2006, formal approvals have been granted for setting up of 585 SEZs out of which 385 have been notified. Out of the total employment provided to 9,45,990 persons in SEZs as a whole, 8,11,286 persons is the incremental employment generated after February, 2006 when the SEZ Act came into force. This is apart from the employment generated by the developers for infrastructure activities. A total of 160 SEZs are engaged in exports activity at present. Out of this 93 are IT/ITES, 17 multi-product and 50 other sector specific SEZs. There are a total of 3622 units set up in the SEZs. Physical exports from the SEZs has increased from ₹ 315,868 crore in 2010-11 to ₹ 364,478 crore in 2011-12, registering a growth of 15.0 per cent. The total exports from SEZs as on 30th September, 2012 i.e. in the first two quarters of the current financial year 2012-13, has been to the tune of ₹ 2,35,629 crore registering a growth of 36 per cent over the corresponding period of the previous year. The total investment in SEZs till 30th September, 2012 is around ₹ 2,18,795 crore, including ₹ 1,99,333 crore in the newly notified SEZs set up after SEZ Act, 2005.

Current Status of India's Free Trade Agreements (FTAs)

1.79 So far India has concluded 10 Free Trade Agreements (FTAs), 5 limited scope Preferential Trade Agreements (PTAs) and is in the process of negotiating / expanding 17 more Agreements. India's important trade engagements in 2012 are the following:

- India - EU Broad Based Trade and Investment Agreement (BTIA): Negotiations launched on 28th June 2007 in the areas of Goods, Services, Investment, Sanitary and Phyto-sanitary Measures (SPS), Technical Barriers to Trade (TBT), Trade Facilitation and Customs Cooperation, Competition, Intellectual Property Rights (IPR) & Geographical Indications (GIs) etc. Fourteen rounds of negotiations have been held till date with the 14th round being held in April, 2012 in New Delhi.
- India - ASEAN Comprehensive Economic Cooperation Agreement (CECA) - Services and Investment Agreement: 14 rounds of ASEAN-India Trade Negotiations Committee - Working Group on Services have been held so far with the last meeting on September 19-21, 2012 in New Delhi. 16 rounds of ASEAN-India Trade Negotiation Committee - Working Group on Investment (AITNC -WGI) have been held. The last meeting was held in Jakarta, Indonesia during 17 - 19 October, 2012.

- India - Thailand CECA: Under the Early Harvest Scheme (EHS), both sides finalized a list of 82 common items for gradual tariff elimination. Tariff was eliminated on these items by both sides, simultaneously, between 1st September 2004 and 31st August 2006. 26th round of India-Thailand Trade Negotiation Committee (ITTNC) was held on November 26-27, 2012 in New Delhi.
- India European Free Trade Association (EFTA) Broad-based Trade and Investment Agreement (BTIA) (Iceland, Norway, Liechtenstein and Switzerland): Negotiations cover areas of Trade in Goods, Trade in Services, Investment, SPS, TBT, Trade Remedies, Government Procurement, Customs Cooperation and Trade Facilitation, Dispute Settlement, Competition and Intellectual Property Rights. Eleventh round of negotiations was held during 5-7 March 2012 in New Delhi. Inter-sessional meetings on Goods, Services and IPRs issues were held during 27-29 August, 2012 in Delhi
- India - New Zealand FTA/CECA: Eighth round was held in June, 2012 in New Zealand.
- India - Israel FTA: Fifth round of negotiation was held during 14-16 August 2012 in New Delhi.
- India - Singapore CECA: Meeting on Second Review of India-Singapore CECA was held on 1-2 November, 2012 in New Delhi at the Chief Negotiator level.
- India - Chile PTA: The PTA was expanded by widening product coverage and deepening preferences. 5th meetings for expansion of the India-Chile PTA was held during 3-4 August, 2012.
- India - Canada Comprehensive Economic Partnership Agreement (CEPA): Sixth round of negotiations was held in November 2012.
- India - Australia: The inaugural round of negotiations was held in July, 2011. Third round of negotiation was held during 24 - 25 May 2012 in Australia and the fourth round was held during 8-9 November, 2012 in New Delhi.

Global Economy

1.80 The global economic climate continues to be fragile with the problem of fiscal cliff in US and uncertainties surrounding the Euro zone. The Euro zone is at particular risk due to worsening Greek debt crisis, fiscal and banking problems in Spain, social unrest in peripheral countries, slow progress in achieving banking union and difficulty in building political consensus on major issues.

1.81 While the Outright Monetary Transactions (OMT) announced by European Central Bank has provided a temporary reprieve, the risk on/ risk off behavior of investors continues to roil markets, contributing to heightened currency and stock market volatility. At the same time, record low interest rates in advanced countries and quantitative easing has contributed to "search-for-yield" behaviour similar to what prevailed immediately prior to the 2008 crisis. The slowdown in emerging economies like China, Brazil and India that grew strongly after the 2008 crisis, is adding to the global economic woes. The uncertain global climate has affected the Indian economy through a decline in exports, a fall in the value of rupee and a slowdown in investment. It has also led to a widening of the trade and current account deficits and an overall deceleration in the growth rate of the economy.

1.82 The IMF in its latest global economic assessment (World Economic Outlook October 2012) indicates the deterioration in the world economic environment and signs of increasing risks. Accordingly, global economy is estimated to grow 3.3 per cent in 2012 and 3.6 per cent in 2013 with advanced economies projected to grow by 1.3 per cent in 2012. Growth of emerging economies has been revised downward further by the IMF to 5.3 per cent in 2012. Leading emerging markets such as China and India are projected to show lower growth in 2012. India's GDP at market prices (2004-05 prices) is projected to grow to 4.9 per cent in 2012 and 6.0 per cent in 2013. China is projected to grow at 7.8 per cent in 2012 and 8.2 per cent in 2013. Growth in the volume of world trade is projected to slump to 3.2 per cent this year from 5.8 per cent in 2011 and 12.6 per cent in 2010 (Table 1.29).

Table 1.29: Global Economic prospects

Sl	Item	2010	2011	2012 P	2013 P
1	**World Output (per cent change) #**	**5.1**	**3.8**	**3.3**	**3.6**
a	Advanced Economies	3.0	1.6	1.3	1.5
b	Emerging Market & developing Countries	7.4	6.2	5.3	5.6
	China	10.4	9.2	7.8	8.2
	India	10.1	6.8	4.9	6.0
II	**Net Capital Flows to Emerging Market and Developing Countries (US$ billion)**				
i	Net Private Capital Flows (a+b+c)	604.7	503.0	268.3	399.6
	a) Net Private Direct Investment	392.0	462.4	393.8	409.0
	b) Net Private Portfolio Investment	240.8	129.7	133.0	150.9
	c) Net Other Private Capital Flows	-28.1	-89.1	-258.6	-1 60.2
ii	Net Official Flows	62.8	-108.3	-51.8	-89.2
III	**World Trade in Goods and Services @**				
i	Trade Volume	12.6	5.8	3.2	4.5
ii	Export Volume				
	a) Advanced Economies	12.0	5.3	2.2	3.6
	b) Emerging Market & developing Countries	13.7	6.5	4.0	5.7
IV	**Current Account Balance (Per cent to GDP)**				
i	US	-3.0	-3.1	-3.1	-3.1
ii	China	4.0	2.8	2.3	2.5
iii	India	-3.2	-3.4	-3.8	-3.3
iv	Middle East and North Africa	7.7	14.2	12.2	10.6

Source: World Economic Outlook, October 2012, International Monetary Fund (IMF)

Note : P – Projections, # growth rates are based on exchange rates at purchasing power parities, @ Average of annual percentage change for world exports and imports of goods and services.

BALANCE OF PAYMENTS

Balance of Payments development during 2011-12

1.83 India's balance of payment was under stress during the fiscal 2011-12, as trade and current account deficits widened. Though the capital inflows increased, they fell short of financing current account deficit, resulting in a reserve drawdown.Exports crossed the US$ 300 billion mark for the first time in 2011-12 and increased by 23.7 per cent to US$ 309.8 billion in 2011-12 from US$ 250.5 billion in 2010-11. The improvement has been accompanied by structural shift in the composition of export basket from labour intensive manufacture to higher value-added engineering and petroleum products as well diversification of exports destinations with developing countries becoming India's largest export market in recent years.Imports also recorded similar increase of 31.1 per cent to reach US$ 499.5 billion in 2011-12 from US$ 381.1 billion in 2010-11. Economic slowdown in advanced countries and its spill over effects in EMEs coupled with rising crude oil and gold prices were responsible for sharp increase in trade deficit. The trade deficit increased in absolute terms to US$ 189.8 billion (10.3 per cent of GDP) in 2011-12 as compared to US$ 130.6 billion (7.8 per cent of GDP) during 2010-11.

1.84 Net invisible balance showed significant improvement, registering a 31.9 per cent increase from US$ 84.6 billion in 2010-11 to US$ 111.6 billion during 2011-12, due to an increase in invisibles receipts while invisible payments declined. Net invisible balance as per cent of GDP improved to 6.0 per cent in 2011-12 from 4.9 per cent in 2010-11. The current account deficit (CAD) widened both in absolute terms as well as a proportion of GDP in 2011-12, reflecting widening trade deficit on account of subdued external demand, relatively inelastic imports of petroleum, oil and lubricant (POL) and higher imports of gold & silver. The CAD in 2011-12 at US$ 78.2 billion was 4.2 per cent of GDP as compared with US$ 45.9 billion, amounting to 2.7 per cent of GDP in 2010-11. Net capital inflows were higher at US$ 67.8 billion in 2011-12 as compared to US$ 62.0 billion in 2010-11, mainly due to higher FDI inflows and NRI deposits.

1.85 The net FDI (inward FDI minus outward FDI) was higher at US$ 22.1 billion in 2011-12 as compared with US$ 9.4 billion in 2010-11, due to higher inward FDI of US$ 33.0 in 2011-12 as against US$ 25.9 billion in 2010-11. As against this, Outward FDI decreased to US$ 10.9 billion in 2011-12 vis-a-vis US$ 16.5 billion in 2010-11. Portfolio investment witnessed marked decline in net inflow and was US$ 17.2 billion during 2011-12 as against of US$ 30.3 billion in 2010-11 due to decline in FII inflows to US$ 16.8 billion in 2011-12 from US$ 29.4 billion in 2010-11. Net external commercial borrowings (ECBs) inflows decreased to US$ 10.3 billion in 2011-12 as against US$ 12.5 billion in 2010-11. Similarly, short term trade credit decreased from US$ 11.0 billion in 2010-11 to US$ 6.7 billion in 2011-12. Further, external assistance decreased from US$ 4.9 billion in 2010-11 to US$ 2.3 billion in 2011-12. Banking capital, including NRI deposits, however, witnessed more than threefold increase to US$ 16.2 billion (inclusive of NRI deposits of US$ 11.9 billion) in 2011-12 as against US$ 5.0 billion (including NRI deposits of US$ 3.2 billion) in 2010-11.

1.86 The Capital Account Balance improved marginally by 9.4 per cent to US$ 67.8 billion during 2011-12 from the level of US$ 62.0 billion in 2010-11. However, as a per cent of GDP, it remained at the same level of 3.7 per cent in 2011-12 as it was in 2010-11.As the capital account surplus fell short of financing current account deficit, there was a drawdown of reserves(on BoP basis) to the extent of US$ 12.8 billion during 2011-12 as against an accretion of US$ 13.1 billion in 2010-11.

Balance of Payments development during first Quarter (April-June 2012) of 2012-13

1.87 During the first quarter of the fiscal 2012-13 (Q1 April -June 2012), exports at US$ 76.7 billion recorded a negative growth of 2.4 per cent over US$ 78.6 billion during Q1 of 2011-12, largely reflecting the impact of slowdown in global economy. Imports at US$ 119.2 billion registered a decline of 3.6 per cent over US$ 123.7 billion during Q1 of 2011-12. This was probably due to slowdown in domestic economic activity and weakening exports. There has also been a moderation in the POL imports. Gold and silver imports declined sharply by 48.6 per cent as against a growth of 123.1 per cent in the corresponding quarter of last year. Similarly, non-oil non-gold imports declined by about 2 per cent over the corresponding quarter of previous year. With sharper decline in imports than in exports growth, the trade deficit moderated to US$ 42.5 billion in Q1 of 2012-13 as compared with US$ 45.0 billion in Q1 of 2011-12.

1.88 Net invisible balance showed marginal deterioration, registering a decline of 5.8 per cent to US$ 25.9 billion during Q1 of 2012-13 from US$ 27.5 billion during Q1 of 2011-12. The decrease was mainly due to decline in services inflows to US$ 14.2 billion in Q1 of 2012-13 as compared to US$ 16.4 billion in Q1 of 2011-12. However, net software services at US$ 15.2 billion during Q1 of 2012-13 (US$ 14.6 billion in Q1 of 2011-12) and private transfers at US$ 16.8 billion in Q1 of 2012-13 (US$ 14.8 billion in Q1 of 2011-12) remained buoyant. The Current Account Deficit (CAD) at US$ 16.6 billion was marginally lower in Q1 of 2012-13 as compared to US$ 17.5 billion during the corresponding quarter of 2011-12,

1.89 Higher level of vulnerability in global financial markets owing to the Eurozone crisis and subdued domestic economic activity continued to impact capital flows to India in Q1 of 2012-13.

1.90 Net capital flows were lower at US$ 17.0 billion in Q1 (April- June 2012) of 2012-13 as compared to US$ 23.9 billion during the corresponding period last year. The net FDI in Q1 (inward FDI minus outward FDI) was significantly lower at US$ 4.2 billion in April-June 2012 as compared with US$ 9.3 billion in April-June 2011, due to lower inward FDI in 2012-13. Portfolio investment witnessed negative flow of US$ 1.9 billion in Q1 of 2012-13 vis-a-vis inflow of US$ 2.5 billion in Q1 of 2011-12. There was a significant reduction in net external commercial borrowings (ECBs) to US$ 1.0 billion in April-June 2012 as against US$ 3.1 billion in April-June 2011. Similarly banking capital inflow declined from US$ 12.7 billion in Q1 of 2011-12 to US$ 9.4 billion in Q1 of 2012-13. However, short term trade credit increased from US$ 3.1 billion in April-June 2011 to US$ 5.4 billion in April-June 2012.

1.91 As a result, the Capital Account Balance has declined from US$ 23.9 billion during Q1 of 2011-12 to US$ 17.0 billion during 2012-13. India's Balance of Payments developments during 2010-11 to 2012-13 (up to Q1 of 2012) are indicated below (Table 1.30):

Table 1.30: Major Items of India's Balance of Payments during Q1 of 2011-12 and 2012-13

(US$ billion)

Sl	Items	2010-11 (PR)	2011-12 (P)	2011-12 (PR)	2012-13 (P)
		Full Year	Full Year	Q1 (April-June)	Q1 (April-June)
1	Exports	250.5	309.8	78.6	76.7
2	Imports	381.1	499.5	123.7	119.2
3	Trade Balance	-130.6	-189.8	-45.0	-42.5
4	Net Invisibles	84.6	111.6	27.5	25.9
5	Goods & Services Balance	-81.8	-125.7	-28.6	-28.3
6	**Current Account Balance**	**-45.9**	**-78.2**	**-17.5**	**-16.6**
7	External assistance (Net)	4.9	2.3	0.3	-0.2
8	Commercial Borrowings (Net)	12.5	10.3	3.1	1.0
9	FDI (Net)	9.4	22.1	9.3	4.2
10	Portfolio	30.3	17.2	2.5	-1.9
11	**Capital Account Balance**	**62.2**	**67.8**	**23.9**	**17.0**
12	Errors & Omissions	-3.0	-2.4	-0.9	0.1
13	Overall Balance	13.1	-12.8	5.4	0.5
14	Change in Reserves (- indicates increase; + indicates decrease) (on BOP Basis)	-13.1	12.8	-5.4	-0.5
	Memo Items/Assumptions				
1	Trade Balance/GDP (per cent)	-7.8	-10.3		
2	Goods & Services Balance / GDP (per cent)	-4.9	-6.8		
3	Invisibles / GDP (per cent)	4.9	6.0		
4	**Current Account Balance/GDP (per cent)**	**-2.7**	**-4.2**		
5	**Net Capital Flows / GDP (per cent)**	**3.7**	**3.7**		

Note: Total may not tally due to rounding off. PR: Partially Revised. P: Preliminary.
Source : RBI.

1.92 As per the latest available information on capital inflows, net FDI inflows were US$12.8 billion during April-September 2012 as compared to US$ 15.4 billion in the corresponding period of 2011-12. FII inflows increased to US$ 6.2 billion during April-September 2012 from US$ 0.9 billion in April-September 2011. ECB approvals stood at US$14.3 billion during April-September 2012 vis-à-vis US$ 18.2 billion a year earlier, NRI deposits amounted to US$ 8.9 billion during April-September 2012 vis-à-vis US$ 3.9 billion during the same period in 2011-12.

Foreign Exchange Reserves

1.93 The foreign exchange reserves stood at US$ 304.8 billion at end March 2011. In the fiscal 2011-12, foreign exchange reserves reached a high of US$ 322.0 billion at end August 2011. However, it declined thereafter and stood at US$ 294.4 billion at end March 2012. In the current fiscal 2012-13, the foreign exchange reserves declined by US$ 4.7 billion to US$ 289.7 billion during the first quarter. At the end of the second quarter (end September 2012), it stood at US$ 294.8 billion. At end October 2012, it stood at US$ 295.3 billion. Country-wise details of foreign exchange reserves reveal that India continues to be one of the largest holders of foreign exchange reserves. India is the seventh largest foreign exchange reserves holder in the world, after China, Japan, Russia, Switzerland,Brazil and China P R Hong Kong (Table1.31) at end September 2012.

Exchange Rate

1.94 The movement of exchange rate in 2011-12 indicates that the average monthly exchange rate of rupee against the US dollar depreciated by 10.6 per cent from ₹ 44.97 per US dollar in March 2011 to ₹ 50.32 per US dollar in March 2012. Similarly, on point-to-point basis, the average exchange rate of rupee (average of buying and selling rate of FEDAI) depreciated by 12.7 per cent from ₹ 44.65 per US dollar on 31 March 2011 to ₹51.16 per US dollar on March 30, 2012.

1.95 In order to reduce the volatility of exchange rate value of the rupee, the RBI had intervened in the foreign exchange market through sale of US dollars amounting to US$ 20.1 billion in 2011-12 Further, in view of the sharp depreciation of the rupee in the later part of 2011, the RBI announced various policy measures that were aimed at curbing speculative behaviour of banks and corporate in the foreign exchange market. A number of steps were also taken to facilitate capital flows and boost exports to augment supply of foreign exchange.

1.96 During the first quarter of current fiscal 2012-13, monthly average exchange rate of rupee again showed a depreciating trend. It has depreciated by 2.9 per cent in April 2012, 4.9 per cent in May and 2.8 per cent in June 2012 over the previous month. In the month of June 2012, the rupee touched a low of ₹ 57.22 per US dollar (RBI's reference rate) on June 27, 2012 indicating 10.6 per cent depreciation over ₹51.16 per US dollar on March 30, 2012.

Table 1.31 : Foreign exchange reserves of some major countries

(US$ billion)

Sl	Country	Foreign exchange reserves at end September, 2012
1	China	3285.0
2	Japan	1277.0
3	Russia	529.9
4	Switzerland	525.0
5	Brazil	378.7
6	China P R Hong Kong (August 2012)	298.2
7	India	294.8
8	Germany	262.9
9	France	190.3
10	Thailand	183.6

Source: IMF except for China. In additional foreign exchange reserves of Taiwan are shown at US$ 391.2 billion (Q2) as per The Economist November 1st , 2012

Table 1.32: Exchange rates of Rupee per foreign currency and RBI's Sale / Purchase of US dollar in the Foreign Exchange Market*

Month	US Dollar	Pound Sterling	Euro	Japanese Yen**	RBI Net Sale (-) / Purchase (+) (US$ million)
2011-12 (annual average)	47.9229	76.3912	65.8939	60.7484	- 20,138
	(-4.9)	(-7.2)	(-8.6)	(-12.3)	
March 2012	50.3213	79.6549	66.5307	61.0259	-
	(-2.3)	(-2.5)	(-2.1)	(2.8)	
2012-13(monthly average)					
April 2012	51.8029	82.9414	68.1617	63.8139	-275
	(-2.9)	(-4.0)	(-2.4)	(-4.4)	
May 2012	54.4735	86.7202	69.6991	68.3286	-485
	(-4.9)	(-4.4)	(-2.2)	(-6.6)	
June 2012	56.0302	87.1349	70.3087	70.6743	-50
	(-2.8)	(-0.5)	(-0.9)	(-3.3)	
July 2012	55.4948	86.5173	68.2520	70.2809	-785
	(1.0)	(0.7)	(3.0)	(0.6)	
August 2012	55.5598	87.2492	68.8750	70.6814	-452
	(-0.1)	(-0.8)	(-0.9)	(-0.6)	
September 2012	54.6055	87.8663	70.1263	69.9084	-10
	(1.7)	(-0.7)	(-1.8)	(1.1)	

* Data upto April 2012 and based on FEDAI indicative Market Rates. Data from May 2012 onwards are based on RBI's reference rates. **Per 100 Yen

Figures in parentheses indicate appreciation (+) and depreciation (-) over the previous month/year in per cent. Some per centage figures may not tally due to rounding off.

Source: RBI

1.97 The decline in rupee indicated among others, supply-demand imbalance in the domestic foreign exchange market due to widening trade and current account deficit and slowdown in FII inflows. The depreciation could also be partly explained by the strengthening of US dollar in the international market and the decline of euro due to unfolding euro zone crisis. Apart from the global factors, there are several domestic factors which have added to the weakening trend of the rupee that included continued high inflation. In the second quarter of 2012-13, the monthly average exchange rate of rupee has appreciated by 1.0 per cent in July 2012 and 1.7 per cent in September over the previous month, while in the month of August it has marginally depreciated by 0.1 per cent (Table 1.32).

1.98 The domestic policy measures for attracting FDI, coupled with the announcement of quantitative easing by the US Federal Reserve and Bank of Japan in September 2012 contributed to an increase in capital inflows to India leading to a strengthening of the rupee. Besides, the Reserve Bank sold nearly US$ 2.1 billion during 2012-13 (April-September 2012). As a result, the rupee recovered to ₹51.62 per US dollar on October 05, 2012. The rupee however, has weakened again since October 08, 2012 due to demand for dollars from oil importing firms and pressure on the trade account.

1.99 It may be noted that the depreciation of the exchange rate in 2012-13 is not specific to India. Most of the emerging market currencies have depreciated due to the uncertain global economic environment. The extent of depreciation for rupee (5.6 per cent) between March 2012 and October 2012 is lower than that of the currencies of major EMEs like South Africa's Rand (11.1 per cent), Brazilian Real (9.8 per cent) and Russian Rouble (6.5 per cent), reflecting the favourable impact of recent policy measures on capital inflows.The 6-currency trade-based REER (base: 2004-05=100) of the Rupee depreciated by 5.5 per cent from 115.97 to 109.59 between March 2011 and March 2012. During 2012-13 so far (up to September 2012), the 6 currency index of 104.24 showed depreciation of 5.6 per cent over the March 2012 index of 109.59 largely reflecting depreciation of rupee in nominal terms (Table1.33).

Table 1.33: Indices of REER and NEER of Indian Rupee (6-Currency Trade Based Weights) Base 2004-05 (April-March)=100				
Monthly	NEER	Appreciation(+) / Depreciation(-) in NEER over previous period / month (per cent)	REER	Appreciation(+)/ Depreciation(-) in NEER over previous period / month (per cent)
March 2011	90.29		115.97	
March 2012	81.60	-9.6	109.59	-5.5
2012-13				
April 2012	79.24	-2.9	107.57	-1.8
May 2012	76.10	-4.0	104.12	-3.2
June 2012	74.67	-1.9	102.24	-1.8
July 2012	75.95	1.7	103.85	1.6
August 2012	75.53	-0.6	104.33	0.5
September 2012	75.67	0.2	104.24	-0.1
Source: Reserve Bank of India.				

External Debt

1.100 India's external debt continues to remain within manageable limits as indicated by the external debt to GDP ratio of 20.0 per cent and debt service ratio of 6.0 per cent during 2011-12. As per the latest data available, India's external debt stood at US$ 349.5 billion at end-June 2012, recording an increase of US$ 3.9 billion (1.1 per cent) over an estimate of US$ 345.6 billion at end-March 2012. The increase in total external debt during the quarter was primarily on account of the rise in NRI deposits and short-term trade credit. The long-term debt increased by US$ 1.6 billion (0.6 per cent) to US$ 269.1 billion, while short-term debt showed an increase of US$ 2.3 billion (2.9 per cent) to US$ 80.4 billion. The long-term debt accounted for 77.0 per cent of total external debt at end-June 2012, while the remaining was short-term debt. The share of Government (Sovereign) external debt in total external debt was 23.0 per cent, while the share of non-Government debt in total external debt was 77.0 at end-June 2012. The share of concessional debt in total external debt stood at 13.5 per cent at end-June 2012 vis-a-vis 13.8 per cent at end-March 2012. The ratio of short-term debt to foreign exchange reserve at 27.8 per cent at end-June 2012 was higher compared to 26.6 per cent at end-March 2012.

1.101 India's key debt indicators compare well with other indebted developing countries. According to the latest Global Development Finance, 2012 of the World Bank, which contains external debt numbers for 2010, India's position was fifth in terms of absolute debt stock among top twenty developing indebted countries in 2010, after China, Russian Federation, Brazil and Turkey, In terms of ratio of external debt to Gross National Income, India's position was the fifth lowest. The share of concessional credit in India's external debt portfolio was the fourth highest after Pakistan, Indonesia and the Philippines. In terms of cover provided by foreign exchange reserves to debt, India's position was the fifth highest after China, Thailand, Malaysia and Russian Federation among the top twenty developing debtor countries.

1.102 The active external debt management policy of the Government of India has helped in containing the growth of accumulation of external debt and maintaining a comfortable external debt position. It continues to focus on monitoring long and short-term debt, raising sovereign loans on concessional terms with longer maturities, regulating external commercial borrowings through end-use and all-in-cost restrictions, rationalizing interest rates on Non-Resident Indian deposits. As a consequence of this, key external debt indicators remained at comfortable levels (Table 1.34).

Table 1.34: India's Key External Debt Indicators (Per cent)

At end March	External Debt (US$ billion)	External Debt to GDP	Debt Service Ratio	Foreign Exchange Reserves to Total External Debt	Concessional Debt to Total External Debt	Short-Term to Foreign Exchange Reserves	Short-Term to Total External Debt
2005-06	139.1	16.8	10.1[a]	109.0	28.4	12.9	14.0
2006-07	172.4	17.5	4.7	115.6	23.0	14.1	16.3
2007-08	224.4	18.0	4.8	138.0	19.7	14.8	20.4
2008-09	224.5	20.3	4.4	112.1	18.7	17.2	19.3
2009-10	260.9	18.3	5.8	106.8	16.8	18.8	20.0
2010-11	305.9	17.8	4.3	99.6	15.5	21.3	21.2
2011-12 PR	345.7	20.0	6.0	85.1	13.8	26.6	22.6
End-June 2012 QE	349.5	-	5.9	82.9	13.5	27.8	23.0

PR: Partially Revised; QE: Quick Estimates.

a: Works out to 6.3 per cent, excluding India Millennium Deposit repayments of US$ 7.1 billion and pre-payment of US$ 23.5 million.

SOCIAL SECTOR: DEVELOPMENTS AND PERFORMANCE OF PROGRAMMES

Falling unemployment

1.103 As stated in the Mid-Year Analysis 2011-12, a comparison of the different unemployment rates like Usual Principal Status (UPS), Usual Status (US), Current Weekly Status (CWS) and Current Daily Status (CDS) as per the 61st round (2004-05) and 66th round (2009-10) of the NSSO Surveys show that there is a fall in unemployment rate in 2009-10 over 2004-2005. Total unemployment rates have fallen from 3.1 per cent to 2.5 per cent (UPS), 2.3 per cent to 2.0 per cent (US), 4.4 percent to 3.6 per cent (CWS) and 8.2 percent to 6.6 percent (CDS). Quarterly quick employment surveys are being conducted by the Labour Bureau since January 2009 for selected sectors. Comparing the results of the last four quarterly surveys (i.e. July, 2011 to June, 2012), overall employment increased by 6.94 lakh in June, 2012 over July, 2011, for the selected sectors with the highest increase of 4.44 lakh in IT/BPO followed by 1.70 lakh in textiles, 0.45 lakh in transport, 0.26 lakh in metals, 0.19 lakh in gems & jewellery and 0.11 lakh in automobiles.

Performance of Programmes

Developmental schemes are proceeding apace

1.104 The progress under major programmes of the Government of India is as under:

- *Mahatma Gandhi National Rural Employment Guarantee Act (MGNREGA):* This scheme has been provided a sum of ₹ 33,000 crore in the Budget 2012-13. During 2012-13 (up to September, 2012) the expenditure incurred by the States/UTs is ₹ 18,148.6 crore, which accounts for 55 per cent of allocated funds and 3.55 crore households have been provided employment during the period. The share of SCs, STs and Women is 23 percent, 15 percent and 54 per cent respectively. The share of women in total persondays generated is well above the stipulation of 1/3 as per the Act.

- *PradhanMantri Gram SadakYojana (PMGSY):* During the current financial year, PMGSY has been allocated a sum of ₹ 24,000 crore for connecting 4,000 habitations and construction of 30,000 KM of roads. Up to September, 2012 connectivity has been provided to 3,155 habitations; 9,256.41 KM length road has been constructed and a total of ₹ 4,260 crore has been released. Since inception of PMGSY 87,567 habitations (73 per cent of the cleared habitations) have been provided with all-weather road connectivity (till August, 2012); 216,635 kms of roads have been constructed for new connectivity and 1,43,123 kms of roads have been upgraded by the States.

- *Indira AwaasYojana (IAY):* During the current financial year, ₹ 11,075 crore has been allocated for rural housing, out of which ₹ 10,513.2 crore were earmarked for release to District Rural Development Agencies under IAY for construction of 30.10 lakh houses. Till September, 2012 ₹ 4,930.32 crore have been released and 7.67 lakh houses have been constructed which is 25.48 per cent of the target.
- *Swarnajayanti Gram SwarozgarYojana (SGSY)/ National Rural Livelihoods Mission (NRLM):* SGSY/NRLM is a self-employment programme which aims at linking bank credit to income generation. Central allocation of SGSY/ NRLM is ₹ 3,915 crore during the financial year 2012-13. Central subsidy for the States and UTs is ₹ 2,196.7 crore. The central release under SGSY & NRLM amounts to ₹ 384.0 crore and ₹ 623.6 crore respectively. Out of the total number of assisted Swarozgaries of 127 lakh, 96 lakh Swarozgaries have been covered under Self-Help Groups (SHGs) and 31 lakh are individually assisted Swarozgaries. The per centage coverage of SCs, STs, Minorities, Women and Physically Challenged is 30.0 percent, 12.6 percent, 9.7 percent, 54.6 percent, and 0.8 percent respectively.
- *National Rural Health Mission (NRHM):*During 2012-13, the budget outlay of the Central Government for health sector has increased to ₹ 34,488 crore with a step up of 13.1 per cent. During 2012-13, the activities of ASHA (Accredited Social Health Activist) under NRHM, is sought to be enlarged to include prevention of Iodine Deficiency Disorder (IDD), ensure 100 per cent immunization and better spacing of children, more active role for ASHA as convener of the Village Health and Sanitation Committee as also to support the initiative on malnutrition. States have also been supported under NRHM to provide free emergency and patient transport services through basic and advanced level ambulances in every nook and corner of the country. More than 15,000 ambulances are integrated all over the country under the network. An amount of ₹ 20,542 crore has been earmarked for programmes/ schemes under NRHM.
- *JananiShishuSurakshaKaryakaram (JSSK):* As an initiative in the direction of universal healthcare, JSSK was introduced in 2011, which entitles all pregnant women deliveries in public health institutions to be absolutely free, even for caesarean cases. The initiative stipulates free drugs, diagnostics, blood and diet, besides free transport from home to institution and between facilities in case of a referral and drop back home. An amount of ₹ 1,301.6 crore has been provided to the States in the current financial year for free drugs. Further, States have been provided with financial assistance for operating Mobile Medical Units (MMUs) with the objective to take health care to door steps of people in the underserved rural and tribal areas. So far 2,013 vehicles are operational as MMUs in 464 districts across the country.
- *Pradhan Mantri Swasthya Suraksha Yojana (PMSSY):* This is being expanded during the year to cover upgradation of more Government Medical Colleges to enhance the availability of affordable tertiary health care services and quality medical

education. An amount of ₹ 1,544.2 crore has been budgeted for PMSSY, during 2012-13. Various initiatives have been taken to reform Medical Education, which inter-alia include relaxation of land requirement, bed strength and bed-occupancy, increase in maximum intake, opening of Medical Colleges. The numbers of MBBS seats have increased by 36 per cent while the number of PG seats has increased by 60 per cent, in last four years. 26 new Medical Colleges have started in 2012-13 including 6 AIIMS like Institutions which commenced functioning in September 2012, with intake of 50 students each. In order to strengthen the Nursing sector, 176 districts have already been supported for establishment of Auxiliary Nurse Midwife (ANM) Schools and General Nursing & Midwifery (GNM) Schools.

- *RashtriyaSwasthyaBimaYojana (RSBY):* Under RSBY over 3.25 crore smart cards have been issued till September, 2012. The scheme has now been extended to construction workers, street vendors, railway porters & vendors, MGNREGA workers who have worked for more than fifteen days during the preceding year, domestic workers and beedi workers. Government is contemplating to extend the benefit of the Scheme to other occupational groups in the unorganized sector in a phased manner.
- *Rajiv Gandhi National Rural Drinking Water Mission:* National Rural Drinking Water Programme (NRDWP) which aims to ensure drinking water supply for all households in rural India, has a plan outlay of ₹ 10,500 crore for 2012-13 out of which ₹ 4,289.83 crore has been released till September, 2012 and 27,273 partially covered and 4,036 quality affected habitations have been covered against the target of 75,000 for partially covered and 25,000 quality affected habitations respectively for the year as a whole.

1.105 Some important programmes in the education sector viz. the Sarva Shiksha Abhiyan (SSA) supported by the Mid-Day Meal Scheme (MDMS), intend to ensure provision of elementary education to all children in the 6-14 age group. Under the MDMS, 10.64 crore children are provided hot cooked meal in 12.31 lakh schools in the country. During 2011-12, 11.86 lakh schools have been provided with kitchen devices and 24.70 lakh cook-cum-helper have been appointed by the State to prepare and serve the mid-day meals to the school children. 5.72 lakh kitchen-cum-stores have been constructed to ensure safety of foodgrains and provisioning of hygienic and nutritious meals to the children. An intensive programme for providing health care to the school children has been undertaken in collaboration with the National Rural Health Mission (NRHM). A sum of ₹ 11,937 crore has been earmarked for the programme in the current financial year. The Government revised the MDMS in 2009-10 to incorporate upward revision of food norm for upper primary children, enhancement of cooking cost for supply of pulses, vegetables, oils, salt & condiments and fuel, separate provision of honorarium of ₹ 1,000 per month to each cook-cum-helper etc. The web enabled Management Information System (MIS) for MDMS has also been launched in July, 2012. The MIS will integrate with Intractive Voice Responsive System (IVRS) to monitor the scheme on real time basis.

1.106 The Right of Children to Free and Compulsory Education (Amendment) Act, 2012 inter-alia provides inclusion of children with disability as stipulated in the Persons with Disabilities (PWD)Act 2005 and the National Trust Act under the purview of RTE Act and provide them free and compulsory education. Option of home based education has also been provided for the children with severe disability. The rights of minorities as provided to them under Article 29 and 30 of the Constitution are protected, educational institutions imparting religious instruction are exempted from the provisions of the RTE Act and School Management Committees constituted under the Act by aided institutions shall perform advisory function, and shall not be required to prepare a School Development Plan.

1.107 A National Vocational Education Qualification Framework for establishing a system of clear education pathways from school through higher education for vocational education stream has been developed and will be implemented in close partnership with the industry/ potential employer so as to enhance the employability of the youth. The Centrally Sponsored Scheme of "Vocationalisation of Higher Secondary Education" was approved by the government on 15th September, 2011. 100 new schools were provided under the revised scheme for the financial year 2011-2012. Of these, 40 schools are being set up in Haryana and 60 in Assam.

1.108 Universalization of Secondary Education is the other important goal in view of the fact that there is an increase in the number of students moving upward from elementary education to secondary level. The goal of universal access by 2017 and universal retention by 2020 is to be achieved through the Rashtriya Madhyamik Shiksha Abhiyan (RMSA). RMSA has been operational from 2009-10. Since inception of the scheme, opening of 9,636 new schools, strengthening of 34,311 existing secondary schools, 40,018 teachers in existing secondary schools and 55,974 teachers for new secondary schools have been sanctioned.

1.109 Saakshar Bharat (SB) is the new variant of the programme format of National Literacy Mission. The principal target of the Mission is to impart, by 2012, functional literacy to 70 million adults in the age group of 15 years and above. Auxiliary target of the mission is to cover 1.5 million adults under Basic Education (Equivalency) programme and equal number under Vocational Training (skill development) programme. The total of 372 districts in 25 States and one in U.T have been covered by the end of September, 2012.

1.110 Higher Education plays a vital role in overall economic development and to have a just and equitable society and a vibrant political system. Government has set a target of increasing the Gross Enrolment Ratio (GER) to 30 per cent by the year 2020. Further, Government has taken several legislative initiatives of which the most important is the establishment of an overarching regulatory body, the National Commission for Higher Education and Research (NCHER) to cover all areas/disciplines of learning; setting up of Educational Tribunals to adjudicate on disputes among stake-holders within institutions and between the institutions; making mandatory accreditation system to ensure quality of higher educational institutions and programmes; creation of a National Accreditation Regulatory Authority and creation of a national electronic database of academic awards through the Academic Depository Bill. To have an inclusive higher education system, the Government launched 89 Virtual labs for quality enhancement so that the learner in distance education system and remotely located & backward areas can reap the benefit of quality and relevant education, through ICT mode. To strengthen comprehensively all issues related to teacher, teaching, teacher preparation and professional development, Government has planned to launch National Mission on Teacher and Teaching which is one of the major thrust areas of action during the 12th Five Year Plan. The scheme of Community College has been initiated in 200 colleges on pilot basis from existing colleges / polytechnics so that they become operational from the academic session 2013.

1.111 The Unique Identification Authority of India (UIDAI) is expected to bring in efficiency in service delivery mechanism and reducing corruption, leakage and wastefulness in it. A total of 22.7 crore enrolment packets have been uploaded into the system out of which 20.6 crore Aadhaar numbers have been generated as on 30th September 2012. The innovative technology embedded in Aaadhar Platform together with the spread of modern banking system will make it possible the direct cash transfer of subsidies and in ensuring that these reach the targeted beneficiaries. Ambitious timelines have been set for a phased use of this platform with 51 districts to be covered by January, 2013, 18 States by April, 2013 and the rest of the country later in 2013.

CHAPTER II

CENTRAL GOVERNMENT FINANCES

REVIEW OF TRENDS IN RECEIPTS AND EXPENDITURE DURING APRIL-SEPTEMBER 2012

2.1 The Budget for 2012-13 was presented against the backdrop of growth slowdown and rising prices that owed to a mix of domestic and global factors. The Budget for 2012-13 estimated fiscal deficit at ₹ 5,13,590 crore (5.1 per cent of estimated GDP for the year) and a revenue deficit of ₹ 3,50,424 crore (3.4 per cent of GDP). The total fiscal deficit upto September, 2012 is ₹ 3,36,904 crore. Revenue deficit upto September, 2012 is ₹ 2,63,284 crore. The total non-debt receipts upto September, 2012 is ₹ 3,57,115 crore where as the total expenditure was ₹ 6,94,019 crore.

2.2 The reduction in fiscal deficit from a level of 5.9 per cent of GDP in RE 2011-12 to 5.1 per cent of GDP in BE 2012-13 was designed with a mix of reduction in total expenditure as percentage of GDP and improvement in gross tax revenue as percentage of GDP. The revenue deficit estimated for the year 2012-13 is also lower than the revenue deficit of 4.3 per cent for the financial year 2011-12. The 'effective revenue deficit', which represents imbalance in revenue account after netting grants used for creation of capital assets has been estimated at 1.8 per cent of GDP in BE 2012-13. Going forward, it would be the endeavor of the Government to eliminate this imbalance in revenue account by 2014-15 as per the Medium Term Fiscal Policy Statement 2012-13.

2.3 The fiscal policy of 2012-13 was calibrated with two fold objectives – first, to aid the economy in growth revival; and second, to bring down the deficit from 2011-12 level so as to leave space for private sector credit as the investment cycle picks up. Being the first year of the 12th Five Year Plan, an ambitious plan outlay which is 22.1 per cent higher than RE 2011-12 has been provided. Even with higher increase in plan allocation, fiscal deficit is estimated to be reduced with appropriate policy measures. It is estimated that non-plan expenditure could be controlled with a growth of 8.7 per cent in BE 2012-13 over RE 2011-12. This would result in overall expenditure increase of 13.1 per cent in BE 2012-13 over RE 2011-12. Thus the bulk of the correction in fiscal deficit has been targeted though revenue augmentation.

2.4 With the macroeconomic performance continuing to be at lower levels, the fiscal outcome in the first half of the financial year was affected. The FRBM Mid-Year benchmarks of a minimum attainment of 40 per cent of BE in terms of non-debt receipts and maximum of 45 per cent of BE in terms of both revenue and fiscal deficits could not be realised in the current financial year.

2.5 Trends in receipts and expenditure at the end of the second quarter of year 2012-13 (April-September, 2012) are summarized in Table 2.1. The figures therein are unaudited and may undergo revision subsequent to audit. The receipts and recoveries, wherever directly linked to expenditure, have been netted out.

Table 2.1- Budgetary Position April-September

	Particulars	(₹ crore)			(Percentage)		
		B.E.	Actuals up to Sept.		Percentage to BE		5 years moving average
		2012-13	2012-13	2011-12	Upto 09/2012	COPPY	
1	**Revenue Receipts**	**935685**	**350888**	**305528**	**37.5**	**38.7**	**43.6**
2	Tax Revenue (Net)	771071	293812	254731	38.1	38.3	40.2
3	Non-Tax Revenue	164614	57076	50797	34.7	40.5	56.7
4	**Capital Receipts (5+6+7)**	**555241**	**343131**	**293565**	**61.8**	**62.7**	**55.6**
	Non Debt Capital Receipts	**41650**	**6227**	**12755**	**15.0**	**23.2**	**52.3**
5	Recovery of Loans	11650	4855	10024	41.7	66.7	74.5
6	Other Receipts	30000	1372	2731	4.6	6.8	97.0
7	**Borrowings and other liabilities**	**513590**	**336904**	**280810**	**65.6**	**68.0**	**56.6**
8	**Total Receipts (1+4)**	**1490925**	**694019**	**599093**	**46.5**	**47.6**	**46.7**
9	**Non-Plan Expenditure**	**969900**	**491279**	**421270**	**50.7**	**51.6**	**48.8**
10	On Revenue Account	865596	446673	376275	51.6	51.3	50.2
11	*of which* Interest payments	319759	131165	122499	41.0	45.7	43.3
12	On Capital Account	104304	44606	44995	42.8	54.5	38.2
13	**Plan Expenditure**	**521025**	**202740**	**177823**	**38.9**	**40.3**	**42.3**
14	On Revenue Account	420513	167499	151033	39.8	41.5	42.4
15	On Capital Account	100512	35241	26790	35.1	34.4	42.1
16	**Total Expenditure (9+13)**	**1490925**	**694019**	**599093**	**46.5**	**47.6**	**46.7**
17	Revenue Expenditure (10+14)	1286109	614172	527308	47.8	48.1	47.7
18	Of which Grants for creation of Capital Assets	164672	50656	51411	30.8	35.0	--
19	Capital Expenditure (12+15)	204816	79847	71785	39.0	44.7	39.1
20	**Revenue Deficit** (17-1)	**350424**	**263284**	**221780**	**75.1**	**72.2**	**77.0**
21	**Effective Revenue Deficit # (20-18)**	**185752**	**212628**	**170369**	**114.5**	**106.2**	**--**
22	**Fiscal Deficit {16 – (1+5+6)}**	**513590**	**336904**	**280810**	**65.6**	**68.0**	**56.6**
23	**Primary Deficit (22 – 11)**	**193831**	**205739**	**158311**	**106.1**	**109.3**	**12.5**

Notes: 1. The figures of Railways have been netted as in Budget Estimates.

2. COPPY – Corresponding Period of Previous Year.

3. # Excluding Grants for creation of Capital Assets

RECEIPTS

Revenue Receipts

2.6 Revenue receipts consist of net tax revenue and non-tax revenue. Revenue receipts were estimated at ₹ 9,35,685 crore in BE 2012-13 reflecting a growth of 23.7 per cent over provisional actuals of 2011-12. Revenue receipts at ₹ 3,50,888 crore during first half of 2012-13 are 37.5 per cent of B.E. 2012-13 (Table 2.2 and Fig 2.1). This is lower than the five year average of 43.6 per cent of respective BE. The growth in total revenue receipts during the first half of 2012-13 is 14.8 per cent over

Table 2.2-Revenue receipts in April-September

(₹ crore)

Sl. No.	REVENUE RECEIPTS	April - September 2007-08	2008-09	2009-10	2010-11	2011-12	2012-13
1	Tax Revenue (Net)	160500	202247	185669	233415	254731	293812
2	Non-Tax Revenue	37456	42651	58802	164819	50797	57076
3	Total Revenue Receipts (TRR)	197956	244898	244471	398234	305528	350888
4	BE for the full year	486422	602935	614497	682212	789892	935685
5	Realised revenue as per cent to BE	40.7	40.6	39.8	58.4	38.7	37.5
6	Rate of Growth of TRR (per cent)	22.6	23.7	-0.2	62.9	-23.3	14.8

the corresponding period in 2011-12. Growth in gross tax revenue in BE 2012-13 was estimated at 21.0 per cent over the actual receipts of 2011-12 (provisional). However, the performance during first half is not in line with BE due to continued economic slowdown affecting revenues.

Gross Tax Revenue

2.7 During the first half of 2012-13 direct tax refunds were ₹46,012 crore as against ₹62,230 crore during the corresponding period of 2011-12 (Table 2.3). The overall growth in gross tax revenue in April-September 2012 has been 15 per cent over last year's actuals of the same period. As percentage of BE, gross tax revenue till September is almost the same level as last year. Trends in year on year growth for different quarters in collection of gross taxes for 2010-11, 2011-12 and 2012-13 is shown in Fig 2.2.

Direct Taxes

2.8 The gross direct tax collection (net of refunds) increased by 16.0 per cent amounting to a sum of ₹ 2,28,072 crore for April-

Fig 2.1: Net Tax Revenue and its rate of growth

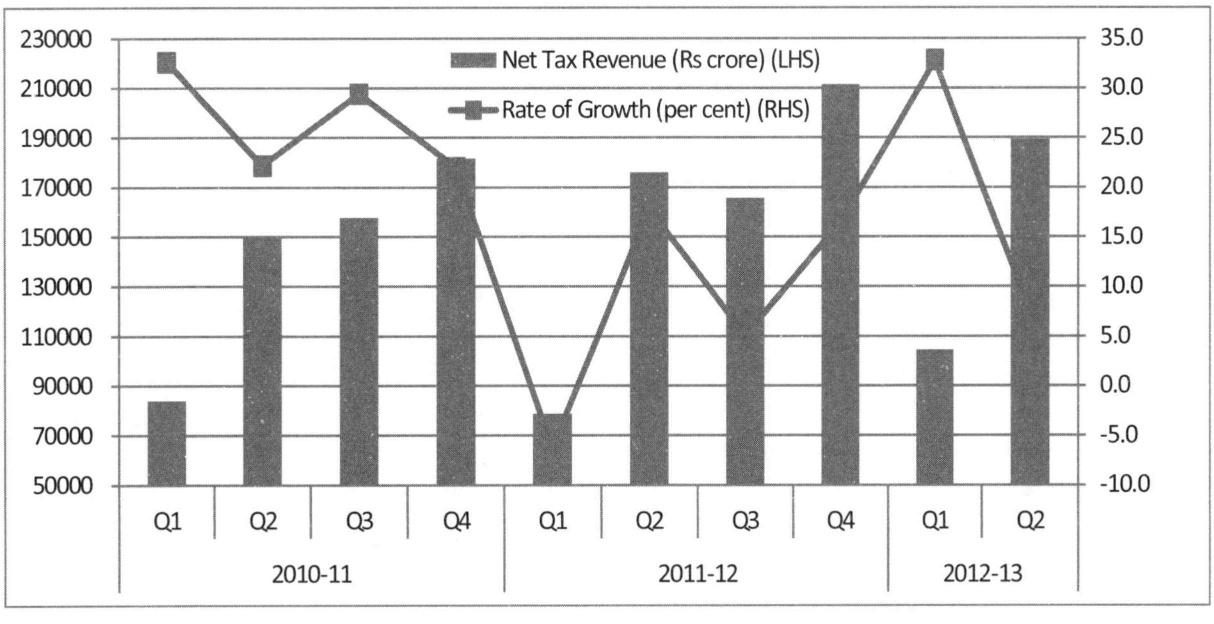

September, 2012 over April-September, 2011 (₹ 1,96,623 crore). Going by the past trends, the target for the fiscal year appears achievable with a pickup in the economic activity in the second half. This is based on the observed fact that there are some seasonalities in both revenue realized as well as GDP growth. However, some downside risks associated with prevailing uncertainty in the global economy and domestic macroeconomic outcome may impact eventual performance. Two major components of Direct Taxes are discussed below. Trends in year on year growth for different quarters in collection of corporation tax and non-corporate direct taxes for 2010-11, 2011-12 and 2012-13 are indicated in Fig 2.3.

Corporation Tax

2.9 Corporation tax at ₹ 1,42,965 crore continues to be the largest component of total taxes. During the first half of 2012-13, it shows a growth of 12.2 per cent over collections during the same period in 2011-12. The BE 2012-13 for this component implies year-on-year growth of 15.5 per cent over the provisional actual receipts in 2011-12.

Income Tax other than Corporation Tax

2.10 Taxes on income other than Corporation tax were estimated at ₹ 1,89,866 crore in BE 2012-13 which is 14.9 per cent higher than provisional actual receipts during 2011-12. Revenue realized at ₹ 82,598 crore during the first half of the year 2012-13 reflects a growth of 24.7 per cent over collections during corresponding period in the previous financial year. In all likelihood, the receipts under this component of tax may exceed BE.

Indirect Taxes

2.11 The gross indirect tax collections during first half of 2012-13 is ₹ 1,96,824 crore. This reflects a growth of 13.9 per cent over the

Table 2.3 Components of Gross Tax Revenue (₹ crore)

Sl. No.	Description	BE 2012-13	Actuals upto Sept. 2012	per cent of BE	Per cent growth over sept. 2011	BE 2011-12	Actuals upto Sept. 2011	per cent of BE
1	Corporation Tax	373227	142965	38.3	12.2	359990	127375	35.4
2	Taxes on income other than Corporation Tax	189866	82598	43.5	24.7	164526	66249	40.3
3	Other Taxes	7165	2509	35.0	-16.3	8135	2999	36.9
	Total Direct Taxes	**570258**	**228072**	**40.0**	**16.0**	**532651**	**196623**	**36.9**
4	Customs	186694	78557	42.1	5.0	151700	74808	49.3
5	Union Excise Duties	194350	67424	34.7	13.7	164116	59315	36.1
6	Service Tax	124000	49103	39.6	32.5	82000	37049	45.2
7	Other Taxes	2310	1740	75.3	11.7	1973	1558	79.0
	Total Indirect Taxes	**507354**	**196824**	**38.8**	**13.9**	**399789**	**172730**	**43.2**
8	**Total Gross Tax Revenue**	**1077612**	**424896**	**39.4**	**15.0**	**932440**	**369353**	**39.6**
Total Gross Tax Revenue (with direct Tax refunds			**470908**				**431583**	

Fig 2.2: Quarterly Gross Tax Revenue Receipts and their growth

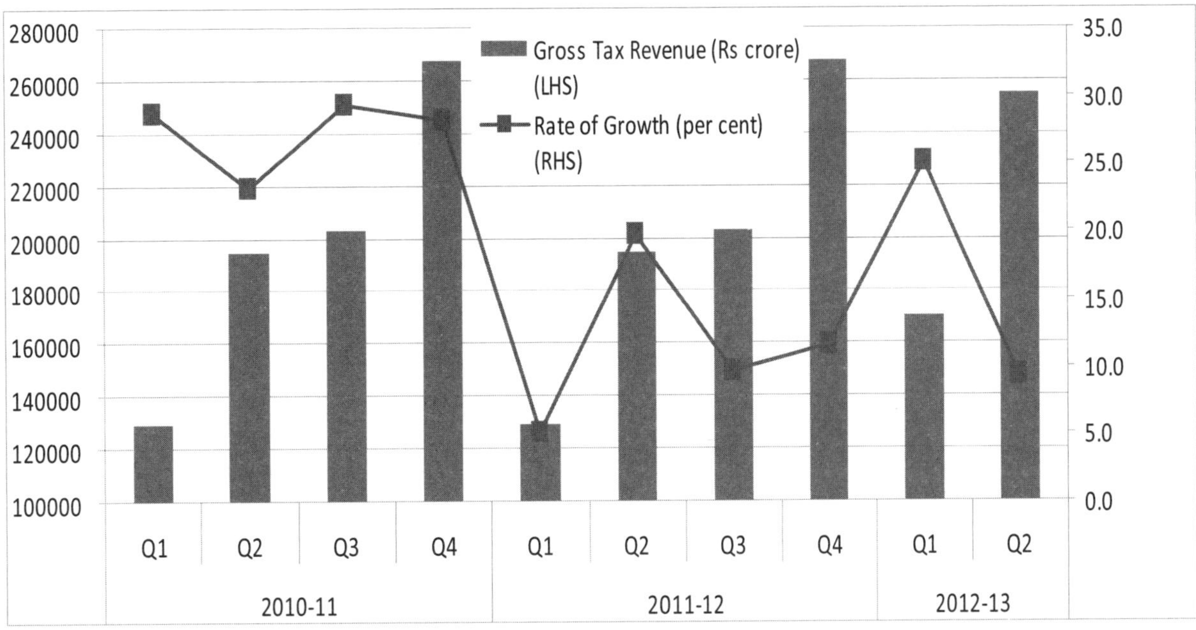

collections during April-September, 2011. However, this is much lower than the estimated growth of 28.2 per cent in BE 2012-13 over provisional actuals of 2011-12. Growth of indirect taxes over last 10 quarters is indicated in Fig 2.4.

Customs

2.12 Customs duties collection during the first half of 2012-13 is on lower side. For this component, BE 2012-13 was estimated at ₹ 1,86,694 crore reflecting a growth of 24.9 per cent over the provisional actuals of 2011-12. Receipts under this component have increased by 5 per cent in the first half of 2012-13 over the corresponding period in 2011-12. Trends in year on year growth for different quarters in collection of customs duties for 2010-11, 2011-12 and 2012-13 are indicated in Fig. 2.4. The collection in the first half of

Fig 2.3: Rate of growth of Direct Taxes

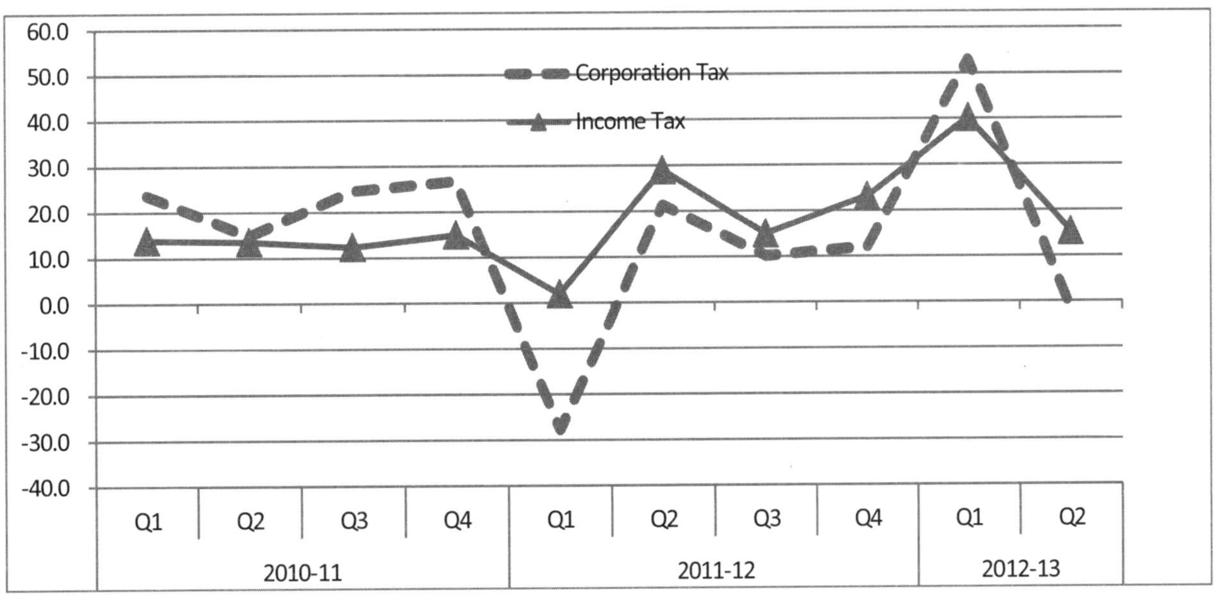

2012-13 is 42.1 per cent of BE 2012-13. As may be seen from the figure, the trends in this year have improved in the second quarter as compared to the previous quarter.

Union Excise Duties

2.13 Revenue from Union excise duties was estimated at ₹ 1,94,350 crore in BE 2012-13 reflecting a growth of 33.8 per cent over the provisional actual collection of 2011-12. This level of increase was estimated on the basis of relative better performance of manufacturing sector and likely demand in the economy. In the first half of 2012-13, the receipts under Union excise duties is ₹ 67,424 crore reflecting a growth of 13.7 per cent over the collections in the corresponding period of 2011-12 (₹59,315 crore) and is 34.7 per cent of BE 2012-13. Lower than estimated growth is also due to moderation in the growth in the manufacturing sector.

Service Tax

2.14 Service Tax in BE 2012-13 was estimated at ₹ 1,24,000 crore reflecting a growth of 27.1 per cent over provisional actual receipts in 2011-12. In the first half of the current fiscal, the receipts are at ₹ 49,103 crore reflecting a growth of 32.5 per cent over the collections made in the corresponding period of 2011-12 (₹ 37049 crore). The amount collected during April – September, 2012 constituted 39.6 per cent of BE 2012-13. The broadened base and higher rate is expected to result in collections exceeding the Budget Estimates.

2.15 On the tax revenue side, the trend growth in the mid-year is lower than estimated. While the targets may be achieved in taxes on income other than Corporation tax and service tax, achieving targets in Corporation tax on the Direct tax side and Customs and Central Excise duty on the Indirect tax side is somewhat difficult given the trend so far. The reason for under achieving target is due to macroeconomic environment being under stress. Slower pace of GDP growth has affected the manufacturing and trade sectors thereby resulting in lower than estimated excise duty collections. Moreover, global economic

Fig 2.4: Rate of Growth of Indirect Taxes

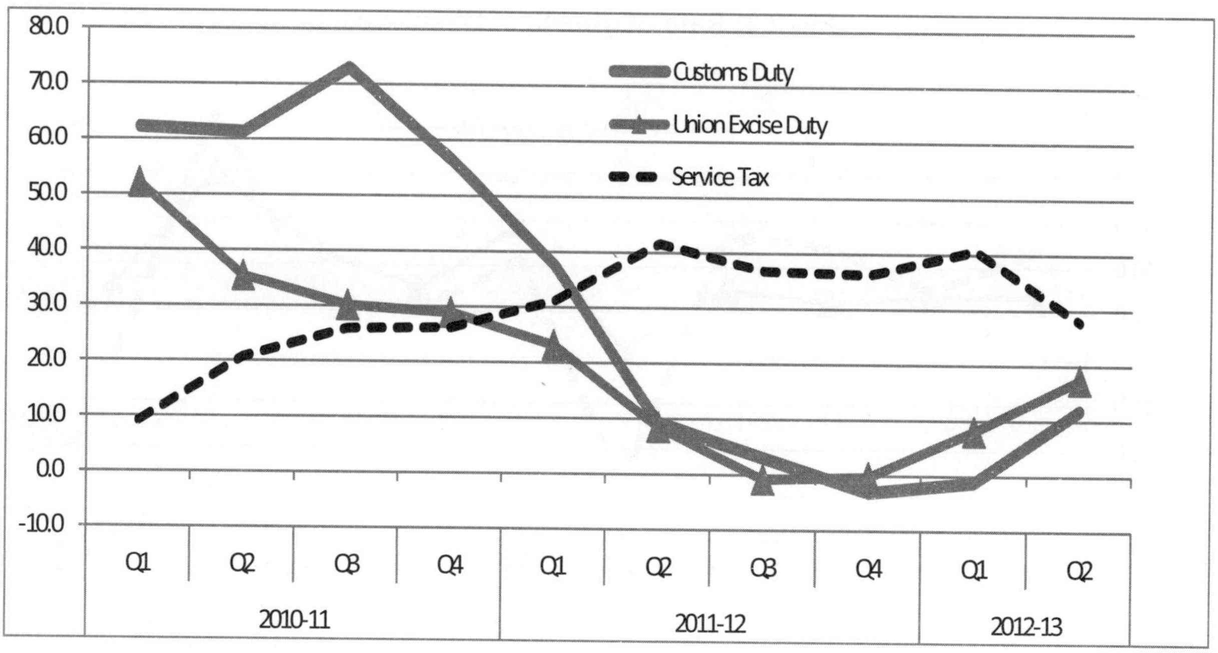

factors and fluctuations in exchange rates have also affected imports other than oil, thereby affecting Customs duty collections. Higher policy rates of the Central bank in effort to contain inflation, has led to an investment downturn and affected corporate profitability. Thus, corporate tax is also lower than estimated. However, based on the proportion of revenue realized in April-September 2012 and observed past trends regarding the proportion of revenue in the first half to total revenue realized for the full year along with the efforts taken to augment revenue, the slippage under overall gross tax revenue may be minimal.

Non-Tax Revenue

2.16 Non tax revenue receipts up to April-September 2012 have been placed at ₹ 57,076 crore amounting to 34.7 per cent of B.E. 2012-13 showing a growth of 12.4 per cent over receipts during corresponding period of previous financial year. The 2G telecom spectrum proceeds are likely to be much lower than budgeted as the response to the auction held in November 2012 was lukewarm and there is likely slippage in terms of receipts on this account as efforts are afoot to reduce the reserve price in the process of auctioning the same afresh.

Non-debt Capital Receipts

2.17 The receipts on account of recoveries of loans in the current fiscal were ₹ 4,855 crore up to September 2012 compared to ₹ 10,024 crore during the corresponding period of previous financial year. This is 41.7 per cent of B.E. 2012-13. Disinvestment receipt and Miscellaneous receipt for current year are ₹ 1,372 crore against ₹ 2,731 crore during the corresponding period of previous financial year. With the present trend and prevailing scenario in the capital market, efforts are there for expeditious divestment; nevertheless achieving the target of ₹ 30,000 crore during the remaining period of 2012-13 would be a challenge.

EXPENDITURE

Total Expenditure

2.18 Total expenditure for 2012-13 is estimated at ₹ 14,90,925 crore in BE 2012-13 (14.7 per cent of GDP), which reflects a growth of 14.8 per cent over actual expenditure of ₹ 12,98,444 crore in 2011-12. Growth in plan expenditure is estimated at 26 per cent over the provisional actuals of 2011-12. However, non-plan expenditure is estimated to increase by 9.6 per cent over the actuals of 2011-12. Total expenditure during April-September 2012 is ₹ 6,94,019 crore as against a level of ₹ 5,99,093 crore during the same period in the previous financial year. As a proportion of BE, total expenditure in April-September 2012 is 46.5 per cent which is in line with the five year average of 46.7 per cent (Table 2.4).Total expenditure in the first half of 2012-13 reflects a growth of 15.8 per cent in expenditure, which is higher by one percentage point over the growth envisaged by BE.

2.19 Revenue expenditure for 2012-13 is estimated at ₹ 12,86,109 crore (12.7 per cent of GDP). This implies a growth of 12.7 per cent over actual expenditure of ₹ 11,40,915 crore in 2011-12. During first half of 2012-13, this has gone up from ₹ 5,27,308 crore in 2011-12 to ₹ 6,14,172 crore implying an year-on-year growth of 16.5 per cent. As a proportion of BE, revenue expenditure upto September 2012 is 47.8 per cent during 2012-13 which is in line with the 5 year average of 47.7 per cent.

2.20 Capital expenditure for 2012-13 is estimated at ₹ 2,04,816 crore (2.0 per cent of GDP), implying a growth of 30 per cent over actual expenditure of ₹ 1,57,529 crore in 2011-12. Capital expenditure during April-September 2012 is ₹ 79,847 crore as against ₹ 71,785 crore during the same period in 2011-12, reflecting a growth of 11.2 per cent. As a proportion of BE, capital expenditure during the first half of 2012-13 is 39 per cent

Table 2.4: Trends in expenditure in April-September

Sl. No.	Expenditure	April - September					
		2007-08	2008-09	2009-10	2010-11	2011-12	2012-13
1	Revenue Expenditure	259080	323211	409454	473155	527308	614172
2	Capital Expenditure	58812*	25870	39394	64822	71785	79847
3	Total Expenditure	317892	349081	448848	537977	599093	694019
4	BE for the full year	680521	750884	1020838	1108749	1257729	1490925
5	Total Expenditure as per cent to BE	46.7	46.5	44.0	48.5	47.6	46.5
6	Rate of growth of Total Expenditure	26.2	9.8	28.6	19.9	11.4	15.8

**This includes one-time expenditure of ₹35,531 crore on account of payment to RBI for acquisition of its stake in SBI*

in 2012-13 and is in line with the five year average of 39.1 per cent.

Plan Expenditure

2.21 Plan expenditure during 2012-13 is estimated at ₹ 5,21,025 crore reflecting a growth of 26.0 per cent over the provisional actuals of 2011-12. Plan expenditure of ₹ 2,02,740 crore during the first half of 2012-13 shows a moderate growth of 14 per cent over the corresponding period during 2011-12 (₹ 1,77,823 crore) and is 38.9 per cent of BE 2012-13. This shows a slower pace of plan expenditure when compared to five year average of 42.3 per cent of respective BE. Details of variations over the previous year performance in Plan expenditure during the first half of fiscal 2012-13 for the Ministries / Departments are shown in Annex II Table 8. Trends in plan expenditure as percentage of B.E. at the end of Q2 of respective financial years are shown in Table 2.5.

Non-Plan Expenditure

2.22 Non-plan expenditure is estimated at ₹ 9,69,900 crore in BE 2012-13 reflecting growth of 9.6 per cent over the provisional actuals of 2011-12 and accounts for 65.1 per cent of the total expenditure in BE 2012-13. Non-plan expenditure during the first half of 2012-13 is at ₹ 4,91,279 crore showing a

Table 2.5: Trends in plan expenditure in April-September

Sl. No.	Plan Expenditure	April - September					
		2007-08	2008-09	2009-10	2010-11	2011-12	2012-13
1	Revenue	71571	93727	108163	144847	151033	167499
2	Capital	15187	14725	18615	24860	26790	35241
3	Total Plan Expenditure	86758	108452	126778	169707	177823	202740
4	BE for the full year	205100	243386	325149	373092	441547	521025
5	Plan expenditure as per cent to BE	42.3	44.6	39.0	45.5	40.3	38.9
6	Rate of growth of Plan Expenditure (per cent)	26.0	25.0	16.9	33.9	4.8	14.0

Table 2.6: Non-Plan Expenditure on key items and growth rates

Non-plan items	Expenditure during the First half (₹ in crore)		Growth during 2012-13 over 2011-12
	2012-13	**2011-12**	
Major Subsidies	141903	95190	**49%**
Defence	84925	75097	**13%**
Interest payment	131165	122499	**7%**
Total	**357993**	**292787**	**22%**

growth of 16.6 per cent over expenditure of ₹ 4,21,270 crore during the same period in the previous financial year. As a proportion of BE, non-plan expenditure in the first half is 50.7 per cent during 2012-13 as against five year average of 48.8 per cent. In absolute terms, there is increase of ₹ 70,009 crore in the non-plan expenditure during the first half of 2012-13 when compared to the same period in 2011-12. This increase is largely on account of three items: namely, interest payment (which has increased by ₹ 8,666 crore); major subsidies (which show increase of ₹ 46,713 crore); and defence (which has increased by ₹ 9,828 crore). Table 2.6 shows the growth in percentage terms of the above three items.

2.23 Higher growth in expenditure on the above three items explains the structural problem of government finances which needs to be addressed through policy initiatives. Trends in non-plan expenditure as percentage of B.E. at the end of Q2 of respective financial years are shown in Table 2.7.

Resources transferred to States/UTs

2.24 Against the B.E. of ₹ 5,21,294 crore for transfers to States/UTs, the actual resources transferred to States/UTs during the first half of 2012-13 is ₹ 2,10,318 crore. This shows a growth of 11.8 per cent over ₹ 1,88,198 crore transferred during the corresponding period in the previous financial year. States' share of Central Taxes as proportion of gross tax receipts during the first half of 2012-13 is 30.5 per cent which is almost equal to 30.6 per cent devolved during the corresponding period of 2011-12.

Table 2.7: Trends in non-plan expenditure in April-September

Sl. No.	Non-Plan Expenditure	2007-08	2008-09	2009-10	2010-11	2011-12	2012-13
1	Revenue Account of which	187509	229484	301291	328308	376275	446673
	Interest Payments	72820	86061	86669	102779	122499	131165
2	Capital Expenditure	43625*	11145	20779	39962	44995	44606
3	Total Expenditure	231134	240629	322070	368270	421270	491279
4	BE for the full year	475421	507498	695689	735657	816182	969900
5	Non-Plan expenditure as per cent to BE	48.6	47.4	46.3	50.1	51.6	50.7
6	Rate of growth of Non-Plan Expenditure (per cent)	26.3	4.1	33.8	14.3	14.4	16.6

**This includes one-time expenditure of ₹35,531 crore on account of payment to RBI for acquisition of its stake in SBI*

DEFICIT

2.25 In the Budget for 2012-13, fiscal deficit for the year is estimated at ₹ 5,13,590 crore amounting to 5.1 per cent of GDP. In April-September 2012 fiscal deficit is ₹ 3,36,904 crore, which is 65.6 per cent of BE 2012-13. Higher levels of fiscal deficit as percentage of BE during the first half of 2012-13 raises some concern when compared with five year average of 56.6 per cent. Trends in tax revenue do not show any significant slippage. Expenditure during the first half is in line with Budget Estimates. However, uncertainty on account of disinvestment receipts and likely higher subsidy requirement does make it a challenging task to adhere to the overall fiscal deficit target during 2012-13.

2.26 Revenue deficit for 2012-13 is estimated in the Budget at ₹ 3,50,424 crore amounting to 3.4 per cent of GDP. During the period April-September, 2012, revenue deficit is ₹ 2,63,284 crore amounting to 75.1 per cent of B.E. 2012-13. Five year average of revenue deficit during the first half as percentage of BE is 77.0 per cent. In the current year, refunds in direct taxes during the first half (₹ 46,012 crore) are lower than the first half of previous year (₹ 62,230 crore in 2011-12). This has resulted in higher availability of net tax resources (post refunds and post devolution to States) for Centre to finance its deficit in the current financial year.

2.27 Trends in various deficit indicators in both absolute terms as well as in terms of percentage of B.E. up to the Q2 of respective financial years are shown in Table 2.8.

FINANCING OF DEFICIT

2.28 The deficit of ₹ 3,36,409 crore on Consolidated Fund of India was financed by raising net Internal Debt of ₹ 3,03,185 crore, net External Assistance of (-)₹ 765 crore, Ways and means advance/ cash draw down of ₹ 18,410 crore and public account (net) of ₹ 1,486 crore as shown in Table 2.9.

2.29 Gross and net market borrowings during the first half of 2012-13 amounted to ₹ 3,55,000 crore and ₹ 2,84,384 crore respectively and accounted for 62.3 per cent and 59.4 per cent of the estimated market

Table 2.8: Trends in Deficit in April-September

		April - September					
Sl. No.	Deficits	2007-08	2008-09	2009-10	2010-11	2011-12	2012-13
1	Revenue Deficit (RD) (Apr-Sep)	61124	78313	164983	74921	221780	263284
2	Revenue Deficit (BE)	71478	55184	282735	276512	307270	350424
3	RD Percentage of BE	85.5	141.9	58.4	27.1	72.2	75.1
4	Fiscal Deficit (Apr-Sep)	81200	102654	197775	133252	280810	336904
5	Fiscal Deficit (FD) (BE)	150948	133287	400996	381408	412817	513590
6	FD Percentage of BE	53.8	77.0	49.3	34.9	68.0	65.6
7	Primary Deficit (PD) (Apr-Sep)	8380	16593	111106	30473	158311	205739
8	Primary Deficit (BE)	-8047	-57520	175485	132744	144831	193831
9	PD Percentage of BE	-104.1	-28.8	63.3	23.0	109.3	106.1

Table 2.9: Financing of Deficit

		April-Sept. 2012	April-Sept. 2011
	Fiscal Deficit	336904	280810
	Sources of Financing		
1	Internal Debt	303185	235399
a	Market Loans & Short Term Borrowings	331839	277074
b	Treasury Bills (14 days)	-27549	-35733
c	Compensation and Other Bonds	-3516	-6803
d	Others	2411	861
2	External Assistance including Revolving Fund	-765	2368
3	Cash Draw Down Decrease(+) Increase (-)	18410	1833
4	Borrowing (-)/Surplus(+) on Public Account*	1486	407

* Includes Suspense & Remittances.

borrowings for the year. During the corresponding period of the previous financial year, gross and net borrowings accounted for 59.9 per cent and 55.6 per cent of budget estimates, respectively. The weighted average maturity of dated securities issued upto the end of first half of the fiscal year 2012-13 (April-September) at 13.55 years was higher than 12.19 years during the corresponding period of the previous year. The weighted average yield of dated securities issued during the same period increased to 8.46 per cent from 8.40 per cent during the first of half of 2011-12.

CASH MANAGEMENT

2.30 The year 2012-13 commenced with surplus cash position of ₹ 26,022 crore and investment surplus of ₹ 50,000 crore. At the end of second quarter, the Government ended with a cash balance of ₹ 10 crore and investment of ₹ 35,412 crore. The net collection under National Small Savings Fund during April-September 2012 continued to be negative; it is (-) ₹ 13,593 crore as against (-) ₹ 6,549 crore during the first half of last year.

ASSESSMENT VIS-À-VIS MID-YEAR FRBM BENCHMARKS

2.31 Under Rule 7 of the FRBM Rules, 2004, Government is required to take appropriate corrective measures in case the outcome of the second quarter review shows that:

I. The total amount of non-debt receipts are less than 40 per cent of budget estimates for that year; or

II. The fiscal deficit is higher than 45 per cent of the budget estimates for that year; or

III. The revenue deficit is higher than 45 per cent of the budget estimates for that year.

The performance in the first half of the fiscal year 2012-13 does not comply with any of the targets in respect of the benchmark of non-debt receipts, fiscal deficit and revenue deficit. It could be seen from Table 2.10 that only in 2010-11 were all the three FRBM Mid-Year bench marks was achieved and this owed to the higher than budgeted receipts from the 3G Broadband Wireless Access spectrum auction.

2.32 The Indian economy was estimated to grow by 6.9 per cent in 2011-12 in terms of gross domestic product at factor cost at constant 2004-05 prices. However, this has been revised to 6.5 per cent mainly on account of lower performance in 'manufacturing' and 'trade hotels, transport and communication' than anticipated. The slowdown in the economy, coupled with rising costs and narrowing profit margins of corporate sector led to a lower than budgeted growth in government revenues. Increasing subsidy bill of three major subsidies viz. Food, Fertilizer and Petroleum, on the other hand has led to rising Non-Plan expenditure. At the time of the presentation of the Budget for 2012-13, it was estimated that growth would recover, particularly in the industrial sector. A continuance of the slowdown well into the second quarter of the current year has led to the slippages in terms of the Mid-Year FRBM benchmarks. The outlook for the second half looks much brighter with a growth of 8.2 per cent in IIP in October 2012, better corporate profit margins, moderation in inflation and better business expectations for the third quarter (outlook section of Chapter 3 provides greater details).

2.33 Government is continuously monitoring the emerging economic developments and the fiscal position. Government appointed a committee headed by Dr. Vijay L Kelkar to suggest roadmap for fiscal consolidation (See Chapter 3 for details). Government has broadly accepted its recommendation with certain reservations on the details of achieving the targets and has initiated action on many of its recommendations.

- Government has announced the roadmap for fiscal consolidation by containing current year's fiscal deficit at 5.3 per cent of the GDP and reducing it to 4.8 per cent next year. The fiscal deficit is targeted to be reduced by 0.6 percentage points each year thereafter (till 2016-17), at 4.2%, 3.6% and 3.0% in the years 2014-15, 2015-16 and 2016-17 respectively.
- To contain the increasing Subsidy burden, Government has revised Diesel prices and capped subsidized LPG cylinders to consumers. Government has also initiated reforms to boost investment.

Table 2.10: Outcome versus mid-year benchmarks under FRBM rules

Outcome versus mid-year benchmarks under FRBM Rules							
S.No.	Variable	Performance benchmarks under FRBM Rules	April-September				
			2012	2011	2010	2009	2008
1	Total Non-Debt Receipts	Not Less than 40 percent	36.5	37.7	55.6	40.5	39.9
2	Fiscal Deficit	Not more than 45 percent	65.6	68.0	34.9	49.3	77.0
3	Revenue Deficit	Not more than 45 percent	75.1	72.2	27.1	58.4	141.9

- Government is taking various steps to boost revenues and limit any slippage therefrom. As indicated earlier the reserve price of 2G telecom Spectrum auction has been revised and a fresh auction would be held soon and efforts are there to expedite the plan for divestment.

- Government has imposed economy measures like rationalization of expenditure and optimization of available resources with a view to improve the macro-economic environment. This include 10 % mandatory cut on Non-Plan expenditure in the current financial year, ban on creation of Plan and Non-Plan posts, restrictions on foreign travel, restrictions on re-appropriation of funds, strict observance of discipline in fiscal transfers to States, Public Sector Undertakings, Autonomous Bodies, etc.

- The measures on the expenditure side would partially offset the higher than budgeted outgo on subsidies and the slippage in non-debt receipts.

2.34 While the fiscal outcome in the first six months of the current financial year raises concerns on the likely fiscal marksmanship this year, it would be instructive to note that in 2005-06 a similar situation obtained; but the actual fiscal outcome was broadly in line with the budget estimates for non-debt receipts and performance in terms of deficit indicators was much better than budgeted. With the likely revival in the economy and the measures already taken and those on the anvil, it is likely that the fiscal deficit for the year would be 5.3 per cent of GDP.

CHAPTER III

ANALYSIS AND OUTLOOK

GROWTH AND INVESTMENT

The Indian economy recovered quickly after the global crisis of 2008-09, which reduced the growth rate of real GDP at factor cost to 3.5 per cent in Q4 of 2008-09. Growth improved to 11.2 per cent by Q4 of 2009-10. However, following the crisis in Eurozone and the slow recovery in several other countries, in combination with certain domestic factors, economic growth began to decelerate thereafter and has averaged 5.8 per cent in last five quarters. A decline in the contribution of the industrial sector to overall GDP growth, from 36.9 per cent in Q4 of 2009-10 to 9.8 per cent in Q4 of 2011-12, has been the key factor in this moderation. Besides the slowdown in growth, the economy has been under pressure on account of elevated levels of inflation, a high fiscal deficit and a widening current account deficit.

Moderation in manufacturing growth-expectations and interest costs

3.2 While the global economic slowdown has adversely affected export dependent sectors, depressed business sentiment, coupled with high interest rates and moderation in credit growth have led to a deceleration in investment growth, as well as some moderation in consumption demand, resulting in slower overall growth. The Reserve Bank of India's quarterly Business Expectation Index (BEI)[1], after recovering from a low of 96.4 in Q1 of 2008-09 to 126.5 in Q3 of 2010-11, has declined steadily thereafter. The index, however, still remains in the growth terrain (i.e., above 100, which is the threshold that separates contraction from expansion). Nearly half of the companies reported production constraints preventing them from attaining their normal production levels during the quarter July-September 2012. They cited lack of domestic demand, uncertainty of the economic environment, shortage of power, lack of export demand and shortage of working capital finance. Deseasonalized IIP growth has generally mirrored the BEI (Fig 3.1).

Fig 3.1: Business Expectation Index and IIP growth (Deseasonalized annualized quarter over quarter)

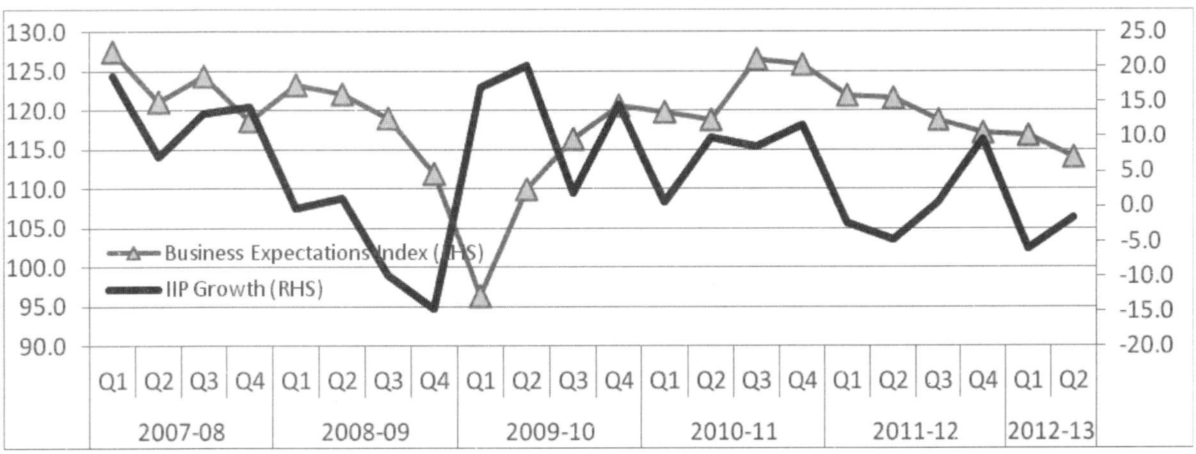

[1] The Business Expectation Index gives a single snapshot of the industrial outlook in each quarter. This index is computed as a weighted average of net responses from all the industries on nine select performance parameters where the weights are the industry's share in Gross Value Added (GVA). The selected parameters are 'overall business situation', 'production', 'order books', 'inventory of raw materials', 'inventory of finished goods', 'profit margin', 'employment', 'exports' and 'capacity utilization'.

3.3 While high interest rates may have been necessary to combat inflation, they have also raised the interest cost for manufacturing industries. Interest as a percentage of operating profits of these companies (non-government non-financial) increased from 15.2 per cent in Q4 of 2009-10 to 30.3 per cent in Q1 of 2012-13. Investment as measured by new projects in the CMIE Capex declined from 28.5 per cent of GDP to 9.7 per cent of GDP over the same period (Fig 3.2). Of course, a substantial portion of the decline in new projects occurred before interest expenses grew substantially, suggesting that other factors such as the difficulty in acquiring various project clearances or land may also have played a part. The proposal for setting up a National Investment Board (NIB) headed by the Prime Minister for fast tracking projects over ₹1000 crore is intended to reduce unnecessary delays in granting such clearances, for delays not only slow growth but also render projects unviable, turning them into NPAs for the banking system.

3.4 The decline in investment affected the production of capital goods. Higher growth of imports of capital goods in 2011-12 (para 1.27 of Chapter 1) also contributed to deceleration in growth of domestic production. Based on an analysis of relationship between production and imports of manufactured goods industries, RBI has also observed a negative association between production and imports in case of electrical machinery (which had a negative growth in last 5 quarters) resulting in substitution of domestic output by imports.

3.5 Some sectors have been affected by high interest rates to a greater extent than others. In interest-sensitive sectors like capital goods and consumer durables (Fig 3.3), there

Fig 3.2: Interest cost of Companies and Investment in industrial projects

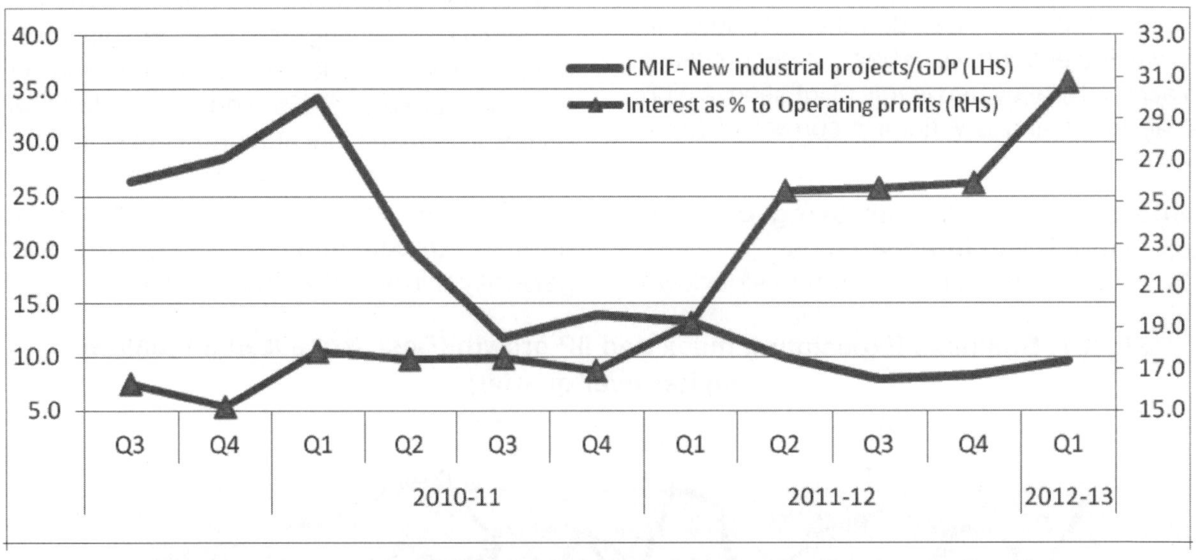

Fig 3.3: Growth of Capital goods and Consumer Durables and Repo rates

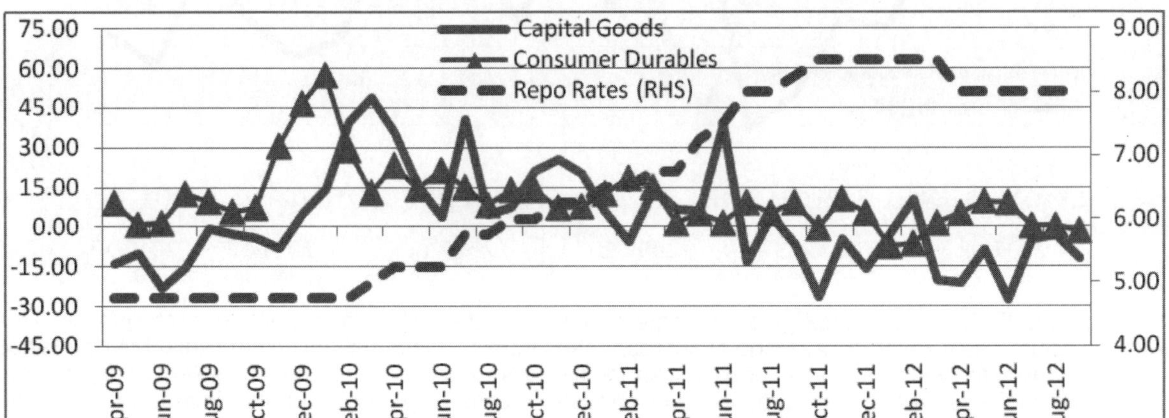

seems to be a strong negative correlation between the growth in production and rising repo rates. Here again, though, high interest rates should be seen as only one of the factors affecting growth.

Cycle of moderation in expectation may have reached its trough

3.6 There are, however, signs that the cycle of moderation of expectation has reached its trough. The confidence building measures announced by Government in September and October, 2012 including liberalization of FDI policy in sectors like multi-brand retail, aviation, power and broadcasting sectors to attract foreign investment, announcing a road map to achieve fiscal consolidation, rationalization of subsidy on diesel, etc. are gradually improving business expectations, though progress on implementing some of the suggested measures, such as the proposed National Investment Board, is needed to consolidate the shift. RBI's business expectation index, after having declined for seven consecutive quarters, moved up in the Oct-Dec, 2012 quarter. HSBC's purchasing managers index (PMI), picked up in November, indicating the fastest rate of expansion in November in the last five months. Companies reported an increase in order book volumes and together with depletion of inventories, this could set the stage for higher output growth.

Some early signs of improved availability of investable funds

3.7 The slowdown in investment was also partly due to financing constraints. As indicated in Chapter 1, growth of aggregate deposits moderated considerably, from an average of 17.8 per cent during Apr-Sep, 2011 to 14.2 per cent during Apr-Sep, 2012. Corporate profitability as reflected in corporate internal accruals (profit after tax and depreciation) also declined sharply from 14.3 per cent of sales in Q1 of 2009-10 to 8.2 per cent in Q3 of 2011-12. There has also been a slowdown in national savings, particularly financial savings since 2007-08 (from 26.0 per cent of GDP in 2007-08 to 19.6 per cent of GDP in 2010-11) due to public dis-savings, fall in corporate savings and shift in household savings towards real assets away from financial assets (even if we do not include gold purchases). The components of household savings clearly indicate that there has been a steady decline in the share of pension and provident funds as real interest rates have declined and a decline in investment in shares and debentures, as real estate and gold have become perceived as more attractive alternatives. In addition to increasing customs duty on gold to reduce its demand - and there is a limit to how much this can be done without encouraging smuggling - - measures to offer gold-linked savings as well as bonds linked to real returns are being considered (see later). Finally, corporate profitability also appears to be reversing its declining trend (Fig 3.4) which suggest that availability of domestic funds for investment may see an increase in subsequent quarters.

3.8 Because of the slowdown and high levels of leverage, some industry and infrastructure sectors are experiencing an

Fig 3.4: Corporate Profitability and Gross Fixed Capital Formation

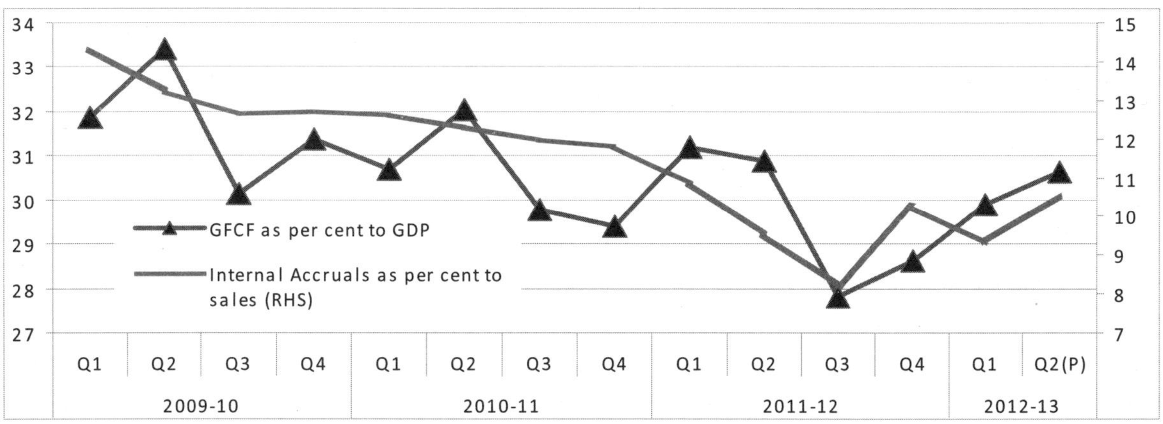

increase in non- performing assets (NPAs). Overall NPAs of the banking sector increased from 2.36 per cent of total credit advanced in March, 2011 to 3.57 per cent of total credit advanced in September, 2012 (Fig 3.5). While there has been across the board increase in NPAs, the increase is particularly sharp for industry and infrastructure sectors, with NPAs as per cent to credit advanced increasing from 1.91 per cent in March, 2011 to 3.44 per cent in September, 2012. Sectors, particularly under stress include textiles, chemicals, iron & steel, food processing, construction and telecommunications. The rapid rise in non-performing bank loans suggests once again the need for a single-minded focus by all stakeholders on reducing unnecessary delays to project completion. Moreover, failing projects need to be restructured rapidly and equitably, drawing in new promoters if the old ones cannot bring in better capabilities and new equity, and requiring greater risk capital up front in future financing, including greater promoter equity to buffer bank claims.

INFLATION

3.9 Headline inflation measured in terms of the Wholesale Price Index (WPI) is still uncomfortably high, albeit at a lower level than what was observed in 2010-12. The frequency distribution of commodities included in the WPI indicates that there has been a sharp reduction in the number of commodities experiencing double digit inflation in the first half of 2012-13 (Table 3.1) along with a corresponding increase in the number and weights of commodities with inflation in the single digits. This distributional shift has not only resulted in the moderation of inflation but suggests more room for adopting commodity focused strategies for containing inflation.

Fig 3.5: Non-Performing Assets of the Banking Sector

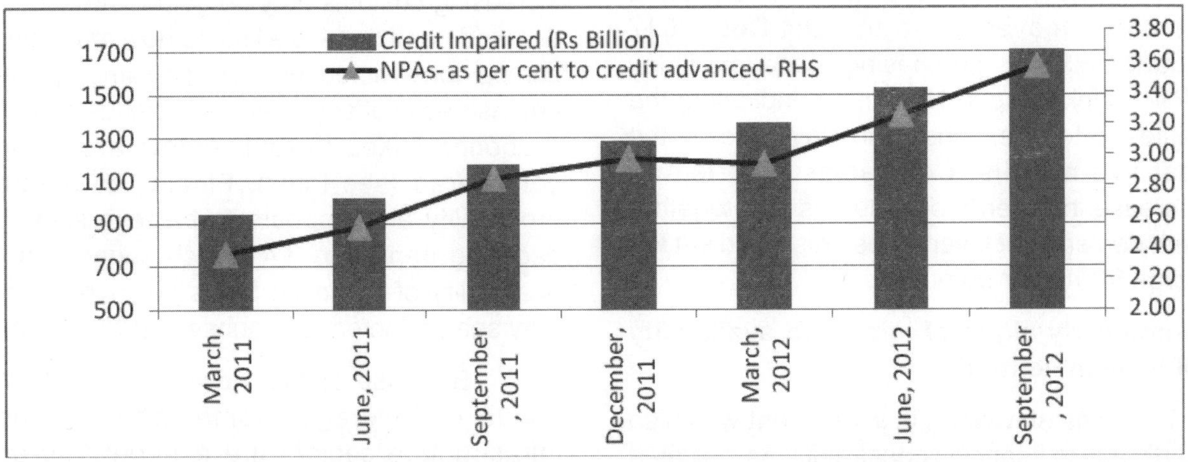

Table 3.1: Frequency distribution of WPI- commodities in terms of inflation range

	2009-10		2010-11		2011-12		2012-13
	Apr-Sep	Oct-Mar	Apr-Sep	Oct-Mar	Apr-Sep	Oct-Mar	Apr-Sep
Headline inflation	**0.64**	**7.01**	**9.90**	**9.24**	**9.66**	**8.24**	**7.66**
Frequency Distribution of commodities by inflation range (Number of Commodities)							
up to 5	492	459	389	394	340	397	449
6-10	81	88	112	113	149	124	137
Above 10	103	129	175	169	187	155	95
Weights of the Commodities (per cent)							
up to 5	75.25	63.66	40.50	47.17	39.37	47.86	49.21
6-10	8.69	12.82	22.81	17.79	30.81	20.94	31.21
Above 10	16.06	23.52	36.69	35.04	29.82	31.20	19.58

Inflation momentum

3.10 Policy decisions to contain inflation are expected to be ahead of the curve. This requires understanding the momentum of inflation along with its current level. Besides headline WPI and CPI inflation, RBI has been monitoring non-food manufacturing (NFM) inflation as the key measure of core inflation that will influence its policy stance. The reason for this emphasis is partly because demand conditions, which can be affected by RBI interest rate policy, are better measured by NFM inflation, and NFM inflation is also relatively sticky. The seasonally adjusted annualized rate of inflation (SAAR) indicates the momentum of NFM inflation is currently on a decline.

3.11 Within core inflation, while the inflation for capital goods has continued to remain muted, inflation for consumer durables has been showing signs of easing recently (Fig 3.7). Inflation for consumer durables generally remained above core inflation and its moderation reflects the impact of monetary policy.

3.12 WPI food inflation has shown a sharper moderation during the period April 2010 to October 2012, because of its initial high levels. Food inflation however is more structural and its response to monetary policy changes is relatively weak. However, the momentum of food inflation is also pointing towards moderation (Fig 3.8).

Fig 3.6: Momentum of WPI Core Inflation

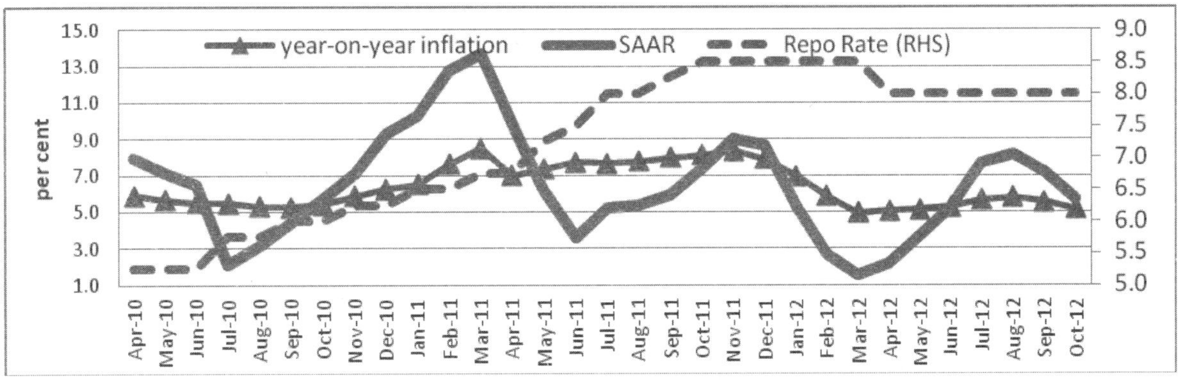

Fig 3.7: Inflation of Consumer Durables and Capital Goods

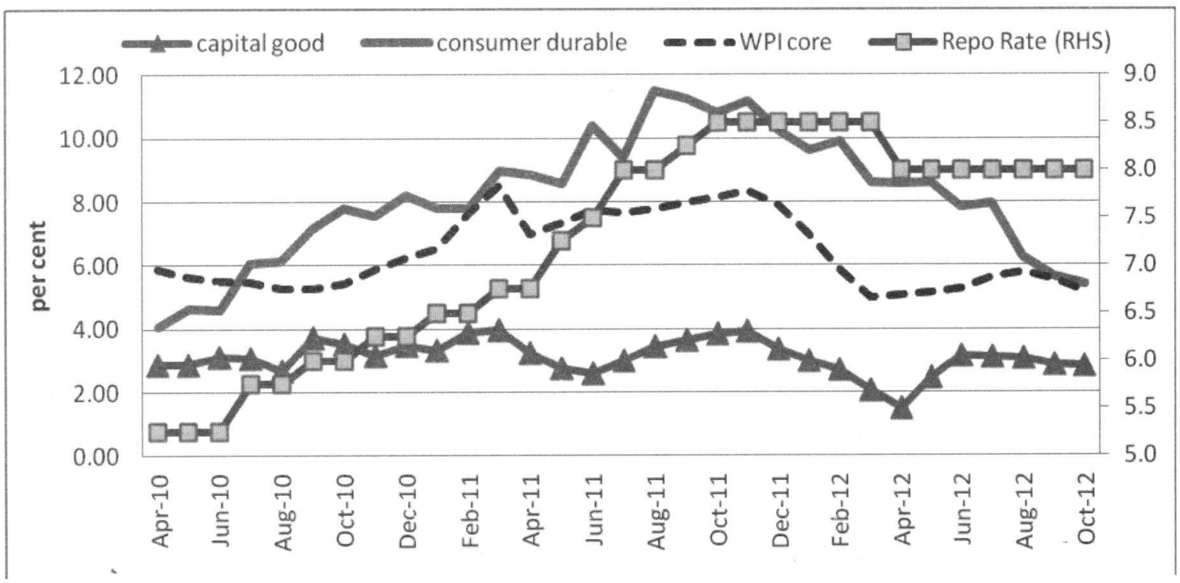

Fig 3.8: Momentum of food inflation

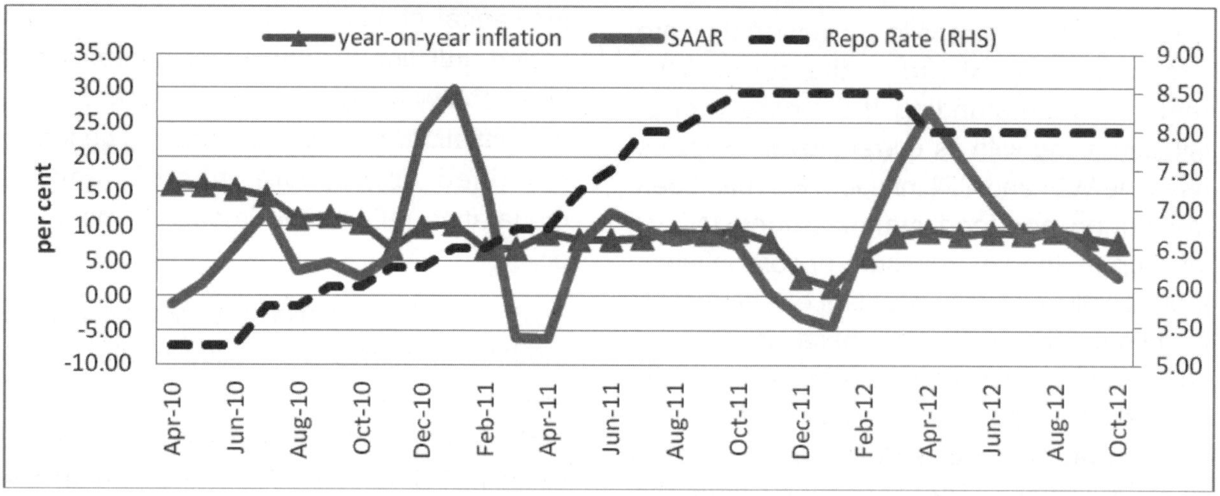

Fig 3.9: Momentum of CPI-IW inflation

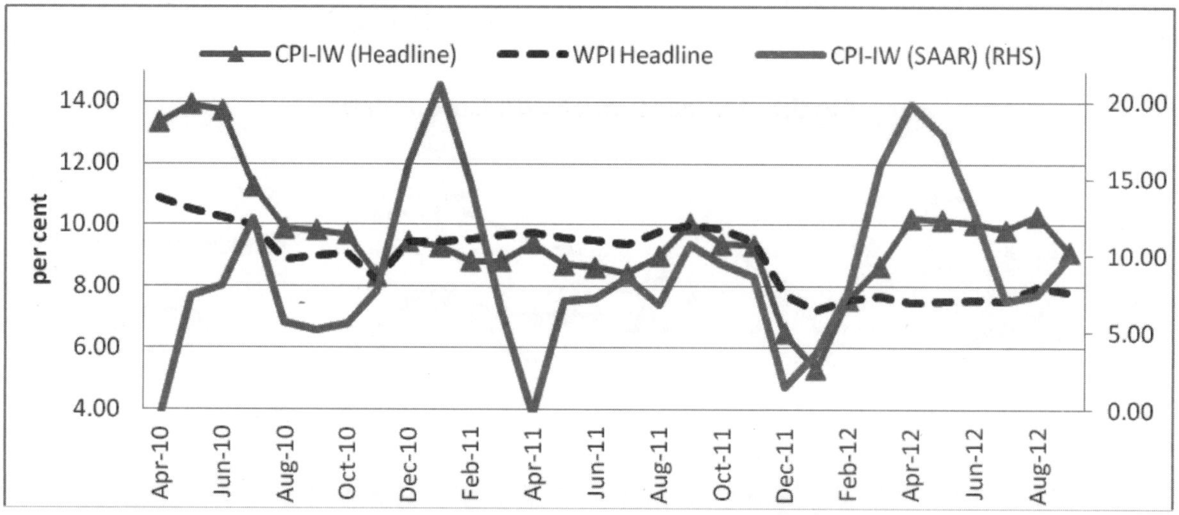

3.13 Some economists prefer the central bank to target consumer price inflation rather than the NFM inflation, because the former is what the person on the street experiences. Moreover, generalized and persistent CPI inflation could entrench high inflationary expectations amongst the public. Though there have been 3 consumer price indices, before the Central Statistical Office launched the new series of CPI in January, 2010, all of these indices have been for a specific class of consumers. CPI for industrial workers, which is primarily used for wage indexation, however, has been the CPI index preferred by many economists. Inflation during August 2010 to March 2012 appears to follow more or less a similar trend irrespective of whether it is measured in terms of WPI or CPI-IW. A nearly 2-percentage point gap has emerged in recent months between these two measures. Momentum of CPI-IW as measured by its deseasonalized series, however indicates moderation in inflation in recent months, consistent with WPI-core and WPI-food (Fig 3.9).

Why has inflation persisted?

3.14 Inflation in protein foods particularly meat, fish and eggs; milk and milk products; and vegetables and fruits has continued to persist because of changes in dietary habits and supply constraints. Data from National Accounts Statistics indicate that while the share of food in total private final consumption expenditure continued to show a decline, expenditure on protein foods increased from 18.6 per cent of total food expenditure in 1980-81 to 29.6 per cent in 2010-11. An increase in income made this desirable shift in consumption feasible. At the national level, per capita income, adjusted for inflation continued to rise. There was also a significant increase in rural wages. Rural wages in nominal terms went up by an average of over 18 per cent since 2008-09. Inflation-adjusted rural wages also went up by 7.5 per cent during this period. (Fig 3.10) The input costs for producers in both food and non-food segment, as reflected in the prices of feed, fodder and other inputs also increased. An increase in MSP, while necessary to ensure remunerative returns to farmers, raised the floor prices and also contributed to rise in input prices.

Commodities under price pressure and policy initiatives

3.15 As indicated earlier, a few commodities have contributed disproportionately to inflation. In Q2 of 2012-13, 19 commodities (commodity groups) with a weight of 28.5 per cent in WPI contributed 67.8 per cent to total inflation (Table 3.2). Contribution of each of these commodities to inflation in Q2 of 2012-13 exceeded 1.5 times of their weight (with the exception of milk).

Fig 3.10: Index of per capita income, rural wages and CPI-IW

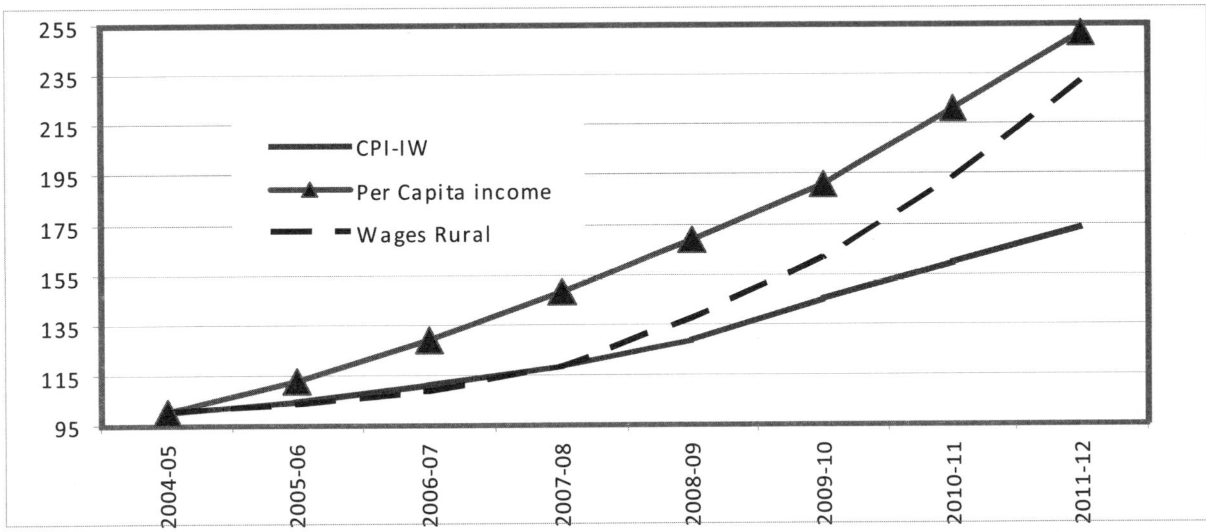

Table 3.2: Contribution to inflation (in per cent): items to be watched

	Weight	2010-11	2011-12				2012-13	
			Q1	Q2	Q3	Q4	Q1	Q2
Rice	1.79	1.33	0.66	0.84	0.68	0.68	1.61	2.79
Wheat	1.12	0.44	-0.01	-0.14	-0.52	-0.47	1.06	1.97
Gram	0.33	-0.06	0.25	0.82	1.77	1.89	2.44	3.01
Arhar	0.14	-0.11	-0.36	-0.29	-0.06	-0.23	-0.12	0.35
Tomatoes	0.27	0.79	0	-0.68	0.85	-0.54	0	0.75
Potatoes	0.20	-1.2	0	0.25	-0.38	-0.08	1.5	1.66
Milk	3.24	7.63	2.84	4.21	4.88	6.78	5.96	3.63
Fish (inland+ marine)	1.30	5.47	2.29	2.96	4.12	6.79	5.64	4.67
Black Pepper	0.03	0.14	0.33	0.31	0.41	0.41	0.36	0.37
Oil seeds+ edible oil+ oilcake	5.32	2.47	6.27	6.89	5.64	6.26	8.84	11.97
Sugar	1.74	-0.25	1.14	1.2	1.35	0.84	1.32	3.67
Minerals	1.52	6.14	7.07	6.7	7.21	11.72	4.72	5.04
Coal	2.09	1.49	3.38	3.29	3.48	7.12	4.68	4.46
Non-Administered Mineral Oil	3.04	6.63	10.92	10.2	13.73	13.18	9.01	7.82
Electricity	3.45	1.59	0.08	-0.09	0.8	1.4	2.89	5.37
Non-Urea Fertilizer	1.08	0.83	1.01	1.39	2.9	3.41	3.33	4.03
Cement & Lime	1.39	0.2	0.32	0.08	1.12	1.27	1.37	2.12
Gold & gold ornaments	0.36	1.75	2.75	3.15	3.66	4.06	3.6	2.78
Guar Seed	0.05	0.04	0.25	0.5	0.68	2.4	3.99	1.3

3.16 Two factors contributed to an increase in inflation in cereals. Besides an increase in the minimum support prices (MSP) for wheat and rice, there has been a mismatch between open market availability and demand, particularly for wheat. Food Corporation of India has already announced a programme of open market sales of 65 lakh tonnes of wheat in next three months which is expected to cool the market and dampen expectation of a price rise. The upsurge in the prices of pulses has largely been due to a persistent mismatch in demand and domestic availability. In the long run, containment of inflation in pulses would require an increase in the supply of pulses through improved productivity.

3.17 Prices of vegetables have remained volatile in recent past. Apart from a demand and supply mismatch, inefficient intermediation and loss in the value of vegetables at different stages of their transactions have contributed to both an increase in prices and its volatility. Both the locational differences in prices and the volatility of prices over time could be considerably reduced with improvement in the supply chain mechanism. The existence of a large number of intermediaries between the farmer and the consumers and time delays due to activities such as packing, sorting, transporting and delivery adds to intermediation costs and value losses. Organised marketing and greater private sector participation is critical for improving this state of affairs but it requires reforming the APMC legislation. The Inter Ministerial Group on Inflation (IMGI) had suggested exempting perishables from the purview of APMC, provide freedom to farmers to make direct sales to aggregators and processors, introduce electronic auction platform for all mandis and replacing licenses of APMC market with an open registration backed by bank guarantees to ensure wider choices to growers and to prevent cartelization by traders. Electronic display of prices for short duration vegetable crops could reduce the asymmetry in information flow and provide appropriate marketing signals to producers.

3.18 There have been some developments along these recommended lines. To develop integrated value chains, the government has also been emphasizing the need for exempting vegetables from the levy of market fees. The States of Madhya Pradesh and West Bengal have recently waived the market fee on fruits and vegetables. Such waivers are expected to promote investment in development of backend infrastructure by private sector. The Ministry of Agriculture in collaboration with Forward Markets Commission is facilitating display of spot and futures prices on Price Ticker Boards in around 1700 mandis in different states. Recently, the government has permitted Foreign Direct Investment (FDI) in multi-brand retail trading. This will help consumers and farmers by improving the logistical facilities connecting the two.

3.19 The persistence of high inflation in milk and animal products has partly been due to the regional concentration of production centres, rising input costs which raised the floor price and lower productivity. While in some cases, there has been an increase in availability, typically it has been at a higher cost. Further, due to limited organized marketing (even in case of milk it is around 15 per cent of total milk produced) back end infrastructure such as a seamless cold chain has not been established, reducing quality and increasing wastage. A number of measures have been announced in Union Budget 2012-13 to augment supply and improve storage and warehousing facilities. Government had launched a National Mission for Protein supplements in 2011-12 with allocation of ₹300 crore. To broaden the scope of production of fish to coastal aquaculture, apart from fresh water aquaculture, the outlay for the mission in 2012-13 is being stepped up to ₹ 500 crore.

3.20 Issues related to sugar industry have been analyzed by the Rangarajan Committee. The Committee has recommended deregulation of sugar industry and dismantling of regulated release mechanism together with the levy obligations. These recommendations are under consideration by the Department of Food and Public Distribution.

3.21 The NFM products except for fertilizers (urea), non-administered petroleum products and edible oils are fully tradeable and none of these products are under administered price regime. Domestic prices for these products are governed both by global commodity prices and the domestic availability of these products. A stable rupee and moderate global prices, both relatively exogenous factors, may be important in keeping the prices of these products stable.

3.22 To summarize, inflation in India stems from a traditional mismatch between demand and supply. The relative magnitude of the imbalance has varied across sectors. For example, demand for consumer durables has remained high till recently, even while the demand for capital goods has remained more muted because of the slowdown in investment.

3.23 The inflation picture is further complicated in India because of shifting consumption basket and the supply of proteins and micro-nutrients like fruits and vegetables has not responded quickly. Interest rates are probably an inappropriate tool to shift people's preferences. This is why it may be reasonable for the RBI to look through the rise in food prices (which is what it does by focusing on NFM inflation, which puts lower emphasis on food prices), while trying to ensure that food inflation does not feed into wages and generalized inflation. Unfortunately, food is a big part of a worker's consumption basket, and higher food prices do feed into higher wage demands. What can be done? Government efforts to create the conditions for greater protein supply (some of which are described earlier) are important. Tempering wage inflation that is not directly linked to productivity increases may also be worth exploring.

CURRENT ACCOUNT DEFICIT (CAD)

3.24 India's current account deficit (CAD) has remained within manageable limits in recent years and has been financed largely by capital flows. During 2011-12 however, the CAD widened to 4.2 per cent of GDP because of the widening trade deficit. This has increased Balance of Payment vulnerability to 'sudden stop' and reversal of capital, especially when sizeable flows comprise of debt, and volatile portfolio investment.

Forecasting inflation in India

Augmented Phillips curve framework lends support that both demand and supply factors are drivers of inflation. Global commodity prices have a strong and quick pass-through and an increase of 10 per cent in global non-fuel commodity prices increases headline WPI inflation by 70-90 basis points in the same quarter, with the long-run impact being double (140-180 basis points). The exchange rate pass-through is 0.06 in the short-run and 0.12 in the long-run, i.e., 10 per cent appreciation (depreciation) of rupee vis-à-vis the US dollar reduces (increases) inflation by 60 basis points in the same quarter, while the long-run pass-through is 120 basis points. A deficiency of 10 per cent in the rainfall in July increases headline inflation by 60 basis points with a lag of three quarters and the long-run impact turns out to be 120 basis points. Minimum support prices have a substantial impact: 10 per cent increase in minimum support prices increase headline WPI inflation by 100 basis points with lag of a quarter, and the long-run impact is 200 basis points. At the same time, minimum support prices are also found to respond to headline WPI inflation with a lag. The finding of demand conditions having a relatively stronger impact on NFMP inflation vis-a-vis headline inflation supports the RBI's policy focus on NFMP as an indicator of demand pressures in the economy. Second, NFMP inflation is more persistent compared to headline inflation. The relatively sticker nature of NFMP also extends support to NFMP being used as a core measure of inflation or an indicator of underlying inflation pressures.

Muneesh Kapur- **Inflation Forecasting: Issues and Challenges in India- Reserve Bank of India, Working Paper series (DEPR):01/2012.**

3.25 The priority has therefore been to reduce CAD through improving trade balances. Efforts have been made to promote exports by diversifying the export commodity basket and export destinations. One way to limit imports is to bring prices up to international levels so that users see the full cost. A recent study commissioned by the Ministry of Finance on "Diesel Price and Under Recoveries: Macro-Economic Impacts" by Integrated Research and Action for Development of the Department of Economic Affairs, Ministry of Finance, suggests that diesel price revision will have a positive impact on curbing inflation over the medium term, enhancing GDP growth and reducing the fiscal deficit (Box 3.2).

3.26 Emphasis has continued on further facilitating remittances and encouraging software exports that have been responsible for the surplus on the invisible account. In recent years, this surplus has lowered the impact of widening trade deficit on CAD significantly. The two components together account for nearly two-third of the trade deficit that was more than 10 per cent of GDP in 2011-12. Remittances particularly are known to exhibit resilience when the country is hit by an external shock, as was evident during the global crisis of 2008.

Box 3.2 Diesel Price and Under Recoveries: Macro-Economic Impacts

A study on the "Diesel Price and Under Recoveries: Macro-Economic Impacts" by Integrated Research and Action for Development commissioned by the Ministry of Finance, suggests that diesel price revision will have a positive impact on curbing inflation, enhancing GDP growth and reducing the fiscal deficit

Impact on inflation

Any increase in price of diesel will lead to higher prices immediately but lower price rise in longer run as the fiscal deficit is reduced. With no change in policy, average inflation 2011-15 will be 7.13 per cent, while with a one shot 30 per cent increase in diesel price, average inflation rate may come down to 5.68 per cent. Even with a 10 per cent increase in diesel prices, the inflation rate expects to come down to an average of 6.66 per cent during 2011-15.

Impact on GDP:

GDP is affected by diesel price policy also. Under the various scenarios studied, GDP is impacted negatively in the immediate quarters following a price rise of diesel. However as the impact of price rise dissipates and inflation falls (compared to the "no change" scenario), GDP increases faster. GDP growth is projected to average 8.23 per cent, 8.92 per cent and 8.46 per cent during 2011-15 with a business as usual, a one shot 30 per cent increase in diesel prices and a partial 10 per cent increase in prices, respectively.

Demand of Petroleum products

Analysis indicates diesel consumption will reach 2681 crore litres, 2445 crore litres and 2549 crore litres with a business as usual, one shot 30 per cent increase in diesel prices and a partial 10 per cent increase in prices, respectively.

Fig 3.11: Quarterly movement of BOP parameters

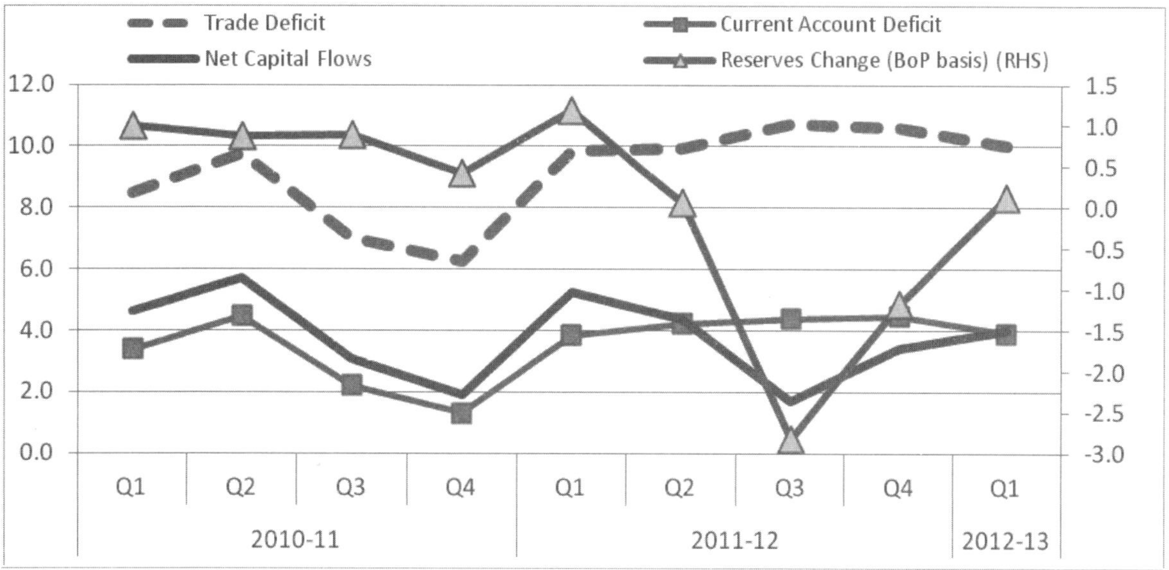

3.27 Gold imports have been one of the major factors in deterioration of CAD. Concerned over the sharp rise in the growth of gold loan companies, RBI has been tightening norms for NBFC's lending against gold and removed in February, 2011 the priority sector tag to such loans that banks used to give to NBFCs for on-lending, thus pushing up the cost of money for such companies. In March, 2012, RBI capped the amount NBFCs can lend against gold at 60 per cent. This was followed by putting banks' exposure to single gold loan NBFCs from 10 per cent to 7.5 per cent of their capital base. Commercial banks were also asked to set an internal ceiling for overall exposure to gold loan NBFCs. In October RBI barred banks from financing the purchase of gold in any form other than working capital finance.

3.28 New gold-backed financial instruments in the form of modified gold deposits and gold accumulation plans, besides gold-linked accounts and pension products linked with the precious metal, are some of the measures being considered to reduce the attraction of a direct investment in bullion and jewellery in the domestic market and check a substantial rise in imports. Gold-backed products will allow investors to gain the benefits of investments in the high-yielding commodity without actually investing in the physical commodity. They will thus provide more choices to investors in the domestic market. Of course, gold-linked instruments will have to be hedged through direct purchases of gold, or in the derivatives markets. Any rollout of gold-linked instruments will have to be monitored carefully to see whether the overall demand for gold actually falls. More generally, however, the demand from the public for financial investments in assets that retain their real value needs to be addressed. Of course, the ideal solution to this problem would be to bring down inflation so that household see good returns from traditional financial instruments.

3.29 Capital flows are driven by both pull (economic fundamentals of recipients) and push (policy stance of source countries) factors and have implications for exchange rate management, overall macroeconomic and financial stability including liquidity conditions. Capital account management needs to emphasize promoting foreign direct investment and reducing dependence on volatile portfolio flows. This would ensure that to the extent current account deficit is bridged through capital surplus, it would be through stable and growth enhancing investment flows. In the prevailing international financial architecture, reserves are the first line of defense against the volatile capital flows. In this context, the decline in reserves as a fraction of GDP, while not an immediate source of concern, needs to be watched closely.

FISCAL CONCERNS

3.30 As has been pointed out earlier, the growth slowdown in the current fiscal and in the previous year owes partly to domestic factors. In an environment where the supply side is constrained, a high fiscal deficit contributes to excess demand. Higher government borrowing can also crowd out private borrowing, and if sustained, lead to concerns about debt sustainability. The fiscal deficit needs therefore to be addressed to ensure that growth is stable and sustainable.

3.31 The fiscal situation started worsening beginning 2008-09, but following the global economic meltdown, it was understandable that fiscal space would be used for stimulating the economy. The Economic Survey 2011-12 pointed out the reasons for the lower-than-budgeted fiscal outcome in 2011-12 due to the sharp slowdown in industry, rising costs and thinning profits, a less-than-conducive financial market inhibiting divestment plans, and continued high subsidy outgo on account of firm global crude petroleum and fertilizer prices. This process has continued through the first half of the current fiscal. Given that these factors are unlikely to reverse substantially over the foreseeable future, it is imperative that the government tackle the fiscal deficit more forcefully, and has indicated its determination to do so.

3.32 Recognizing the concerns with public finances, the Government set up a committee headed by Dr. Vijay L. Kelkar to suggest an appropriate medium term roadmap for fiscal consolidation. The Committee suggested immediate steps to minimize the resources' shortfall and to keep expenditures under control. These include: a comprehensive strategy on tax policy and administration; new instruments to overcome concerns on the disinvestment front; progressive alignment of prices of diesel to the international market, eliminating half the diesel subsidy in the current fiscal, and a medium term policy for all fuel subsidies including movement towards direct cash transfer in lieu of LPG subsidy as well as regular increases in urea prices. The Committee also suggested improved monitoring of plan expenditure focusing on outcomes.

3.33 Immediately prior to the submission of the report of the Kelkar Committee, the government had to take measures to restrain the mounting under-recoveries of the oil marketing companies (OMCs) on account of non-revision of prices of subsidized fuel. Diesel prices were increased on September 13, 2012 by ₹ 5 per litre and the supply of subsidized LPG cylinders to each consumer was capped at 6 per annum which were expected to lower the under-recovery on these products by ₹20,300 crore for the remaining part of the fiscal. The Kelkar Committee recommended the following roadmap for the Central Government (Table 3.3).

Fig 3.12: Gross Tax Receipts, Fiscal Deficit and Expenditure on Interest & Subsidies as per cent to GDP

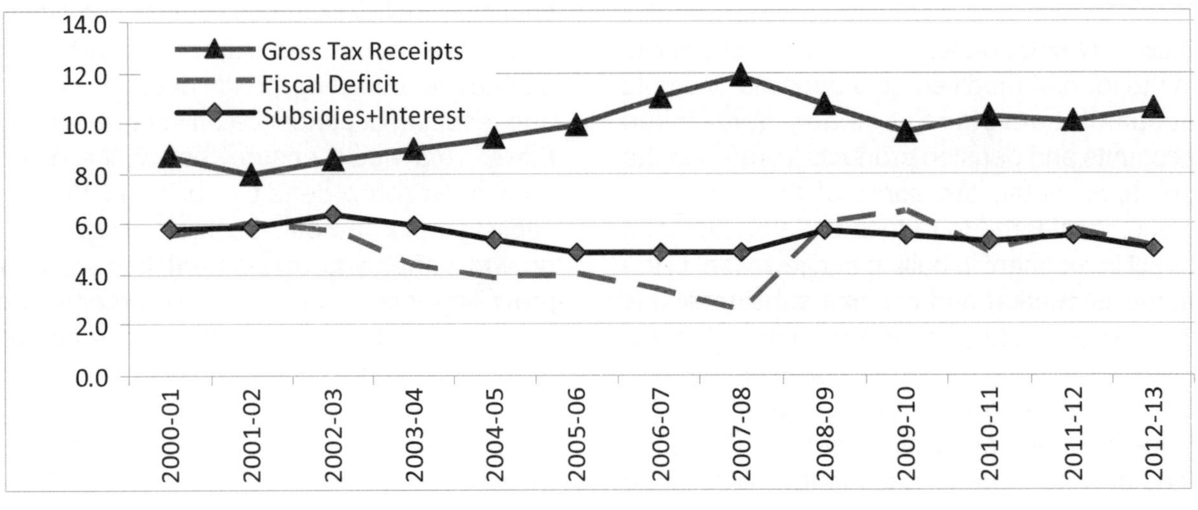

Table 3.3 Fiscal Roadmap (per cent to GDP)

	2012-13			2013-14	2014-15
	Budget	No Reform	Reform	Projections	
Gross Tax Revenue	**10.6**	**10.1**	**10.3**	**10.6**	**11.1**
Net-Centre's Tax Revenue	7.6	7.2	7.4	7.6	7.9
Non-Tax Revenue	1.6	1.6	1.6	1.4	1.3
Total-Revenue Receipts	**9.2**	**8.9**	**9.0**	**9.0**	**9.2**
Non-debt Capital Receipts	0.4	0.2	0.4	0.3	0.3
TOTAL- RECEIPTS	**9.6**	**9.1**	**9.4**	**9.3**	**9.5**
Non-Plan Expenditure	**9.5**	**10.2**	**9.8**	**9.1**	**8.5**
On Revenue Account	8.5	9.3	8.9	8.2	7.6
of which Subsidies	1.9	2.6	2.2	1.7	1.5
On Capital Account	1.0	0.9	0.9	0.9	0.9
Plan Expenditure	**5.1**	**5.0**	**4.8**	**4.9**	**4.9**
On Revenue Account	*4.1*	*4.0*	*3.8*	*3.6*	*3.6*
On Capital Account	*1.0*	*1.0*	*1.0*	*1.3*	*1.3*
TOTAL EXPENDITURE	**14.7**	**15.2**	**14.6**	**13.9**	**13.4**
On Revenue Account	*12.7*	*13.3*	*12.7*	*11.7*	*11.2*
Grants in aid for CapEx	*1.6*	*1.6*	*1.6*	*1.9*	*2.0*
On Capital Account	*2.0*	*1.9*	*1.9*	*2.2*	*2.2*
Deficits					
Revenue Deficit	3.4	4.4	3.7	2.8	2.0
Effective Revenue Deficit	1.8	2.8	2.1	0.9	0.0
Fiscal Deficit	5.1	6.1	5.2	4.6	3.9
Primary Deficit	1.9	2.9	2.0	1.4	0.9
Debt	45.5	46.7	46.1	44.9	42.9

Table 3.4 Fiscal roadmap for the Twelfth Plan

Year	Fiscal deficit to GDP (per cent)
2012-13	5.3
2013-14	4.8
2014-15	4.2
2015-16	3.6
2016-17	3.0

3.34 After examining the report of the Kelkar Committee, the Union Finance Minister announced in his press statement on October 29, 2012 that the Kelkar Committee had rightly cautioned against a business-as-usual scenario for the current year, which would entail grave consequences for the economy. Further, the recommendations on tax policy, tax administration, expenditure management and new models of disinvestment were meritorious and have been accepted by the Government. The statement also announced the intent to realize required revenues and contain expenditure, both on the plan and non-plan side. The statement also indicated the roadmap of fiscal consolidation for the Twelfth Plan based on the steps taken, being taken and those on the anvil (Table 3.4).

3.35 The Finance Minister in his Statement on October 29, 2012 has indicated that with sound policies and determination the goals can be achieved and that as fiscal consolidation takes place and investors' confidence increases, the economy is expected to return to the path of high investment, higher growth, lower inflation and long term sustainability.

Box 3.2: Report of the Committee on roadmap for fiscal consolidation.

The Union Finance Minister Shri P. Chidambaram in his Press Statement on August 6, 2012 indicated the proposed steps for economic recovery and announced the intent to unveil a path for fiscal consolidation. To this effect a Committee headed by Dr. Vijay L. Kelkar was set up with Dr. Indira Rajaraman and Dr. Sanjiv Mishra as Members. The Committee was charged with the task of introducing Mid-term corrections in the current fiscal and to chart a medium term framework in this regard.

In its report, the Committee cautioned that fiscal consolidation was imperative and serious adverse macro-economic consequences would result if corrective action was not taken. The Committee made an assessment of the trends in the Union public finances for the current fiscal and observed that in a business-as-usual scenario fiscal deficit could reach 6.1 per cent of GDP. With certain policy interventions, the Committee observed that this could be brought down to 5.2 per cent of GDP in 2011-12 and in the medium term to 3.9 per cent of GDP (2014-15).

The following summarises the recommendations of the Committee.

The Direct Taxes Code Bill 2010 should be comprehensively reviewed before it is enacted into law for implementation giving due consideration to the fact that in the current conjecture when tax-GDP ratio was low, there is not much fiscal space to accommodate any loss of revenue.

Tax departments need to harness the large volume of information collected by them. They have to develop data mining skills, ensuring improved compliance through proper risk management system, on line verification of Permanent Account Number for all high value transactions and 360 degree profiling of all tax payers.

The standard rate of 12 per cent in Union excise duties and service tax is to be progressively reduced to align with the goods and services tax (GST) rate of 8 per cent proposed for the Central GST.

The lower rate of 6 per cent in respect of Union excise duties will be limited only to merit goods and further pruning negative list of services under service tax.

The exemption granted to railways for transportation of goods and passengers (of higher class) should not be extended beyond 30.09.2012.

A comprehensive model for cross-verification of claims for input tax credit should be put in place by the Central Board of Excise and Customs.

The Government should consider the new mechanism of 'offer for sale' created by SEBI for facilitation divestment of stake in public sector undertakings by using the secondary market mechanism of stock exchanges either through 'call option' model or the model of 'Exchange Traded Fund'.

The use of technology in managing expenditure needs to be carried forward through the setting up of Expenditure Information Network. The committee suggested the use of direct cash transfers increasingly in lieu of certain subsidies.

Administered prices on a number of products need to be raised progressively to rein in subsidies to obviate the key fiscal risk.

OUTLOOK FOR ECONOMY

3.36 A slowdown in economic growth in the recent times, with the growth moderating to 5.4 per cent in the first half of 2012-13 indicate that the growth for the year as a whole will fall short of 7.6 per cent as was envisaged in the Economic Survey in March 2012. There are, however, reasons to believe that the slowdown has bottomed out and the economy is headed towards higher growth in the second half of 2012-13. A positive upturn in the Business Expectation Index in Oct-Dec quarter, higher PMI in November, visible buoyancy in capital markets, improved internal accruals of the corporate sector in July-Sept. quarter and resurgence of the growth in the manufacturing sector suggest that the economy is poised for a moderate acceleration in growth in the second half of 2012-13. Eight core sectors of industry with a weight of 38 per cent in IIP recorded a growth of 6.5 per cent in October, 2012, compared to an average growth of 3.2 per cent in the first half of 2012-13. Manufacturing sector has also reported a growth of 9.6 per cent in October 2012, compared to a contraction of 0.3 per cent in first half of 2012-13.

3.37 Agriculture is also expected to improve because of better prospects with rabi crops benefiting from greater moisture content in the soil and dominance of irrigated wheat and rice crops. Most services, particularly the trade, transport, communication, financial services, etc., being largely driven by the performance of real sectors will also have a better growth.

3.38 The assessment about the Union finances as made in Chapter 2 indicates that fiscal deficit would be contained to 5.3 per cent of GDP, compared to a level of 5.1 per cent as indicated at the Budget stage. A fiscal consolidation road map announced by the Government on October 29, 2012, has considerably improved business expectations and perception of the domestic and global investors. A further moderation in inflation, likely to commence from the fourth quarter of the current year, together with benign global commodity prices, will also facilitate softening of the monetary policy stance of RBI. Inflation as at the end of March 2013 is expected to moderate to 6.8-7.0 per cent level. Trade deficit in the first seven month of the year 2012-13 has been somewhat higher than what it was in the corresponding period of previous year. However, given the present indications, it is expected that the trade deficit in the current year would not be significantly higher than what it was last year. Consequently, it is reasonable to expect that the current account deficit as a ratio of GDP would be lower than what it was in 2011-12.

3.39 Given such an emerging scenario, it should be possible for the economy to improve the overall growth rate of GDP to around 5.7 to 5.9 percent for the year 2012-13. This would imply that the growth rate for the second half of the year 2012-13, would be close to around 6 per cent. To achieve this, both fiscal and monetary policies, however, would need to be supportive to sustain investor confidence. The government will also have to address the concerns relating to structural supply side bottlenecks.

Annex I

Status of Implementation of Major Budget Announcements

Sl. No.	Para No.	Summary of Budget Announcement	Status of Implementation
1.	20	Streamlining and reducing the number of Centrally Sponsored Schemes while implementing the 12th Five Year Plan and expanding the Central Plan Scheme Monitoring System to facilitate better tracking and utilisation of funds released by the Central Government.	Streamlining and reducing the number of Centrally Sponsored Schemes (CSS) is a policy issue and would be kept in view during the appraisal of new schemes proposed during the course of implementation of the XII Plan. So far as the ongoing schemes are concerned, the report of the B.K. Chaturvedi (BKC) Committee on "Restructuring of Centrally Sponsored Schemes" has been deliberated upon in the Planning Commission. Based on the deliberations, the Planning Commission has come up with its recommendations on rationalization of the Centrally Sponsored Schemes for 12th Plan. These recommendations, which draw upon the suggestions/ recommendations of BKC Committee report, will be placed before the Cabinet for approval. A proposal to expand the Central Plan Scheme Monitoring System has been prepared by the Planning Commission, which will be taken up for consideration by the Expenditure Finance Committee shortly.
2.	22	To restrict the expenditure on Central subsidies to under 2 per cent of GDP in 2012-13, and further bringing it down to 1.75 per cent of GDP over the next three years through better targeting and leakage proof delivery to improve the quality of public spending.	The committee constituted under the chair of Sh. Vijay Kelkar to formulate the fiscal consolidation roadmap has submitted its report and further appropriate action shall be taken based on the recommendations to keep the overall subsidy outgo of Government of India to the minimum possible level.
3.	23	Rolling out a mobile- based Fertiliser Management System (mFMS) designed to provide end-to-end information on the movement of fertilisers and subsidies, from the manufacturer to the retail level during 2012, and implementing a direct transfer of subsidy to the retailer, and eventually to the farmer in subsequent phases.	The Department of Fertilizers (DOF), with the technical support of National Informatics Centre (NIC) has developed a mobile and web application named mobile Fertilizers Monitoring System (m-FMS) which provides information about stock position, sale and receipt of fertilizers till the last retail point. Fertilizers companies, retailers and wholesalers can update the data on mFMS portal (http://mfms.nic.in) through web or mobile application. With the help of the system, it would be possible to track fertilizers movement from plant/port up to retailer level. Hitherto tracking of fertilizer movement was monitored up to wholesaler level only. This Phase I of the Direct transfer of subsidy to farmers has come into effect from 1st

Annex continued

Sl. No.	Para No.	Summary of Budget Announcement	Status of Implementation
			November, 2012. Further, DOF would be doing pilots in 10 districts spread over nine States to track the movement of fertilizers from retailer to farmer under Phase-III (A). This pilot will start from January 2013. In these pilot districts, part of the subsidy to manufacturers will be linked to sales of fertilizers to farmers by retailers, thereby accounting for the subsidized fertilizers from plant/port to consumers in the supply chain management of fertilizers. After successful implementation of Phase-III (A) in these 10 pilot districts, next phase, i.e., Phase III (B) in which cash subsidy will be transferred to farmers would commence from 1st April, 2013. Simultaneously, Phase-III (A) would be rolled out in the whole country.
4.	24	Implementing a pilot project in Alwar district of Rajasthan on direct transfer of subsidy for kerosene into the bank accounts of beneficiaries on the lines of a pilot project in Mysore for selling LPG at market price and reimbursing the subsidy directly into the beneficiary's bank account	The pilot project has been undertaken in the Kotkasim tehsil of the Alwar district. As on 30th September, 2012, a total of 15,020 bank accounts have been opened as against 25,843 card holders. Till that date an amount of ₹52.06 lakh has been deposited in those accounts as subsidies. Against the cumulative quota of 792 KL for 10 months (average 80 KL/month) in Kotkasim, only 96 KL (average 10.67 KL/Month) has been lifted by the cardholders. This is 12% of the quota fixed for Kotkasim. The project has been extended till 31.12.12 to enable the State to put in the last mile mechanism in PDS shops.
5.	25	To scale up and roll out Aadhaar enabled payments for various government schemes in at least 50 selected districts within the next six months.	51 districts have been identified and the social sector schemes in most of these identified districts have also been selected for implementation of the pilot projects. As a first step, efforts have been directed toward completing Aadhaar enrolments in these identified districts and substantial enrolment penetration has been achieved. As on 30.09.2012, Aadhaar enrolments have covered 75% or more of the resident population in 22 out of the 51 districts, while in 13 other districts the enrolments have covered a population in excess of 50%. The technology framework and infrastructure for rolling out Aadhaar Enabled Payment System (AEPS) at UIDAI's Technology Centre has been put in place. The social sector schemes in most of these 51 identified districts have also been selected for integration with

Annex continued

Sl. No.	Para No.	Summary of Budget Announcement	Status of Implementation
			Aadhaar. Aadhaar seeding in the beneficiary databases in these districts is underway and up to the end of September 2012, about 31% of the beneficiary population of the various Government schemes in these districts has been seeded with Aadhaar. The linkage of bank accounts of the beneficiaries with Aadhaar is also in progress.
6.	26	Enacting the Direct Taxes Code (DTC) Bill at the earliest.	The Direct Tax Code (DTC) Bill, 2010 shall be introduced in the Lok Sabha for consideration after examination of the recommendations of the Standing Committee.
7.	27	Finalizing the Constitution Amendment Bill, as a preparatory step in implementation of the Goods and Services Tax (GST) after examining the recommendations of the Parliamentary Standing Committee, and drafting of model legislation for Centre and State GST in concert with States.	The Constitution Amendment Bill is under examination by the Standing Committee. A discussion paper on key concepts underlying GST is being finalized. The drafting of Model GST legislation for the Centre and the State will be taken up after the discussion paper is finalized.
8.	28	To set up and operationalise the Goods and Service Tax Network (GSTN) as a National Information Utility by August 2012.	The proposal relating to the incorporation of the company has been approved by the Empowered Committee of State Finance Ministers on 13.07.2012 with suggestions. These suggestions are under examination in the Department of Revenue.
9.	30	Raising ₹30,000 crore during 2012-13 through disinvestment, while retaining at least 51 per cent ownership and management control of CPSEs with the Government.	Disinvestment proceeds from the Initial Public Offer (IPO) of National Building Construction Corporation Limited (NBCC) amounting to ₹124.97 crore and ₹24.51 lakh as interest have been credited to Government account as on 30.09.2012.
10.	32	Achieving a broad consensus in respect of allowing FDI in multi-brand retail trade up to 51 per cent in consultation with the State Governments.	**Announcement implemented** Press Note 5 of 2012 has been issued by Department of Industrial Policy and Promotion on 20.9.2012.
11.	33	Advancing implementing the Advance Pricing Agreement (APA) by introducing it in the Finance Bill, 2012 to significantly bring down tax litigation and provide tax certainty to foreign investors.	**Announcement implemented** Advance Pricing Agreement (APA) Rules have been notified vide Notification No. 36/2012, S.O. 2005(E) dated 30th August, 2012. The Rules have become effective from the same date.

Annex continued

Sl. No.	Para No.	Summary of Budget Announcement	Status of Implementation
12.	35	To introduce a new scheme called Rajiv Gandhi Equity Savings Scheme to allow for income tax deduction of 50 per cent to new retail investors, who invest up to ₹50,000 directly in equities and whose annual income is below ₹10 lakh.	The broad provisions of the scheme and the income tax benefits under it have been incorporated as Section 80CCG of the Income Tax Act, 1961, as amended by the Finance Act, 2012. The Scheme has been finalised and sent to DoR for notification and SEBI for operationalisation.
13.	37	Deepening the reforms in Capital market by:- • Allowing Qualified Foreign Investors (QFIs) to access Indian Corporate Bond market;	**Announcement implemented** RBI and SEBI have issued circulars dated 16th July 2012 and 18th July 2012 respectively. A separate sub-limit of USD 1 billion has been created for QFIs investment in corporate bonds and mutual fund debt schemes.
		• Simplifying the process of issuing Initial Public Offers (IPOs), lowering their costs and helping companies reach more retail investors in small towns; inter alia, by making it mandatory for companies to issue IPOs of ₹10 crore and above in electronic form through nationwide broker network of stock exchanges;	**Announcement implemented** SEBI has issued the required Circular on 4th October 2012.
		• Providing opportunities for wider shareholder participation in important decisions of the companies through electronic voting facilities, besides existing process for shareholder voting, which would be made mandatory initially for top listed companies; and	**Announcement implemented** On 13th July 2012 SEBI has come out with necessary amendments to be made to equity listing agreement by stock exchanges. The main features of the scheme are as under;- a. Electronic voting is made mandatory for top 500 listed companies at Bombay Stock exchange (NSE), chosen based on market capitalization in respect of those businesses to be transacted through postal ballot. b. Listed companies may chose any one of the two agencies (Central Depository Services (India) Ltd. (CDSL) and National securities Depositories Ltd.(NSDL) which are currently providing the e-voting platform. These platforms permit any shareholder holding shares in physical or demat form, to cast their votes electronically irrespective of which depository he holds his shares with. c. This shall be applicable for the shareholders' meetings, for which noticed are issued on or after October 01,2012. However, the listed companies are at liberty to provide e-voting

Annex continued

Sl. No.	Para No.	Summary of Budget Announcement	Status of Implementation
			facility to their shareholders in the meeting for which notices have been sent prior to October 01,2012.
		• Permitting two-way fungibility in Indian Depository Receipts subject to a ceiling with the objective of encouraging greater foreign participation in Indian capital market.	**Announcement implemented** RBI and SEBI have already issued final Circulars on implementation of two-way fungibility of Indian Depository Receipts (IDRs) on 28th August 2012. Ministry of Corporate Affairs has issued notification on Companies (Issue of Indian Depository Receipts) Amendment Rules, 2012 on 01 October 2012.
14.	38	To move official amendments to the "The Pension Fund Regulatory and Development Authority Bill, 2011", "The Banking Laws (Amendment) Bill, 2011" and "The Insurance Laws (Amendment) Bill, 2008" in the Budget Session in pursuance to the recommendations of the Standing Committee.	The official amendments in "The Banking Laws (Amendment) Bill, 2011" will be moved in the Winter session of the Parliament. Amendments to the remaining two Bills have been approved by the Cabinet on 4.10.2012.
15.	39	To move the following Bills in the Budget Session of the Parliament:	
		• The Micro Finance Institutions (Development and Regulation) Bill, 2012;	**Announcement implemented** Bill introduced in Parliament on 22.05.2012.
		• The National Housing Bank (Amendment) Bill, 2012;	**Announcement implemented** Bill introduced in Lok Sabha on 30.04.2012.
		• The Small Industries Development Bank of India (Amendment) Bill, 2012;	**Announcement implemented** Bill introduced in Lok Sabha on 22.05.2012.
		• National Bank for Agriculture and Rural Development (Amendment) Bill, 2012;	Legal vetting of the draft Bill is in progress.
		• Regional Rural Banks (Amendment) Bill, 2012;	Legal vetting of the draft Bill is in progress.
		• Indian Stamp (Amendment) Bill, 2012; and	The draft Bill was sent to the Legislative Department for vetting. As advised by them, further opinion of Department of Legal Affairs is being sought on certain issues.
		• Public Debt Management Agency of India Bill, 2012.	Note for consideration of the Cabinet is under preparation.

Annex continued

Sl. No.	Para No.	Summary of Budget Announcement	Status of Implementation
16.	41	To provide ₹15,888 crore for capitalisation of Public Sector Banks, Regional Rural Banks and other financial institutions including NABARD to protect the financial health of Public Sector Banks and financial institutions, and also to create a financial holding company which will raise resources to meet the capital requirements of Public Sector Banks.	**Capitalization of RRBs** **Announcement implemented**. Cabinet has approved the proposal for capitalization of RRBs. An amount of ₹200 crore has been released to 11 RRBs on 08.07.2012. Further release will be made after finalization of revised estimate and subject to release of proportionate share by concerned State Governments and Sponsor Banks. **Capitalization of NABARD** **Announcement implemented**. An amount of ₹108.20 crore has been released on 08.07.2012. **Capitalization of Public Sector banks:** A cabinet note is under preparation. **Creating a Financial Holding Company to meet capital requirements of PSBs,** A cabinet note is under preparation.
17.	42	Implementing a comprehensive action plan during 2012-13 to bring banking payment structure at par with global standards, and also to develop a central Know Your Customer (KYC) depository in 2012-13 to avoid multiplicity of registration and data upkeep.	**Bringing banking payment structure at par with global standards** The Key Advisory Group constituted on this issue has submitted their recommendations. A Committee constituted, vide order dated 17.07.2012, under the chairmanship of Secretary (FS) is now seized with implementation of the recommendations on Payment Structure. **Know your customer (KYC) depository** The report of the Committee on developing KYC depository is under preparation.
18.	43	Issuance of revised guidelines on priority sector lending after stakeholder consultation, based on the recommendations of a Committee set up by the RBI.	**Announcement implemented** Revised guidelines on priority sector lending have been released by RBI on 20.07.2012.
19.	44	To cover the all identified habitations under the "Swabhimaan" campaign by March 31, 2012, and also to set up ultra small branches at these habitations as a next step, where the Business Correspondents would deal with cash transactions.	As against the 74398 habitations with population over 2000 identified for coverage under Swabhiman, banking facilities to 74194 habitations have been provided till 31st March, 2012 through Branches, Business Correspondent Agents (BCAs), Mobile branches etc, More than 62,000 BCAs have been appointed and about 3.16 crore Financial Inclusion Accounts opened.

Annex continued

Sl. No.	Para No.	Summary of Budget Announcement	Status of Implementation
20.	45	To extend the "Swabhimaan" campaign in 2012-13 to habitations with population of more than 1000 in North Eastern and hilly States and to other habitations which have crossed population of 2,000 as per Census 2011.	**Announcement implemented** Since the village level Census data for 2011 is not available, it has been decided to cover villages with population 1600-2000 (as per 2001 Census) as it is expected that these villages would have crossed the population of 2000 in 2011 Census. Necessary instruction for identification, allocation and coverage of these villages, as well as villages with population between 1000 and 2000 in the Hilly and North Eastern region states have been issued in May, 2012.
21.	47	To extend the scheme of capitalisation of weak RRBs by another 2 years to enable all the States to contribute their share.	**Announcement implemented** Extension of the scheme on capitalization of weak RRBs has been approved by the Cabinet.
22.	49	This year it has been decided to make irrigation (including dams, channels and embankments), terminal markets, common infrastructure in agriculture markets, soil testing laboratories and capital investment in fertiliser sector eligible for Viability Gap Funding (VGF) under this scheme. Oil and Gas/LNG storage facilities and oil and gas pipelines, fixed network for telecommunication and telecommunication towers will also be made eligible sectors for VGF.	The following sub-sectors have been notified as eligible for Viability Gap Funding under the Scheme for Support to PPP in Infrastructure on 24.03.2012: a. Oil/Gas/Liquefied Natural Gas (LNG) storage facility (includes city gas distribution network) b. Oil and Gas pipelines (includes city gas distribution network) c. Irrigation (dams, channels, embankments etc.) d. Telecommunication (Fixed Network) (includes optic fibre/wire/cable networks which provide broadband/internet) e. Telecommunication towers, f. Terminal Markets g. Common infrastructure in agriculture markets; and h. Soil testing laboratories. In respect of the Fertilizer sector, the Department of Fertilizer has been advised to make a comprehensive presentation before the Empowered Committee on the requirements of the Fertilizer sector, and the regime that is proposed to be followed to incentivize production of fertilizers in the country to ensure food security.
23.	52	To raise ₹60,000 crore through tax-free bonds for financing infrastructure projects in 2012-13, including ₹10,000 crore for NHAI, ₹10,000 crore for IRFC,	An aggregate amount of ₹53,500 crores have been approved for tax-free bonds issues in Financial Year 2012-13 as against ₹60,000 crores proposed in the Budget. These bonds are now

Annex continued

Sl. No.	Para No.	Summary of Budget Announcement	Status of Implementation
		₹10,000 crore for IIFCL, ₹5,000 crore for HUDCO, ₹5,000 crore for National Housing Bank, ₹5,000 crore for SIDBI, ₹5,000 crore for ports and ₹10,000 crore for power sector.	ready to hit the market following issue of notification by the Central Board of Direct Taxes on 06.11.2012.
24.	53	To notify a harmonised master list of infrastructure sector to remove ambiguity in the policy and regulatory domain and encourage investment in the infrastructure sector.	**Announcement implemented** The notification for a harmonized master list of infrastructure sectors has since been issued on 28.3.2012. An institutional mechanism for the updation of the harmonized master list has also been set up.
25.	57	Signing of fuel supply agreements by Coal India Limited (CIL) with power plants that have entered into long-term Power Purchase Agreements with DISCOMs and constitution of an inter-ministerial group to undertake periodic review of the allocated coal mines and make recommendations on de-allocations, if so required.	As on 30.09.2012, Fuel Supply Agreements (FSAs) with 30 Power Plants out of 118 Power Plants commissioned after 31.07.2012, have been concluded. Remaining FSAs is under consideration by Coal India Limited (CIL) in consultation with Ministry. An Inter-Ministerial Group (IMG) to review allocation of Coal Mines was constituted on 21.6.2012, which has taken up for review of 58 cases where show cause notices were issued earlier, and 18 other cases where it was decided to deduct Bank Guarantee based on earlier reviews. The IMG has recommended de-allocation of 13 coal blocks allocated to 29 companies, deduction of Bank Guarantee in the cases of 14 blocks allocated to 19 companies and imposition of Bank Guarantee in case of 1 coal block. No action has been recommended in cases of 3 coal blocks allocated to 2 companies. The recommendations of the IMG have been accepted by the competent authority and action is initiated accordingly.
26.	58	To permit External Commercial Borrowings (ECB) to part finance Rupee debt of existing power projects.	**Announcement implemented** Press Release was issued by the Government on 18th April, 2012, and the Reserve Bank of India (RBI) issued circular on 20th April, 2012.
27.	59	To award projects covering a length of 8,800 kms under NHDP during 2012-13.	A total of 81 projects were identified for award up to September 2012. Out of this, 6 projects with a total road length of 561.31 Kilometer and total project cost of ₹5259.56 crore have been awarded as on 30.09.2012.

Annex continued

Sl. No.	Para No.	Summary of Budget Announcement	Status of Implementation
28.	60	Allowing ECB for capital expenditure on the maintenance and operations of toll systems for roads and highways to encourage public private partnerships in road construction projects,.	**Announcement implemented** Press Release issued by the Government on 18th April, 2012, and the Reserve Bank of India (RBI) issued circular on 20th April, 2012.
29.	62	Permitting ECB for working capital requirements of the airline industry for a period of one year, subject to a total ceiling of US Dollar 1 billion to address the immediate financing concerns of the Civil Aviation sector	**Announcement implemented** Press Release issued by the Government on 18th April, 2012, and the Reserve Bank of India (RBI) issued circular on 20th April, 2012.
30.	63	Allowing foreign airlines to participate up to 49 per cent in the equity of an air transport undertaking engaged in operation of scheduled and non-scheduled air transport services.	**Announcement implemented** Press Note No.6 (2012 series) was issued by the Department of Industrial Policy and Promotion (DIPP) on 20.9.2012.
31.	64	The Delhi Mumbai Industrial Corridor (DMIC) is being developed on either side along the alignment of the Western Dedicated Rail Freight Corridor. The project has made significant progress. In September 2011, Central assistance of ₹18,500 crore spread over a period of 5 years has been approved. The Japanese Prime Minister has announced US$ 4.5 billion as Japanese participation in DMIC project.	**Announcement implemented** The Deed of Public Trust of the DMIC Project Implementation Trust Fund has been executed on 27.9.2012 and the first meeting of the Trust was also held on the same day. An amount of ₹411.4 crore has been allocated under BE 2012-13 for the project. Department of Industrial Policy and Promotion (DIPP) as settler of the DMIC Project Implementation Trust Fund has contributed ₹312.4 crore as initial contribution to the main corpus of the Trust and another ₹99 crore as additional corpus to the Trust.
32.	65	In view of the shortage of housing for low income groups in major cities and towns, it was proposed to:-	
		• Allow ECB for low cost affordable housing projects;	Work is in progress. The framework, draft guidelines and monitoring mechanism are being decided.
		• Set up Credit Guarantee Trust Fund to ensure better flow of institutional credit for housing loans;	**Announcement implemented** Ministry of Housing and Urban Poverty Alleviation has set up the Credit Guarantee Trust Fund.
		• Enhance provisions under Rural Housing Fund from ₹3000 crore to ₹4000 crore;	**Announcement implemented** The Fund amount has been increased and allocation of banks has been made on the basis of the shortfall of Priority Sector Lending targets as on last reporting Friday of March 2012 by RBI.
		• Extend the scheme of interest subvention of 1 per cent on housing	**Announcement implemented** Release order was issued by Department of Financial Services on 24.09.2012.

Annex continued

Sl. No.	Para No.	Summary of Budget Announcement	Status of Implementation
		loan up to ₹15 lakh where the cost of the house does not exceed ₹25 lakh for another year; and	
		• Enhance the limit of indirect finance under priority sector from ₹5 lakh to ₹10 lakh.	**Announcement implemented** Notification on Priority Sector Lending was issued by the RBI on 20.7.2012 and clarifications on targets and classifications issued on 17.10.2012.
33.	66	To reduce India's import dependence in urea, and to encourage use of single super phosphate (SSP), which is produced domestically to reduce dependence on potassic-phosphatic (P&K) fertiliser.	To enhance indigenous production of urea and to reduce import of urea in the country, the inter Ministerial consultations have been completed on a revised draft CCEA Note on New Investment Policy 2012. In order to encourage usage of single super phosphate (SSP), following steps have been taken: (i) SSP has been included under Nutrient Based Subsidy (NBS) policy wherein subsidy on SSP has been given based on its nutrient content and MRP has been left open. (ii) Apart from indigenous source of Rock Phosphate, a number of grades of rock phosphate and their blending combinations have been notified to be used by SSP units for production of SSP. (iii) Low Grade Rock Phosphate has also been allowed for Beneficiated Rock Phosphate in order to produce SSP as per FCO standard. (iv) New SSP plants have been inducted under NBS policy in order to increase the production of SSP. As on date, 85 SSP units are registered under NBS Policy. Four new SSP units are under process for induction under NBS Policy. It has been observed that the production of SSP has increased as compared to production of SSP in pre NBS regime.
34.	67	Implementation of the financial package of ₹3,884 crore for waiver of loans of handloom weavers and their cooperative societies.	This is a centrally sponsored plan scheme of which Government of India share is ₹3137 crore and that of State Governments is ₹747 crore. National Implementation, Monitoring & Review Committee (NIMRC) has been meeting from time to time. As on 30.9.2012, 27 States have given letters of commitment to sign MOU and to provide for State share, and 20 States have signed the MoU.

Annex continued

Sl. No.	Para No.	Summary of Budget Announcement	Status of Implementation
35.	68	To set up two more mega handloom clusters, one to cover Prakasam and Guntur districts in Andhra Pradesh and the other for Godda and neighbouring districts in Jharkhand, and to provide assistance in setting up of dormitories for women workers in the 5 mega clusters relating to handloom, power loom and leather sectors.	Advertisement for inviting Expression of Interest (EOI) was published on 6th June, 2012 for appointment of Cluster Management and Technical Agency (CMTA) for Prakasam & Guntur Districts in Andhra Pradesh and Godda & neighboring Districts in Jharkhand. The technical bids were opened on 13.7.2012, and Stage II of technical evaluation is currently underway. So far as setting up of dormitories for women workers in 5 mega clusters relating to handloom, power-loom and leather sector is concerned, Ministry of Textile (MOT) has requested for flexibility to set up the dormitories in projects under the Scheme for Integrated Textile Park (SITP). This is under examination. As regards the dormitory in leather sector, Department of Industrial Policy and Promotion (DIPP) has informed that this would require modifications in the existing 'Mega Leather Cluster' scheme and therefore appraisal of EFC and approval of CCEA again.
36.	69	To set up three Weavers' Service Centres, one each in Mizoram, Nagaland and Jharkhand, and also to launch a pilot scheme in the Twelfth Plan for promotion and application of Geo-textiles in the North East Region.	State Governments of Mizoram, Nagaland and Jharkhand have been requested to provide land for setting up of new Weavers' Service Centres (WSCs) in their States. Simultaneously, SFC/EFC proposals for the setting up of WSCs and Geo textile schemes have been prepared. As regards the pilot scheme for promotion and application of Geo-textiles in the North East Region, a budget line has been created for this scheme. A draft EFC note has also been circulated to the Planning Commission. Several rounds of consultations have been held with stakeholders in the North East Region.
37.	70	To set up a powerloom mega cluster in Ichalkaranji in Maharashtra with a Budget allocation of ₹70 crore to address the need of the local artisans and weavers.	Expression of Interest (EOI) was published on 23.8.2012 for appointment of Cluster Management and Technical Agency (CMTA) for setting up a Powerloom Mega Cluster in Ichalkaranji in Maharashtra. Last date for submission of the EOI was 24.9.2012, and Stage I of technical evaluation is currently underway.
38.	71	To set up a ₹5,000 crore India Opportunities Venture Fund with SIDBI.	**Announcement implemented** India Opportunities Venture Fund has been set up in August 2012.

Annex continued

Sl. No.	Para No.	Summary of Budget Announcement	Status of Implementation
39.	76	To allocate ₹300 crore to Vidarbha Intensified Irrigation Development Programme under RKVY, which seeks to bring in more farming areas under protective irrigation.	Operational guidelines for the scheme have been approved and sent to the State Government of Maharashtra. State Level Sanctioning Committee (SLSC) of Maharashtra has approved Action Plans for ₹300 crore under the scheme and ₹150 crore have already been released as first installment.
40.	77	To merge the remaining activities into a set of missions to address the needs of agricultural development in the Twelfth Five Year Plan. These Missions are: (i) *National Food Security Mission* which aims to bridge the yield gap in respect of paddy, wheat, pulses, millet and fodder. The ongoing Integrated Development of Pulses Villages, Promotion of Nutri-cereals and Accelerated Fodder Development Programme would now become a part of this Mission; (ii) *National Mission on Sustainable Agriculture including Micro Irrigation* is being taken up as a part of the National Action Plan on Climate Change. The Rainfed Area Development Programme will be merged with this; (iii) *National Mission on Oilseeds and Oil Palm* aims to increase production and productivity of oil seeds and oil palm; (iv) *National Mission on Agricultural Extension and Technology* focuses on adoption of appropriate technologies by farmers for improving productivity and efficiency in farm operations; and (v) *National Horticulture Mission* aims at horticulture diversification. This will also include the initiative on saffron.	In-principle approval for all the five Missions has been obtained from Planning Commission, and the memoranda for obtaining the approval of EFC are under preparation.
41.	79	To raise the target for agricultural credit in 2012-13 to ₹5,75,000 crore.	**Announcement implemented** The enhanced target of ₹575,000 crore for agricultural credit has been communicated to Banks/NABARD.

Annex continued

Sl. No.	Para No.	Summary of Budget Announcement	Status of Implementation
42.	80	To provide an additional subvention of 3 per cent to the prompt paying farmers under the interest subvention scheme for providing short term crop loans to farmers at 7 per cent interest per annum, which is to be continued during 2012-13.	**Announcement implemented.** Approval of the Cabinet has been obtained and instruction has been communicated to the Banks on 18.09.2012.
43.	81	To allocate ₹10,000 crore to NABARD for refinancing the RRBs through RRB Credit Refinance Fund to disburse short term crop loans to the small and marginal farmers.	**Announcement implemented.** Necessary allocation has been made to the NABARD. RBI has allocated funds on 24.07.2012.
44.	82	To modify the Kisan Credit Card (KCC) scheme to make KCC a smart card which could be used at ATMs.	**Announcement implemented.** Revised Kisan Credit Card (KCC) guidelines have been issued by the RBI on 11.05.2012.
45.	83	To set aside a sum of ₹200 crore for incentivising research with rewards, both for institutions and the research team responsible for scientific breakthroughs such as developing plant and seed varieties that yield more and can resist climate change .	Seven high priority research projects have been identified for incentivizing research:· • Efficient photosynthesis and yield improvement in rice· • Development of C4rice • Biological Nitrogen Fixation in cereals. • Molecular breeding platform for multiple stress resistance in rice, wheat, mustard and chickpea.· • Breeding and culture of hilsa • Semen sexing in cattle and buffalo.· • Camel immunology. The concept note along with procedure for implementation is under preparation.
46.	84	Revising the Accelerated Irrigation Benefit Programme (AIBP) to maximise the flow of benefits from investments in irrigation projects.	The Cabinet Note to restructure the Accelerated Irrigation Benefit Programme (AIBP) including Command Area Development and Waste Management (CADWM) programme during 12th Plan is under finalization. However, during 2012-13, total grant amounting to ₹850.45 crore has been released to the states for completion of major and minor irrigation projects under AIBP up to September, 2012. A component micro irrigation to cover at least 10% cultivable command area of each CADWM project is proposed to be implemented during the 12th Plan.
47.	85	To operationalise a Government owned Irrigation and Water Resource Finance Company in 2012-13 to mobilise large resources to fund irrigation projects.	**Announcement implemented.** Irrigation and Water Resource Finance Corporation Limited has been operationalised. It has sanctioned one project of ₹28 crore and disbursed an amount of ₹8 crore.

Annex continued

Sl. No.	Para No.	Summary of Budget Announcement	Status of Implementation
48.	86	To fund a flood management project for Kandi sub-division of Murshidabad District by the Ganga Flood Control Commission under the Flood Management Programme.	After appraisal by Ganga Flood Control Commission (GFCC), the techno-economic viability of the scheme namely, "Improvement of embankments and ancillary woks in Kandi and other adjoining areas in district, Murshidabad, West Bengal" with estimated cost of ₹438.94 crore, was accepted by the Advisory Committee of the Ministry of Water Resources for Irrigation Flood Control and Multi-purpose Projects in March, 2012. The Planning Commission accorded investment approval to the scheme in June, 2012. The formal request from the State Government for funding of the above project under Flood Management Programme is awaited. Action is also at hand to obtain requisite approvals for the State Sector Scheme "Flood Management Programme" during XII Plan. On approval of Flood Management Programme during XII Plan and on receipt of request along with mandatory documents from the State Government, the above project will be placed before competent authority for consideration of its inclusion for funding under "Flood Management Programme" during XII Plan.
49.	87	*National Mission on Food Processing* To start a new centrally sponsored scheme titled "National Mission on Food Processing", in cooperation with the State Governments in 2012-13	**Announcement implemented** The Cabinet Committee on Economic Affairs (CCEA) in its meeting held on 23.08.2012 has approved the launching of a new Centrally Sponsored Scheme- National Mission on Food Processing (NMFP) to be implemented by states / UTs. In pursuance of approval of CCEA, Ministry of Food Processing Industries had also issued guidelines for implementation of NMFP during the 12th Five Year Plan vide letter dated 28.8.2012. ₹179.39 crores had been released to States/UTs for taking up preparatory activities and implementation of NMFP scheme.
50.	88	Creation of 2 million tonnes of storage capacity in the form of modern silos has already been approved. Nearly 15 million tonnes capacity is being created under the Private Entrepreneur's Guarantee Scheme, of which 3 million tonnes of storage capacity will be added by the end of 2011-12 and 5 million would be added next year.	Under the Private Entrepreneurs Guarantee (PEG) Scheme, a capacity of about 181.08 lakh tonnes is to be created in 19 states through private entrepreneurs and Central and State Warehousing Corporations. Approvals have already been given for creation of storage capacity of 128 lakh tonnes. A total of 31 lakh tonnes has been completed under PEG out of which 20.55 lakh tonnes has been taken over

Annex continued

Sl. No.	Para No.	Summary of Budget Announcement	Status of Implementation
			as on 30.9.2012 and the balance is expected to be taken over shortly. It is expected that by March, 2013 a cumulative capacity of 73 lakh tonnes will be completed and taken over under the scheme. The EGOM in its meeting held on 7.2.2012 had approved the proposal to construct 2 million tonnes of storage capacity in the form of silos through the PPP mode, within the overall storage requirements of FCI. The capacities to be created in the different States have been finalized, and the locations have been decided in consultation with the State Governments. An Inter Ministerial Group (IMG) has also been constituted to give its recommendations on all aspects of the project. The Planning Commission is drafting the Model Concession Agreements (MCA) through Viability Gap Funding (VGF) route. FCI has also invited bids for appointment of Transaction Advisor.
51.	91	To create a National Information Utility for the computerisation of PDS and to operationalize it by December 2012.	Necessary steps for setting up of National Information Utility i.e. PDS Network (PDSN) for computerisation of PDS will be taken by the Department of Food and Public Distribution in due course.
52.	92	To roll out a multi-sectoral programme to address maternal and child malnutrition in selected 200 high burden districts during 2012-13.	The framework for the multi-sectoral programme to address maternal and child malnutrition in 200 high burden districts has been under consideration of a Committee, as suggested by the Planning Commission. The EFC memo is also under preparation in Ministry of Women and Child Development.
53.	93	To strengthen and re-structure the Integrated Child Development Services (ICDS) scheme.	**Announcement implemented.** The proposal for Strengthening and Restructuring of Integrated Child Development Services (ICDS) Scheme has been approved by the Cabinet Committee on Economic Affairs in its meeting held on 24.9.2012. Administrative approval for the scheme has been issued on 22.10.2012.
54.	98	To strengthen Panchayats across the country through the Rajiv Gandhi Panchayat Sashaktikaran Abhiyan (RGPSA) by expanding on the existing schemes for Panchayat capacity building.	Draft Guidelines of the proposed new scheme, Rajiv Gandhi Panchayat Sashaktikaran Abhiyan (RGPSA) have been prepared and shared with the States/ UTs. Based on the inputs received from the States/ UTs and also the consultation

Annex continued

Sl. No.	Para No.	Summary of Budget Announcement	Status of Implementation
			held with Planning Commission, the guidelines are being finalized. Besides, a draft EFC memo on this newly proposed scheme has also been circulated for the comments of concerned Ministries since the new scheme will require approval of the Cabinet.
55.	99	To carry the Backward Regions Grant Fund (BRGF) scheme into the Twelfth Plan with an enhanced allocation of ₹12,040 crore in 2012-13, including the State component of projects in backward areas in Bihar, West Bengal and the Kalahandi-Bolangir-Koraput region of Odisha, development projects for drought mitigation in the Bundelkhand region and projects under the Integrated Action Plan to accelerate the pace of development in selected tribal and backward districts.	It is proposed to restructure the BRGF in the Twelfth Five Year Plan. Until the completion of this exercise, it is proposed to implement BRGF in 2012-13 in its present form. The District Component of BRGF as well as the Special Plan for West Bengal and the Integrated Action Plan (IAP) are already approved for implementation in 2012-13. The CCEA Note containing the proposal to continue the Special Plan for Bihar, Special Plan for the Kalahandi-Bolangir-Koraput (KBK) districts of Odisha and the Bundelkhand Package in 2012-13 has been submitted for consideration by the CCEA. ₹300 crore has been approved as the additional allocation to cover 22 additional districts included in BRGF district component.
56.	100	To enhance the allocation under Rural Infrastructure Development Fund (RIDF) to ₹20,000 crore, with ₹5,000 crore exclusively earmarked for creating warehousing facilities under RIDF.	**Announcement implemented.** RBI has allocated the necessary funds on 24.07.2012. Necessary earmarking has also been made towards warehousing facilities.
57.	104	To set up a Credit Guarantee Fund to ensure better flow of credit to deserving students.	A draft Cabinet note for this purpose is at the stage of inter-ministerial consultations.
58.	105	To modernize existing vaccine manufacturing and research facilities and setting up a new integrated vaccine unit near Chennai.	**Modernization of existing units** (i) The upgradation of DPT group of vaccine manufacturing facility at Central Research Institute (CRI) Kasauli has been completed and the upgraded facility has been taken over by the CRI, Kasauli in August 2012 on provisional basis. (ii) The recommendations of the Expenditure Finance Committee (EFC) for upgradation of the DPT manufacturing facility at PII, Coonoor have been approved and the Hill Area Conservation Authority Committee (HACA), Chennai has also cleared the construction of the new structure on hill area conservation aspect. The proposal has now been referred for relaxation of building

Annex continued

Sl. No.	Para No.	Summary of Budget Announcement	Status of Implementation
			height to 12 meters which is above the permissible height of 7.00 metres as per Tamil Nadu District Municipalities (Hill Station) Building Rules, 1993. (iii) So far as the BCG Vaccine Laboratory, Guindy is concerned, civil works have started after obtaining all the required approvals from the Chennai Metropolitan Development Authority (CMDA). **Setting up of a new Vaccine Unit** The Cabinet Committee on Economic Affairs (CCEA) has approved establishment of Integrated Vaccine Complex (IVC) at Chengalpattu, Tamil Nadu in public sector by M/s. HLL Life Care Ltd. The financial bids of the civil tender have been finalized and work order shall be placed shortly.
59.	106	To enlarge the scope of ASHA's activities by including prevention of Iodine Deficiency Disorders, better immunisation and better spacing of children, and envisaging a more active role for ASHA at community level as convener of the Village Health and Sanitation Committee.	**Announcement implemented** Accredited Social Health Activist – 'ASHA' is a community health volunteer who acts as a link between community and health facilities. It has been decided to expand the scope of ASHA's activities by giving following additional incentives: **Immunisation** • ₹100/- for each ASHA per child completing all vaccination upto 1 year under full immunization coverage. • An additional ₹50/- to ASHA on ensuring complete immunization beyond 1st and upto 2nd year of age of the child **National Iodine Deficiency Disorder (IDD) control Programme** ₹25/- per month to each ASHA on testing of at least 50 salt samples per month in 303 endemic districts where the prevalence of total IDD is more than 10% in the country. **Family Planning** Financial incentive to each ASHA of: • ₹500/- for ensuring spacing of 2 years after marriage. • ₹500/- for ensuring spacing of 3 years after the birth of 1st child. **Conducting meeting of Village Health Sanitation & Nutrition Committee (VHSNC)** ₹150/- as incentive to ASHA for facilitating the VHSNC meeting followed by meetings of women and adolescent girls every month. Orders have been issued to the States for the implementation of the above decisions.

Annex continued

Sl. No.	Para No.	Summary of Budget Announcement	Status of Implementation
60.	107	To launch National Urban Health Mission and to expand the Pradhan Mantri Swasthya Suraksha Yojana (PMSSY) to cover upgradation of 7 more Government medical colleges to enhance the availability of affordable tertiary health care.	**National Urban Health Mission(NUHM)** Expenditure Finance Committee (EFC) has considered the proposal on 09.10.2012. Action is at hand to obtain the approval of the Cabinet. **Upgradation of 7 existing Government Medical Colleges** The Central team has visited Government Medical College, Kozhikode, Jhansi Medical College and Gorakhpur Medical College to conduct gap analysis for taking up their upgradation. Detailed Project Reports based on the recommendations of Central team are yet to be submitted by the concerned State Governments. The remaining four Government Medical Colleges identified for upgradation are: Government Medical College, Rewa, Government Medical College, Dharbhanga, Government Medical College, Muzzafarpur, and Vijaya Institute of Medical Services, Bellary, Karnataka. Site visits to conduct gap analysis are yet to be made for these Medical Colleges.
61.	110	To enlarge the corpus of 'Women's SHG's Development Fund' housed in NABARD to ₹300 crore from ₹200 crore, and to provide additional interest subvention at 7 percent per annum to women SHGs availing loans up to ₹ 3 lakh and an additional subvention of 3 percent per annum to Women SHGs repaying loan in time. This is to be implemented in select 600 blocks of 150 districts in the first phase.	Release of additional ₹200 crore towards 'Women's SHG's Development Fund' will be processed after Utilization Certificate for the ₹100 crore released last year is received from NABARD. In order to operationalise the interest subvention to Women SHGs to avail loan up to ₹3 lakh at 7 percent per annum and additional 3 percent subvention for prompt repayment of loan in select 600 blocks of 150 districts, including the Left Wing Extremism affected districts, an EFC note is under finalization.
62.	111	To establish a Bharat Livelihoods Foundation of India through Aajeevika to support and scale up civil society initiatives and interventions particularly in the tribal regions covering around 170 districts.	The note for consideration of the Expenditure Finance Committee (EFC) is at the stage of inter-Ministerial consultations.
63.	114	To allocate ₹1000 crore to National Skill Development Fund (NSDF).	**Action complete** In view of the present fund position of the NSDF, it has been decided not to allocate any additional fund to NSDF in the current fiscal.

Annex continued

Sl. No.	Para No.	Summary of Budget Announcement	Status of Implementation
64.	115	To set up separate Credit Guarantee Fund in order to improve the flow of institutional credit for skill development.	A draft Cabinet note for this purpose is at the stage of inter-ministerial consultations.
65.	117	To increase the monthly pension amount per person from ₹200 to ₹300 under the ongoing Indira Gandhi National Widow Pension Scheme and Indira Gandhi National Disability Pension Scheme for BPL beneficiaries,	**Announcement implemented** Cabinet has approved the proposal on 18.10.2012, and necessary guidelines have been issued to States/UTs on 08.11.2012.
66.	118	To double the lumpsum grant of ₹10,000 presently provided on the death of the primary breadwinner of a BPL family, in the age group 18 to 64 years under the National Family Benefit scheme, to ₹20,000.	**Announcement implemented** Cabinet has approved the proposal on 18.10.2012, and necessary guidelines have been issued to States/UTs on 08.11.2012.
67.	120	*Institutions that are being given grants* The driving force of a modern nation is research and the creation of new knowledge. With this in mind I propose to provide:	
		• ₹25 crore to the Institute of Rural Management, Anand;	Action is at hand to obtain the approval of Standing Finance Committee (SFC) to sanction ₹25 crore to Institute of Rural Management, Anand. New budget heads are being created to accommodate the release.
		• ₹50 crore to establish a world-class centre for water quality with focus on arsenic contamination in Kolkata;	Detailed project report is under preparation to seek appraisal and subsequently approval of the competent authority. Additional fund is being arranged through Supplementary Grants for 2012-13.
		• ₹100 crore to Kerala Agricultural University;	The proposal for consideration of the EFC has been prepared and will be circulated for inter-ministerial consultations shortly.
		• ₹50 crore for University of Agricultural Sciences Dharwad, Karnataka;	The proposal for consideration of the EFC has been prepared and will be circulated for inter-ministerial consultations shortly.
		• ₹50 crore to Chaudhary Charan Singh Haryana Agricultural University, Hissar;	The proposal for consideration of the EFC has been prepared and will be circulated for inter-ministerial consultations shortly.
		• ₹ 50 crore to Orissa University of Agriculture and Technology;	The proposal for consideration of the EFC has been prepared and will be circulated for inter-ministerial consultations shortly.
		• ₹100 crore to Acharya N. G. Ranga Agricultural University in Hyderabad;	The proposal for consideration of the EFC has been prepared and will be circulated for inter-ministerial consultations shortly.

Annex continued

Sl. No.	Para No.	Summary of Budget Announcement	Status of Implementation
		• ₹15 crore to National Council for Applied Economic Research;	Administrative approvals have been obtained. Grant will be released after additional funds are arranged through supplementary demand.
		• ₹10 crore to Rajiv Gandhi University, Department of Economics, Itanagar; and	Administrative approvals have been obtained. Grant will be released after additional funds are arranged through supplementary demand.
		• ₹10 crore to Siddharth Vihar Trust Gulbarga, to establish a Pali Language Research Centre	Rashtriya Sanskrit Sansthan (RSkS), which has been entrusted with the work of promotion of Pali language, had deputed a team to Gulbarga to work out the modalities of establishing a Pali Language Research Centre in consultation with Siddharth Vihar Trust, Gulbarga. RSkS are in process of finalizing the modalities in consultation with the Trust. Simultaneously, Ministry of HRD has taken up the proposal to grant ₹10.00 crores to RSkS through Supplementary/RE under the appropriate head.
68.	122	To construct nearly 4,000 residential quarters for Central Armed Police Forces in 2012-13 and to construct office buildings including land acquisition and barracks to accommodate 27,000 personnel.	The target for residential quarters and barracks have been revised based on information received from Central Armed Police Forces (CAPFs) and fixed at 6665 houses and 149 barracks for accommodating approximately 20,259 personnel. The physical achievement up to September, 2012 for Residential Building is 1871 and for Barracks is 71.
69.	123	To complete the National Population Registrar (NPR) within two years and to issue Resident Identity Cards bearing the Aadhaar numbers to all residents who are of age 18 years and above to help in the e-governance initiatives.	**National Population Registrar (NPR)** The demographic data for NPR (in paper format) has been collected for the entire country (approx. 1.2 billion population).The filled-in NPR Schedules (approx. 27 crore) have been scanned. The Data Entry (in English and the Regional language) from the scanned images has been completed for more than 92.17 crore records. The NPR biometric enrolment is in progress by organising camps in the local areas and biometrics have been captured for more than 7.18 crore persons. **Resident Identity Cards (RICs)** The proposal for issuance of RICs to all the usual residents of 18 years and above, under the scheme of NPR in the country, has been appraised by the Expenditure Finance Committee (EFC). The EFC has recommended the scheme at an estimated cost of ₹552.5 crore. Action is at hand to obtain the approval of the Cabinet.

Annex continued

Sl. No.	Para No.	Summary of Budget Announcement	Status of Implementation
70.	126	To lay a white paper on Black Money on the table of the House during the Budget session of Parliament.	**Announcement implemented** The 'White Paper on Black Money' has been laid before the Parliament on 21st May, 2012.
71.	127	To introduce a Bill on Public Procurement legislation in the Budget session of the Parliament to enhance confidence in public procurement and to ensure transparency and efficiency in the process.	**Announcement implemented** Public Procurement Bill, 2012 was introduced in Lok Sabha on 14.5.2012.
72.	142	To reduce the rate of withholding tax on interest payments on external commercial borrowings from 20 per cent to 5 per cent for three years in the following sectors:power; airlines; roads and bridges; ports and shipyards; affordable housing; fertilizer; and dams	**Announcement implemented** The provisions have come in to effect with the passage of the Finance Bill, 2012.
73.	152	To reduce Securities Transaction Tax (STT) by 20 per cent (from 0.125 per cent to 0.1 per cent) on cash delivery transactions in order to reduce transaction costs in the capital markets.	**Announcement implemented** The provision relating to reduction in STT has come into effect from the 1st July, 2012.
74.	154	To introduce a General Anti Avoidance Rule (GAAR) in order to counter aggressive tax avoidance schemes, while ensuring that it is used only in appropriate cases, by enabling a review by a GAAR panel.	General Anti Avoidance Rules have been incorporated in the Income-tax Act, through Finance Act, 2012. These provisions were deferred by one year through Government Amendment and now will be applicable only in respect of income accruing or arising on or after 1.4.2013. Recommendations of the GAAR panel on the implementation of GAAR are under active discussion with stakeholders before finalization.
75.	155	• Introduction of compulsory reporting requirement in case of assets held abroad. • Allowing for reopening of assessment upto 16 years in relation to assets held abroad. • Tax collection at source on purchase in cash of bullion or jewellery in excess of ₹ 2 lakh. • Tax deduction at source on transfer of immovable property (other than agricultural land) above a specified threshold.	**Announcement implemented** These series of measures have been introduced in the Finance Bill, 2012 and are finally part of the Finance Act, 2012 except the provisions of the tax deduction at source on immovable property which has been dropped from the Finance Bill during the official amendments while passing the Bill as Finance Act, 2012.

Annex continued

Sl. No.	Para No.	Summary of Budget Announcement	Status of Implementation
		• Tax collection at source on trading in coal, lignite and iron ore. • Increasing the onus of proof on closely held companies for funds received from shareholders as well as taxing share premium in excess of fair market value. • Taxation of unexplained money, credits, investments, expenditures etc., at the highest rate of 30 per cent irrespective of the slab of income.	
76.	168	To introduce a common simplified registration form and a common return for Central Excise and Service Tax, to be named EST-1 as a measure of harmonisation between Central Excise and Service Tax. This common return will comprise only one page, which will be a significant reduction from the 15 pages of the two returns at present.	A common registration form and a common return for Central Excise & Service Tax have been placed in the public domain. The responses from public and departmental officers have been invited. The Central Board of Excise & Customs has appointed a committee headed by DG, Service Tax to go into all aspects of this issue. Further action would be taken on receipt of the report of the Committee.
77.	169	Introducing Revision Application Authority and Settlement Commission in Service Tax to help resolve disputes with far greater ease.	**Announcement implemented** These are Budget changes. Statutory provision relating to Revision Application Authority is effective since 28th May, 2012, the date of enactment of the Finance Act, 2012. For Settlement Commission, notification no. 16/2012-ST dated 29.05.2012 prescribing rules has been issued.
78.	171	Notifying the Place of Supply Rules, that will determine the location where a service shall be deemed to be provided. These rules will also provide a possible backdrop to initiate an informed debate to assess all the issues that may arise in the taxation of inter-state services for the eventual launch of GST.	**Announcement implemented** Notification 28/2012-ST dated 20/06/2012 issued. Place of Provision of Services Rules have come into effect from 1st July, 2012.
79.	172	To set up a Study Team to examine the possibility of a common tax code for service tax and central excise.	**Announcement implemented** A Study team to examine the possibility of a common tax code for service tax and central excise has been constituted.

Annex continued

Sl. No.	Para No.	Summary of Budget Announcement	Status of Implementation
80.	173	To implement a new scheme that will simplify tax refunds to exporters of goods without resorting to voluminous documentation or verification. Such refunds will also be admissible for taxes on taxable services that have been exempted.	**Announcement implemented** The scheme was made operational through notification no. 27/2012-CE(NT) dated 18.06.2012 prescribing the safeguards, conditions, limitations and the procedure for the refund claims.
81.	174	Rationalising rules pertaining to the Point of Taxation, providing greater clarity and removing the irritants, and restoration of Cenvat credits in a number of areas.	**Announcement implemented** Notifications 04/2012-ST dated 17/03/2012 and 37/2012-ST dated 20/06/2012 issued in respect of Point of Taxation Rules. Notifications 18/2012-CE(NT) dated 17/03/2012 and 28/2012-CE(NT) dated 20/06/2012 have been issued in respect of Cenvat Credit Rules. Notification 26/2012-ST dated 20/06/2012 has been issued in respect of abatements in the case of certain taxable services.

Annex continued

Annex II

1. KEY INDICATORS

	Items	2010-11	2011-12	per cent change 2010-11	per cent change 2011-12	2011-12	2012-13	Period	per cent change 2011-12	per cent change 2012-13
	(1)	(2)	(3)	(4)	(5)	(6)	(7)	(8)	(9)	(10)
1a	GDP at factor cost at current prices- ₹ '000 crore	7157Q	8233R	17.5	15.0	3842	4363	Apr-Sep	17.0	13.5
1b	Implicit Price Deflator	146.5	158.2	8.4	8.0	155.7	167.8	Apr-Sep	9.0	7.8
1c	GDP at factor cost at 2004-05 prices- ₹ '000 crore	4886Q	5203R	8.4	6.5	2468	2600	Apr-Sep	7.3	5.4
2	Agriculture and allied sectors at 2004-05 prices - ₹ '000 crore	709Q	729R	7.0	2.8	304	311	Apr-Sep	3.4	2.1
3	Index of Industrial Production (IIP)	165.5	170.3	8.2	2.9	166.1	166.3	Apr-Sept HI	5.1	0.1
4	Electricity generated (in billion kwh)	811.1	876.9	5.7	8.1	435.1	455.5	Apr-Sept HI	9.5	4.7
5	Wholesale price index(point-to-point) 2004-05=100	143.3	156.1	9.6	8.9	153.8	165.6	Apr-SepP	9.7	7.7
6	Consumer price index(for industrial workers) 2001=100	179.8	194.8	10.4	8.4	191.0	210.0	Apr-Sep	9.0	9.9
7	Money Supply (M3) (₹ '000 crore) 1,2	6,504	7,359	16.1	13.1	7,034	7,965	Mid-Nov.	15.5	13.2
8	Imports at current price 3 (in ₹ Crore)	16,83,467	23,44,772	23.4	39.3	11,01,683	12,82,774	Apr-SepP	35.7	16.4
	(in US$ million)	3,69,769	4,89,181	28.2	32.3	2,43,517	2,34,706	Apr-SepP	38.1	-3.6
9	Exports at current prices 3 (in ₹ Crore)	11,42,922	14,59,281	35.2	27.7	6,97,873	7,76,480	Apr-SepP	38.0	11.3
	(in US$ million)	2,51,136	3,04,624	40.5	21.3	1,54,185	1,42,066	Apr-SepP	40.4	-7.9
10	Foreign currency assets (in ₹ Crore)	1225999	1333954	6.5	8.8	1350855	1374066	Apr-Sep	13.3	1.7
	(in US$ million)	274580	260742	7.7	-5.0	276079	260748	Apr-Sep	4.0	-5.6
11	Exchange rate (₹/US$) 4&5	45.56	47.92	4.1	-4.9	45.23	54.66	Apr-Sep	1.8	-17.3

Q: Quick estimate; R : Revised estimate; P : Provisional Data 1: Units only for columns 2,3,6 and 7; 2: Figures in column 2 and 3 are for end March of the respective financial year; 3: As per DGCI&S; 4 (+) indicates appreciation and (-) indicates depreciation of the Rupee vis-à-vis the US Dollar. 5. Yearly /Half yearly average exchange rate {average of buying & selling by Foreign Exchange Dealers Association of India (FEDAI)}. Exchange Rate from May 2012 onwards are RBI's reference rates.

Annex continued

2. MAJOR ITEMS OF INDIA'S BALANCE OF PAYMENTS DURING Q1 OF 2011-12 AND 2012-13

(in US$ billion)

	Items	2010-11 (PR)	2011-12 (P)	2011-12 (PR)	2012-13 (P)
		Full Year	Full Year	Q1 (April-June)	Q1 (April-June)
1	Exports	250.5	309.8	78.6	76.7
2	Imports	381.1	499.5	123.7	119.2
3	**Trade Balance**	**-130.6**	**-189.8**	**-45.0**	**-42.5**
4	Net Invisibles	84.6	111.6	27.5	25.9
5	Goods & Services Balance	-81.8	-125.7	-28.6	-28.3
6	**Current Account Balance**	**-45.9**	**-78.2**	**-17.5**	**-16.6**
7	External assistance (Net)	4.9	2.3	0.3	-0.2
8	Commercial Borrowings (Net)	12.5	10.3	3.1	1.0
9	FDI (Net)	9.4	22.1	9.3	4.2
10	Portfolio	30.3	17.2	2.5	-1.9
11	**Capital Account Balance**	**62.0**	**67.8**	**23.9**	**17.0**
12	Errors & Omissions	-3.0	-2.4	-0.9	0.1
13	Overall Balance	13.1	-12.8	5.4	0.5
14	Change in Reserves (- indicates increase; + indicates decrease) (on BoP Basis)	-13.1	12.8	-5.4	-0.5
	Memo Items/Assumptions				
1	Trade Balance/GDP (%)	-7.8	-10.3		
2	Goods & Services Balance / GDP (%)	-4.9	-6.8		
3	Invisibles/GDP (%)	4.9	6.0		
4	**Current Account Balance/GDP (%)**	**-2.7**	**-4.2**		
5	**Net Capital Flows / GDP (%)**	**3.7**	**3.7**		

P: Preliminary, PR: Partially Revised

Source: Reserve Bank of India

Annex continued

3. MONETARY SURVEY

	Items	Outstanding Balances				Per cent variation			
		2010-11 (₹ crore)	2011-12 (₹ crore)	Nov 18, 2011 (₹ crore)	Nov 16, 2012 (₹ crore)	Full year 2010-11	Full year 2011-12	year-on-year Nov 18, 2011	year-on-year Nov 16, 2012
I	**Broad Money**	65,04,116	73,59,200	70,34,363	79,65,064	16.1	13.1	15.5	13.2
	Components of Money Stock								
1)	Currency with the Public	9,11,836	10,26,500	9,77,878	11,08,116	18.8	12.6	12.2	13.3
2)	Aggregate deposits with Banks	55,88,627	63,29,878	60,55,326	68,55,566	15.7	13.3	16.1	13.2
3)	Other deposits with RBI	3,653	2,822	1,159	1,382	-4.0	-22.7	-67.2	19.2
	Sources of M3								
I.	**Net Bank Credit to Government (1+2)**	19,83,896	23,69,547	22,23,555	26,52,974	18.9	19.4	22.1	19.3
1)	Net RBI Credit to Govt.	3,96,555	5,35,738	4,16,903	5,77,798	-	-	-	-
2)	Other Banks Investment in Govt. Securities	15,87,341	18,33,809	18,06,652	20,75,176	8.9	15.5	15.7	14.9
II.	**Bank Credit to Commercial Sector (1 + 2)**	42,36,676	49,59,426	45,14,980	52,58,116	21.3	17.1	17.6	16.5
1)	RBI credit to Commercial sector	2,164	3,960	1,908	4,178	-	-	-	-
2)	Other Bank credit to Commercial sector	42,34,512	49,55,467	45,13,072	52,53,939	21.3	17.0	17.6	16.4
III.	**Net Foreign Exchange Assets of the banking sector**	13,93,343	15,43,780	15,89,439	16,30,376	8.7	10.8	15.2	2.6
IV.	**Govt's Net Currency Liability to the public**	12,724	14,273	13,716	15,046	12.9	12.2	11.9	9.7
V.	**Other items (net)**	11,22,523	15,27,826	13,07,326	15,91,449	32.0	36.1	36.2	21.7
	Memorandum items								
1)	NDA	51,10,773	58,15,420	54,44,924	63,34,688	18.3	13.8	15.6	16.3
2)	Reserve Money(M0)	13,76,821	14,27,172	14,01,667	14,78,997	19.1	3.7	13.8	5.5

Please note item V on the sources side is net non-monetary liabilities of the banking sector. On the sources side, M3 is derived by summing items I, II, III and IV and deducting item V.

Annex continued

Table 4: Trends in Growth Rates of Infrastructure Sectors and Universal Intermediaries

(Per cent)

	Industry	Weight	2009-10	2010-11	2011-12	April-September 2011-2012	April-September 2012-13
I.	**Core infrastructure industries**						
i	Electricity generation	10.3	6.2	5.5	8.1	9.3	4.7
ii	Coal	4.4	8.1	-0.3	1.2	-4.8	8.3
iii	Steel	6.7	6.0	8.9	7.0	9.5	2.6
iv	Crude oil	5.2	0.5	11.9	1.0	5.1	-0.8
v	Refinery products	5.9	-0.4	3.0	3.2	4.6	5.4
vi	Cement	2.4	10.5	4.5	6.7	3.8	7.4
vii	Natural Gas	1.7	44.6	10.0	-8.9	-8.5	-12.5
viii	Fertilizers	1.3	12.7	0.0	0.4	0.6	-5.6
	overall index	***37.9***	***6.6***	***5.7***	***4.4***	***5.0***	***3.2***
II.	**Transport and Communications**						
1.	Cargo handled at major ports		5.8	1.6	-1.7	3.1	-3.3
2.	Railway revenue earning freight traffic		6.6	3.8	5.2	4.8	4.8
3.	Civil Aviation						
a.	Export cargo handled		11.4	13.4	-2.2	-0.7	-1.6
b.	Import cargo handled		8.1	20.6	-1.6	4.1	-9.2
c.	Passenger handled at International Terminals		5.7	11.5	7.6	7.8	2.6
d.	Passengers handled at Domestic Terminals		14.5	16.1	15.0	18.8	-3.1
4.	Telecommunications						
a.	Cellular Mobile Phones		47.4	18.0	-52.7	-40.0	0.0

Source: (i). O/o the Economic Adviser, DIPP, Ministry of Commerce & Industry

(ii). Ministry of Statistics & Programme Implementation.

Annex continued

5. TAX REVENUE

(₹ *in crore)*

	DESCRIPTION	2012-2013 BE	2012-2013 ACTUALS upto 09/2012	2012-2013 %	2011-2012 BE	2011-2012 ACTUALS upto 09/2011	2011-2012 %
1	Corporation Tax	373227.00	142965.05	38%	359990.00	127374.70	35%
2	Taxes on Income	195786.00	84611.46	43%	172026.00	68861.95	40%
	(a) Taxes on Income other than Corporation Tax	189866.00	82597.68	44%	164526.00	66249.04	40%
	(b) Fringe Benefit Tax	0.00	-62.05	...	0.00	109.04	...
	(c) Securities Transaction Tax	5920.00	2075.83	35%	7500.00	2503.81	33%
	(d) Banking Cash Transaction Tax	0.00	0.00	...	0.00	0.06	...
3	Wealth Tax	1244.00	483.84	39%	635.00	379.52	60%
4	Customs	186694.00	78556.73	42%	151700.00	74808.21	49%
5	Union Excise Duties	194350.34	67423.60	35%	164115.66	59314.62	36%
6	Service Tax	124000.00	49102.88	40%	82000.00	37049.46	45%
7	Other taxes	2310.45	1752.44	76%	1973.22	1564.18	79%
	(a) Direct Taxes	...	**11.90**	...	...	**6.23**	...
	(b) Indirect Taxes	...	**1740.54**	...	...	**1557.95**	...
	GROSS TAX REVENUE	**1077611.79**	**424896.00**	**39%**	**932439.88**	**369352.64**	**40%**
	Of which netted against expenditure (Surcharge for financing National Calamity Contigency Fund)	4620.00	1689.53	37%	4525.00	1447.89	32%
	Balance Gross Tax Revenue	**1072991.79**	**423206.47**	**39%**	**927914.88**	**367904.75**	**40%**
	<u>**Less**</u> *Assignment to States*	301920.76	129394.64	43%	263457.74	113174.03	43%
	NET TAX REVENUE	**771071.03**	**293811.83**	**38%**	**664457.14**	**254730.72**	**38%**

Annex continued

6. NON-TAX REVENUE

(₹ in crore)

DESCRIPTION	2012-2013 BE	2012-2013 ACTUALS upto 09/2012	2012-2013 %	2011-2012 BE	2011-2012 ACTUALS upto 09/2011	2011-2012 %
A. Interest receipts	25230.68	16972.87	67%	29821.89	19374.86	65%
Less - *i) Receipts incidential to Market Borrowing taken in reduction of cost of borrowing*	5010.00	9698.27	194%	4344.11	5537.70	127%
ii) Waiver of Interest	990.00	0.00	...	5900.00	5900.00	100%
Net Interest Receipts	**19230.68**	**7274.60**	**38%**	**19577.78**	**7937.16**	**41%**
B. Dividends and Profits	50152.55	27525.75	55%	42623.68	22867.27	54%
C. Non-Tax Revenue of U.T.s	1135.78	515.02	45%	1169.35	410.85	35%
D. Other Non-Tax Revenue						
Fiscal Services	119.32	18.09	15%	127.82	41.44	32%
Other General Services	22988.94	8656.80	38%	22001.31	7928.29	36%
Less: Other Receipts utilised to write-off loans etc.	1106.60	5.18	0%	1506.95	6.95	0%
Net - Other General Services	21882.34	8651.62	40%	20494.36	7921.34	39%
Social Services	1371.55	756.11	55%	2353.90	529.28	22%
Economic Services	91147.49	18356.78	20%	57606.69	17229.72	30%
Less - *(I) Other Receipts utilised to write-off loans*	3.00	0.00	...	0.00	0.00	...
Net Economic Services	91144.49	18356.78	20%	57606.69	17229.72	30%
Grants-in-Aid and Contributions	2887.20	254.31	9%	2172.96	451.77	21%
Total Other Non-Tax Revenue	**117404.90**	**28036.91**	**24%**	**82755.73**	**26173.55**	**32%**
Less : Commercial Departments	23310.30	6276.25	27%	20691.42	6592.00	32%
Net Other Non-Tax Revenue	**94094.60**	**21760.66**	**23%**	**62064.31**	**19581.55**	**32%**
Net Non-Tax Revenue (A+B+C+D)	**164613.61**	**57076.03**	**35%**	**125435.12**	**50796.83**	**40%**

Annex continued

7. CAPITAL RECEIPTS

(₹ in crore)

	DESCRIPTION	2012-2013 BE	2012-2013 ACTUALS upto 09/2012	2012-2013 %	2011-2012 BE	2011-2012 ACTUALS upto 09/2011	2011-2012 %
1	(a) Market Loans including Short term borrowings	488000.00	331839.22	68%	358000.00	277074.39	77%
	(b) Receipt under MSS (Net)	20000.00	0.00	0%	20000.00	0.00	0%
	(c) Treasury Bills(14 days)	0.00	-27549.47		0.00	-35732.91	
2	Securities against Small Savings	1197.52	-545.04	-46%	24182.46	-621.61	-3%
3	(i) External Loans						
	Gross Borrowings	26047.94	7369.09	28%	26820.13	8749.25	33%
	Less Repayments	15899.74	8126.10	51%	12320.13	6368.19	52%
	Net Borrowings	10148.20	*-757.01*	-7%	14500.00	2381.06	16%
	(ii) Revolving Fund		-8.45			-12.87	
	Non-Debt Capital Receipts (4&5)						
4	Recoveries of Loans and Advances						
	Gross Recoveries	23095.20	5053.93	22%	26510.00	10245.59	39%
	Less Recoveries of Ways & Means Advances and Loans to Govt. Servants	11445.00	198.75	2%	11490.00	221.26	2%
	Net Recoveries of Loans & Advances	11650.20	4855.18	42%	15020.00	10024.33	67%
5	Miscellaneous Capital Receipts	30000.00	1371.82	5%	40000.00	1144.55	3%
	(i) Disinvestment of Govt.'s Equity Holdings	30000.00	1371.82	5%	40000.00	1144.55	3%
	(ii) Issue of Bonus Shares	0.00	0.00		0.00	1585.74	
	(iii) Other Misc. Receipts	0.00	0.00		0.00	0.00	
6	National Small Savings Fund	5005.48	13593.00	272%	94.21	8598.10	
	(a) Small Savings, Public Provident Funds	0.00	-1267.23		65000.00	-6548.24	-10%
	(b) Investment in Securities	12122.24	11669.84	96%	-58350.00	2304.77	-4%
	(c) Income & Expenditure of NSSF	-7116.76	3190.39	-45%	-6555.79	12841.57	-196%
7	State Provident Funds	12000.00	746.41	6%	10000.00	2161.73	22%
8	Public Accounts (other than SPF& NSSF)	313.57	-12853.00	-4099%	-9783.58	-10353.06	106%
9	Other Internal Debt Receipts	-3074.32	-559.94	18%	-4176.52	-5321.01	127%
10	Ways & Means Advances		0.00			24387.00	
11	Investment (-)/disinvestment (+) of Surplus Cash		14588.00			16416.00	
12	Decrease in Cash Balance (Including difference between RBI & A/C)		18410.14		20000.00	1833.46	
13	Cash held under MSS	-20000.00	0.00	0%	-20000.00	0.00	0%
	TOTAL	**555240.65**	**343130.86**	**62%**	**467836.57**	**291979.16**	**62%**

Annex continued

8. PLAN EXPENDITURE

(₹ in crore)

GRANT NO.	MINISTRY/ DEPARTMENT	2012-2013 BE	2012-2013 ACTUALS upto 09/2012	2012-2013 %	2011-2012 BE	2011-2012 ACTUALS upto 09/2011	2011-2012 %
(1)	(2)	(3)	(4)	(5)	(6)	(7)	(8)
MINISTRY OF AGRICULTURE		**25338.00**	**12471.38**	**49%**	**21522.87**	**10508.53**	**49%**
1	Department of Agriculture and Cooperation	20208.00	9891.59	49%	17122.87	8602.77	50%
2	Department of Agricultural Research and Education						
	Gross:	3220.00	1584.24	49%	2808.54	1302.54	46%
	Less : Recoveries:	0.00	0.00		8.54	48.50	568%
	Net	3220.00	1584.24	49%	2800.00	1254.04	45%
3	Department of Animal Husbandry , Dairying and Fisheries	1910.00	995.55	52%	1600.00	651.72	41%
DEPARTMENT OF ATOMIC ENERGY		**5600.00**	**872.64**	**16%**	**5600.00**	**1391.58**	**25%**
4	Atomic Energy	4601.73	867.19	19%	3991.00	988.07	25%
5	Nuclear Power Schemes	998.27	5.45	1%	1609.00	403.51	25%
MINISTRY OF CHEMICALS AND FERTILISERS		**2201.00**	**1595.97**	**73%**	**1200.00**	**821.23**	**68%**
6	Department of Chemicals and Petro-Chemicals	1757.00	1577.39	90%	800.00	713.62	89%
7	Department of Fertilisers	256.00	0.83	0%	225.00	98.91	44%
8	Department of Pharmaceuticals	188.00	17.75	9%	175.00	8.70	5%
MINISTRY OF CIVIL AVIATION		**4500.00**	**3718.58**	**83%**	**1700.00**	**1255.97**	**74%**
9	Ministry of Civil Aviation	4500.00	3718.58	83%	1700.00	1255.97	74%
MINISTRY OF COAL		**450.00**	**135.93**	**30%**	**420.00**	**131.16**	**31%**
10	Ministry of Coal	450.00	135.93	30%	420.00	131.16	31%
MINISTRY OF COMMERCE AND INDUSTRY		**3465.00**	**1758.15**	**51%**	**3300.00**	**1634.95**	**50%**
11	Department of Commerce	2100.00	1002.13	48%	2000.00	1064.50	53%
12	Department of Industrial Policy & Promotion	1365.00	756.02	55%	1300.00	570.45	44%
MINISTRY OF COMMUNICATIONS AND INFORMATION TECHNOLOGY		**8600.00**	**3131.42**	**36%**	**7218.00**	**2296.41**	**32%**
13	Department of Posts	800.00	49.61	6%	800.00	50.32	6%
14	Department of Telecommunications						
	Gross	7800.00	2371.73	30%	5518.00	2829.61	51%
	Less : Recoveries	3000.00	106.07	4%	2100.00	1322.72	63%
	Net	4800.00	2265.66	47%	3418.00	1506.89	44%
15	Department of Information Technology	3000.00	816.15	27%	3000.00	739.20	25%
MINISTRY OF CONSUMER AFFAIRS, FOOD AND PUBLIC DISTRIBUTION		**367.00**	**16.31**	**4%**	**345.00**	**75.88**	**22%**
16	Department of Consumer Affairs	241.00	13.66	6%	225.00	38.63	17%
17	Department of Food and Public Distribution	126.00	2.65	2%	120.00	37.25	31%
MINISTRY OF CORPORATE AFFAIRS		**32.00**	**2.00**	**6%**	**28.00**	**13.03**	**47%**
18	Ministry of Corporate Affairs	32.00	2.00	6%	28.00	13.03	47%

Annex continued

(1)	(2)	(3)	(4)	(5)	(6)	(7)	(8)
MINISTRY OF CULTURE		**864.00**	**441.55**	**51%**	**785.00**	**386.21**	**49%**
19	Ministry of Culture	864.00	441.55	51%	785.00	386.21	49%
MINISTRY OF DEVELOPMENT OF NORTH EASTERN REGION		**1905.00**	**805.95**	**42%**	**1741.00**	**865.02**	**50%**
28	Ministry of Development of North Eastern Region						
	Gross	2075.00	844.46	**41%**	1911.00	865.02	**45%**
	Less : Recoveries	170.00	38.51	23%	170.00	0.00	0%
	Net	1905.00	805.95	**42%**	1741.00	865.02	**50%**
MINISTRY OF EARTH SCIENCES		**1281.00**	**451.36**	**35%**	**1220.00**	**364.94**	**30%**
29	Ministry of Earth Sciences	1281.00	451.36	35%	1220.00	364.94	30%
MINISTRY OF ENVIRONMENT AND FORESTS		**2430.00**	**760.00**	**31%**	**2300.00**	**526.87**	**23%**
30	Ministry of Environment and Forests						
	Gross	2630.00	760.29	29%	2300.00	526.87	23%
	Less : Recoveries	200.00	0.29	0%	0.00	0.00	
	Net	2430.00	760.00	31%	2300.00	526.87	23%
MINISTRY OF EXTERNAL AFFAIRS		**1500.00**	**1052.24**	**70%**	**800.00**	**421.71**	**53%**
31	Ministry of External Affairs	1500.00	1052.24	70%	800.00	421.71	53%
MINISTRY OF FINANCE		**119675.00**	**32069.90**	**27%**	**90636.61**	**29654.46**	**33%**
32	Department of Economic Affairs						
	Gross	5142.45	1195.18	23%	3080.63	1114.46	36%
	Less : Recoveries	1102.45	551.22	50%	1040.63	520.30	50%
	Net	4040.00	643.96	16%	2040.00	594.16	29%
33	Department of Financial Services	16088.00	1300.00	8%	7850.00	74.42	1%
35	Transfers to State and UT Governments						
	Gross	106908.00	30129.01	28%	88473.61	28984.65	33%
	Less : Recoveries	7365.00	4.07	0%	7732.00	0.00	0%
	Net	99543.00	30124.94	30%	80741.61	28984.65	36%
38	Department of Expenditure	4.00	1.00	25%	5.00	1.23	25%
MINISTRY OF FOOD PROCESSING INDUSTRIES		**660.00**	**424.90**	**64%**	**600.00**	**108.89**	**18%**
45	Ministry of Food Processing Industries	660.00	424.90	64%	600.00	108.89	18%
MINISTRY OF HEALTH AND FAMILY WELFARE		**30477.00**	**14042.29**	**46%**	**26760.00**	**10044.12**	**38%**
46	Department of Health and Family Welfare	27127.00	12643.95	47%	23560.00	8789.06	37%
47	Department of Ayurveda, Yoga & Naturopathy, Unani, Siddha and Homoeopathy (AYUSH)	990.00	294.58	30%	900.00	142.62	16%
48	Department of Health Research	660.00	291.23	44%	600.00	265.11	44%
49	Department of Aids Control	1700.00	812.53	48%	1700.00	847.33	50%
MINISTRY OF HEAVY INDUSTRIES AND PUBLIC ENTERPRISES		**566.00**	**345.85**	**61%**	**410.00**	**362.52**	**88%**
50	Department of Heavy Industry	553.00	342.65	62%	399.00	356.10	89%
51	Department of Public Enterprises	13.00	3.20	25%	11.00	6.42	58%
MINISTRY OF HOME AFFAIRS		**12140.89**	**3507.35**	**29%**	**11562.29**	**2047.13**	**18%**
52	Ministry of Home Affairs	2139.01	671.11	31%	3237.00	165.18	5%
54	Police	8045.99	2064.43	26%	6435.00	1586.68	25%
55	Other Expenditure of the Ministry of Home Affairs	315.00	95.73	30%	328.00	21.29	6%
56	Transfers to UT Govts.	1640.89	676.08	41%	1562.29	273.98	18%

Annex continued

(1)	(2)	(3)	(4)	(5)	(6)	(7)	(8)
	MINISTRY OF HOUSING AND URBAN POVERTY ALLEVIATION	**1155.00**	**389.50**	**34%**	**1100.00**	**291.76**	**27%**
57	Ministry of Housing and Urban Poverty Alleviation	1155.00	389.50	34%	1100.00	291.76	27%
	MINISTRY OF HUMAN RESOURCE DEVELOPMENT	**61407.00**	**33007.67**	**54%**	**52057.00**	**29153.38**	**56%**
58	Department of School Education and Literacy						
	Gross	64584.08	26545.49	41%	57483.33	23342.66	41%
	Less : Rec. (prarambik shiksha kosh/National Inv. Fund	18615.08	0.00	0%	18526.33	0.00	0%
	Net	45969.00	26545.49	58%	38957.00	23342.66	60%
59	Department of Higher Education	15438.00	6462.18	42%	13100.00	5810.72	44%
	MINISTRY OF INFORMATION AND BROADCASTING	**905.00**	**313.59**	**35%**	**861.00**	**336.93**	**39%**
60	Ministry of Information and Broadcasting	905.00	313.59	35%	861.00	336.93	39%
	MINISTRY OF LABOUR AND EMPLOYMENT	**2403.88**	**904.33**	**38%**	**1248.25**	**645.44**	**52%**
61	Ministry of Labour and Employment						
	Gross	2522.44	904.33	36%	1988.25	645.44	32%
	Less : Recoveries	118.56	0.00	0%	740.00	0.00	0%
	Net	2403.88	904.33	38%	1248.25	645.44	52%
	MINISTRY OF LAW AND JUSTICE	**1050.00**	**500.51**	**48%**	**1000.00**	**203.00**	**20%**
63	Law and Justice	1050.00	500.51	48%	1000.00	203.00	20%
	MINISTRY OF MICRO, SMALL AND MEDIUM ENTERPRISE	**2835.00**	**960.91**	**34%**	**2700.00**	**1053.50**	**39%**
65	Ministry of Micro, Small and Medium Enterprises	2835.00	960.91	34%	2700.00	1053.50	39%
	MINISTRY OF MINES	**232.00**	**121.57**	**52%**	**214.00**	**177.65**	**83%**
66	Ministry of Mines	232.00	121.57	52%	214.00	177.65	83%
	MINISTRY OF MINORITY AFFAIRS	**3135.00**	**539.92**	**17%**	**2850.00**	**760.56**	**27%**
67	Ministry of Minority Affairs	3135.00	539.92	17%	2850.00	760.56	27%
	MINISTRY OF NEW AND RENEWABLE ENERGY	**1383.00**	**650.26**	**47%**	**1198.00**	**674.56**	**56%**
68	Ministry of New and Renewable Energy						
	Gross	1423.43	654.68	46%	1198.00	674.56	**56%**
	Less : Recoveries	40.43	4.42	11%			
	Net	1383.00	650.26	47%	1198.00	674.56	56%
	MINISTRY OF PANCHAYATI RAJ	**5350.00**	**1173.10**	**22%**	**5250.00**	**1183.63**	**23%**
70	Ministry of Panchayati Raj	5350.00	1173.10	22%	5250.00	1183.63	23%
	MINISTRY OF PERSONNEL, PUBLIC GRIEVANCES & PENSIONS	**279.00**	**69.48**	**25%**	**260.00**	**41.83**	**16%**
72	Ministry of Personnel, Public Grievances and Pensions	279.00	69.48	25%	260.00	41.83	16%
	MINISTRY OF PETROLEUM AND NATURAL GAS	**43.00**	**0.00**	**0%**	**40.00**	**0.00**	0%
73	Ministry of Petroleum and Natural Gas	43.00	0.00	0%	40.00	0.00	0%

Annex continued

(1)	(2)	(3)	(4)	(5)	(6)	(7)	(8)
MINISTRY OF PLANNING		**2100.00**	**588.71**	**28%**	**1600.00**	**193.84**	**12%**
74	Ministry of Planning	2100.00	588.71	28%	1600.00	193.84	12%
MINISTRY OF POWER		**9642.00**	**1492.94**	**15%**	**9642.00**	**1415.26**	**15%**
75	Ministry of Power						
	Gross	15123.04	1776.00	12%	14694.00	1569.21	11%
	Less : Recoveries	5481.04	283.06	5%	5052.00	153.95	3%
	Net	9642.00	1492.94	15%	9642.00	1415.26	15%
MINISTRY OF ROAD TRANSPORT AND HIGHWAYS		**25359.91**	**10964.05**	**43%**	**22247.75**	**10353.06**	**47%**
81	Ministry of Road Transport and Highways						
	Gross	41568.13	13490.86	32%	36400.01	12368.75	34%
	Less : Recoveries (Central Road fund & Bridge fee fund)	16208.22	2526.81	16%	14152.26	2015.69	14%
	Net	25359.91	10964.05	43%	22247.75	10353.06	47%
MINISTRY OF RURAL DEVELOPMENT		**90376.00**	**35071.18**	**39%**	**87800.00**	**36766.85**	**42%**
82	Department of Rural Development						
	Gross	129876.20	27947.40	22%	138418.00	31281.23	23%
	Less : (i) Recoveries (National Emp. Gur fund/CR fund)	56701.20	551.22	1%	64318.00	520.36	1%
	(ii) Receipts						
	Net	73175.00	27396.18	37%	74100.00	30760.87	42%
83	Department of Land Resources	3201.00	2007.44	63%	2700.00	1419.89	53%
84	Department of Drinking Water Supply	14000.00	5667.56	40%	11000.00	4586.09	42%
MINISTRY OF SCIENCE AND TECHNOLOGY		**5975.00**	**3004.17**	**50%**	**5679.00**	**2651.92**	**47%**
85	Department of Science and Technology	2477.00	1336.21	54%	2349.00	1059.40	45%
86	Department of Scientific and Industrial Research	2013.00	901.82	45%	1930.00	948.74	49%
87	Department of Bio-Technology	1485.00	766.14	52%	1400.00	643.78	46%
MINISTRY OF SHIPPING		**812.00**	**164.11**	**20%**	**743.00**	**52.41**	**7%**
88	Ministry of Shipping	812.00	164.11	20%	743.00	52.41	7%
MINISTRY OF SOCIAL JUSTICE & EMPOWERMENT		**5915.00**	**1836.14**	**31%**	**5375.00**	**2652.44**	**49%**
89	Ministry of Social Justice & Empowerment	5915.00	1836.14	31%	5375.00	2652.44	49%
DEPARTMENT OF SPACE		**5615.00**	**1271.44**	**23%**	**5700.00**	**1185.75**	**21%**
90	Department of Space						
	Gross	5615.04	1271.44	23%	5700.04	1185.75	21%
	Less : Recoveries	0.04	0.00	0%	0.04	0.00	0%
	Net	5615.00	1271.44	23%	5700.00	1185.75	21%
MINISTRY OF STATISTICS AND PROGRAMME IMPLEMENTATION		**4586.00**	**1615.28**	**35%**	**2180.00**	**1096.08**	**50%**
91	Ministry of Statistics and Programme Implementation	4586.00	1615.28	35%	2180.00	1096.08	50%
MINISTRY OF STEEL		**46.00**	**10.47**	**23%**	**40.00**	**7.84**	**20%**
92	Ministry of Steel	46.00	10.47	23%	40.00	7.84	20%
MINISTRY OF TEXTILES		**7000.00**	**1554.77**	**22%**	**5000.00**	**1778.85**	**36%**
93	Ministry of Textiles	7000.00	1554.77	22%	5000.00	1778.85	36%

Annex continued

(1)	(2)	(3)	(4)	(5)	(6)	(7)	(8)
MINISTRY OF TOURISM		**1210.00**	**432.96**	**36%**	**1100.00**	**516.97**	**47%**
94	Ministry of Tourism	1210.00	432.96	36%	1100.00	516.97	47%
MINISTRY OF TRIBAL AFFAIRS		**4090.00**	**2172.89**	**53%**	**3723.01**	**1980.32**	53%
95	Ministry of Tribal Affairs	4090.00	2172.89	53%	3723.01	1980.32	53%
U.T.s WITHOUT LEGISLATURE		**4015.20**	**1294.47**	**32%**	**3140.22**	**1207.23**	38%
96	Andaman & Nicobar Islands	1701.43	575.51	34%	1430.45	472.35	33%
97	Chandigarh	737.23	172.10	23%	661.89	335.09	51%
98	Dadra & Nagar Haveli	607.68	317.02	52%	334.14	149.67	45%
99	Daman & Diu	568.25	137.84	24%	324.95	107.50	33%
100	Lakshadweep	400.61	92.00	23%	388.79	142.62	37%
MINISTRY OF URBAN DEVELOPMENT		**7012.12**	**2407.01**	**34%**	**6279.75**	**3120.55**	**50%**
101	Department of Urban Development	6783.25	2331.18	34%	6068.76	3071.36	51%
102	Public Works	228.87	75.83	33%	210.99	49.19	23%
MINISTRY OF WATER RESOURCES		**1500.00**	**281.96**	**19%**	**720.00**	**239.69**	**33%**
104	Ministry of Water Resources						
	Gross	1512.00	286.77	19%	732.00	244.86	33%
	Less : Recoveries	12.00	4.81	40%	12.00	5.17	43%
	Net	1500.00	281.96	19%	720.00	239.69	33%
MINISTRY OF WOMEN AND CHILD DEVELOPMENT		**18500.00**	**9777.78**	**53%**	**12650.00**	**6650.33**	**53%**
105	Ministry of Women and Child Development	18500.00	9777.78	53%	12650.00	6650.33	53%
MINISTRY OF YOUTH AFFAIRS & SPORTS		**1041.00**	**564.81**	**54%**	**1000.00**	**345.08**	**35%**
106	Ministry of Youth Affairs and Sports	1041.00	564.81	54%	1000.00	345.08	35%
RAILWAYS		**24000.00**	**12000.00**	**50%**	**20000.00**	**8175.27**	**41%**
	Ministry of Railways						
	Gross		12108.59			8188.51	
	Less : Exp.met from Receipts		10.87			13.24	
	Exp. Met from Reserve Funds		97.72			0.00	
	Net	24000.00	12000.00	50%	20000.00	8175.27	41%
	GRAND TOTAL	**521025.00**	**202739.75**	**39%**	**441546.75**	**177822.59**	**40%**

Annex continued

9. NON-PLAN EXPENDITURE

(₹ *in crore*)

GRANT NO.	MINISTRY/ DEPARTMENT	2012-2013 BE	2012-2013 ACTUALS upto 09/2012	2012-2013 %	2011-2012 BE	2011-2012 ACTUALS upto 09/2011	2011-2012 %
(1)	(2)	(3)	(4)	(5)	(6)	(7)	(8)
MINISTRY OF AGRICULTURE		**2593.59**	**1413.60**	**55%**	**2653.85**	**1458.32**	**55%**
1	Department of Agriculture and Cooperation	322.22	102.77	32%	400.00	99.58	25%
2	Department of Agricultural Research and Education	2172.00	1256.75	58%	2157.60	1255.55	58%
3	Department of Animal Husbandry, Dairying and Fisheries						
	Gross	451.37	222.11	49%	437.95	252.18	58%
	Less : Receipts	352.00	168.03	48%	341.70	148.99	44%
	Net	99.37	54.08	54%	96.25	103.19	107%
DEPARTMENT OF ATOMIC ENERGY		**3632.00**	**2939.83**	**81%**	**3752.46**	**2156.74**	**57%**
4	Atomic Energy						
	Gross	4786.60	2819.49	59%	5096.26	2466.58	48%
	Less : Receipts	1601.60	649.11	41%	1331.00	690.36	52%
	Recoveries	136.00	40.28	30%	153.85	31.05	20%
	Net	3049.00	2130.10	70%	3611.41	1745.17	48%
5	Nuclear Power Schemes						
	Gross	3523.00	931.41	26%	7787.38	6763.57	87%
	Less : Receipts	2940.00	121.68	4%	7646.33	6352.00	83%
	Net	583.00	809.73	139%	141.05	411.57	292%
MINISTRY OF CHEMICALS AND FERTILISERS		**61088.71**	**45002.40**	**74%**	**50080.00**	**31445.05**	**63%**
6	Department of Chemicals and Petro-Chemicals	45.62	34.34	75%	22.00	10.82	49%
7	Department of Fertilisers						
	Gross	65618.00	46463.54	71%	53612.00	33016.29	62%
	Less : Recoveries	4618.00	1515.93	33%	3592.00	1597.22	44%
	Net	61000.00	44947.61	74%	50020.00	31419.07	63%
8	Department of Pharmaceuticals	43.09	20.45	47%	38.00	15.16	40%
MINISTRY OF CIVIL AVIATION		**738.80**	**47.27**	**6%**	**693.88**	**213.20**	**31%**
9	Ministry of Civil Aviation						
	Gross	738.84	47.27	6%	693.92	213.20	31%
	Less : Recoveries	0.04	0.00	0%	0.04	0.00	0%
	Net	738.80	47.27	6%	693.88	213.20	31%
MINISTRY OF COAL		**48.35**	**12.61**	**26%**	**48.72**	**-6.67**	**-14%**
10	Ministry of Coal						
	Gross	78.35	42.51	54%	78.72	22.33	28%
	Less : Recoveries	30.00	29.90	100%	30.00	29.00	97%
	Net	48.35	12.61	26%	48.72	-6.67	-14%
MINISTRY OF COMMERCE AND INDUSTRY		**3125.25**	**2030.47**	**65%**	**4700.58**	**874.37**	**19%**
11	Department of Commerce						
	Gross	2927.50	1948.34	67%	4516.08	795.66	18%
	Less : Recoveries	4.50	10.35	230%	4.50	6.87	153%
	Net	2923.00	1937.99	66%	4511.58	788.79	17%

Annex continued

(1)	(2)	(3)	(4)	(5)	(6)	(7)	(8)
12	Department of Industrial Policy and Promotion						
	Gross	202.25	92.48	46%	189.01	85.59	45%
	Less : Recoveries	0.00	0.00		0.01	0.01	100%
	Net	202.25	92.48	46%	189.00	85.58	45%
MINISTRY OF COMMUNICATIONS AND INFORMATION TECHNOLOGY		**11082.16**	**8200.59**	**74%**	**9332.06**	**7137.35**	**76%**
13	Department of Posts						
	Gross	14195.48	7519.00	53%	13240.48	6675.25	50%
	Less : Receipts	7793.31	2047.33	26%	7517.70	1725.30	23%
	Recoveries	665.05	16.78	3%	695.11	38.88	6%
	Net	5737.12	5454.89	95%	5027.67	4911.07	98%
14	Department of Telecommunications	5294.04	2716.97	51%	4255.78	2210.46	52%
15	Department of Information Technology	51.00	28.73	56%	48.61	15.82	33%
MINISTRY OF CONSUMER AFFAIRS, FOOD AND PUBLIC DISTRIBUTION		**76502.45**	**67766.50**	**89%**	**61841.57**	**53063.35**	**86%**
16	Department of Consumer Affairs						
	Gross	383.09	233.26	61%	375.36	135.77	36%
	Less :Recoveries	21.80	0.00	0%	19.80	0.00	0%
	Net	361.29	233.26	65%	355.56	135.77	38%
17	Department of Food & Public Distribution						
	Gross	86835.66	67790.16	78%	72211.32	53102.38	74%
	Less: Receipts	10000.00	0.00	0%	10000.00	0.00	0%
	Recoveries	694.50	256.92	37%	725.31	174.80	24%
	Net	76141.16	67533.24	89%	61486.01	52927.58	86%
MINISTRY OF CORPORATE AFFAIRS		**213.50**	**98.98**	**46%**	**210.94**	**100.22**	**48%**
18	Ministry of Corporate Affairs	213.50	98.98	46%	210.94	100.22	48%
MINISTRY OF CULTURE		**583.00**	**339.26**	**58%**	**553.00**	**325.08**	**59%**
19	Ministry of Culture	583.00	339.26	58%	553.00	325.08	59%
MINISTRY OF DEFENCE		**238205.53**	**104938.64**	**44%**	**202572.30**	**96286.21**	**48%**
20	Ministry of Defence						
	Gross	16598.24	6763.85	41%	13156.81	7152.47	54%
	Less : Receipts	10800.00	3012.98	28%	9000.00	3144.92	35%
	Net	5798.24	3750.87	65%	4156.81	4007.55	96%
21	Defence Pensions	39000.00	16263.15	42%	34000.00	19041.86	56%
DEFENCE SERVICES		**193407.29**	**84924.62**	**44%**	**164415.49**	**73236.80**	**45%**
22	Defence Services-Army						
	Gross	80025.82	39749.71	50%	65985.05	34692.64	53%
	Less : Receipts	1869.64	814.40	44%	1695.62	887.18	52%
	Recoveries	41.82	0.00	0%	37.88	0.00	0%
	Net	78114.36	38935.31	50%	64251.55	33805.46	53%
23	Defence Services-Navy						
	Gross	12748.02	5894.98	46%	10789.06	5434.99	50%
	Less : Receipts	200.00	82.67	41%	200.00	59.38	30%
	Net	12548.02	5812.31	46%	10589.06	5375.61	51%
24	Defence Services-Air Force						
	Gross	18325.19	8203.34	45%	16520.87	7158.67	43%
	Less : Receipts	619.38	329.15	53%	592.92	270.43	46%
	Net	17705.81	7874.19	44%	15927.95	6888.24	43%
25	Defence Ordnance Factories						
	Gross	1801.68	3070.45	170%	795.88	1905.87	239%
	Less : Receipts	1836.77	654.87	36%	1647.63	599.66	36%
	Recoveries	500.00	0.00	0%	325.00	0.00	0%
	Net	-535.09	2415.58	-451%	-1176.75	1306.21	-111%

Annex continued

(1)	(2)	(3)	(4)	(5)	(6)	(7)	(8)
26	Defence Services - Research and Development						
	Gross	6035.56	2296.75	38%	5659.87	1953.95	35%
	Less : Receipts	40.00	19.63	49%	35.00	54.95	157%
	Net	5995.56	2277.12	38%	5624.87	1899.00	34%
27	Capital Outlay on Defence Services	79578.63	27610.11	35%	69198.81	23962.28	35%
MINISTRY OF DEVELOPMENT OF NORTH EASTERN REGION		**24.33**	**15.09**	**62%**	**21.58**	**12.36**	**57%**
28	Ministry of Development of North Eastern Region	24.33	15.09	62%	21.58	12.36	57%
MINISTRY OF EARTH SCIENCES		**387.00**	**205.70**	**53%**	**347.00**	**188.69**	**54%**
29	Ministry of Earth Sciences						
	Gross	391.39	207.33	53%	349.22	188.86	54%
	Less :Recoveries	4.39	1.63	37%	2.22	0.17	8%
	Net	387.00	205.70	53%	347.00	188.69	54%
MINISTRY OF ENVIRONMENT AND FORESTS		**199.41**	**110.14**	**55%**	**191.97**	**94.86**	**49%**
30	Ministry of Environment and Forests						
	Gross	452.41	136.40	30%	441.97	105.11	24%
	Less :Receipt	253.00	26.26	10%	250.00	10.25	4%
	Net	199.41	110.14	55%	191.97	94.86	49%
MINISTRY OF EXTERNAL AFFAIRS		**8161.97**	**3849.45**	**47%**	**6306.00**	**3237.62**	**51%**
31	Ministry of External Affairs	8161.97	3849.45	47%	6306.00	3237.62	51%
MINISTRY OF FINANCE		**435380.00**	**171212.84**	**39%**	**374130.52**	**162010.00**	**43%**
32	Department of Economic Affairs						
	Gross	62899.98	5587.54	9%	18551.59	8814.66	48%
	Less :Recoveries	1651.65	0.23	0%	1590.60	0.00	0%
	Receipts	42123.32	0.00	0%	8767.75	0.00	0%
	Net	19125.01	5587.31	29%	8193.24	8814.66	108%
33	Department of Financial Services						
	Gross	8349.24	3539.36	42%	15855.94	329.27	2%
	Less : Recoveries	0.01	259.05		6000.00	24.82	0%
	Net	8349.23	3280.31	39%	9855.94	304.45	3%
34	Interest Payments						
	Gross	324769.43	140863.02	43%	272330.28	128036.33	47%
	Less : Receipts	5010.00	9698.27	194%	4344.11	5537.70	127%
	Net	319759.43	131164.75	41%	267986.17	122498.63	46%
35	Transfers to State and UT Governments						
	Gross	69022.46	19961.52	29%	60173.62	18692.22	31%
	Less : Receipts	5720.00	1689.53	30%	6025.00	1447.89	24%
	Recoveries	4620.00	1002.50	22%	4525.00	455.26	10%
	Net	58682.46	17269.49	29%	49623.62	16789.07	34%
36	Loans to Govt. Servants etc.						
	Gross	250.00	79.33	32%	300.00	94.81	32%
	Less : Receipts	445.00	198.75	45%	490.00	221.26	45%
	Net	-195.00	-119.42	61%	-190.00	-126.45	67%
37	Repayment of Debt						
	Gross (Excluding MSS)	3786074.35	1679744.89	44%	3155216.93	1767652.94	56%
	Less : Receipts	3786074.35	1679744.89	44%	3155216.93	1767652.94	56%
	Net	0.00	0.00		0.00	0.00	
38	Department of Expenditure	131.25	46.03	35%	96.97	52.71	54%
39	Pensions						
	Gross	19800.00	8970.99	45%	17000.00	8213.15	48%
	Less : Receipts	1000.00	0.00	0%	1000.00	0.00	0%
	Net	18800.00	8970.99	48%	16000.00	8213.15	51%

Annex continued

(1)	(2)	(3)	(4)	(5)	(6)	(7)	(8)
40	Indian Audit and Accounts Department						
	Gross	2568.49	1407.94	55%	2398.56	1248.37	52%
	Less :Recoveries	152.79	116.12	76%	145.48	87.15	60%
	Net	2415.70	1291.82	53%	2253.08	1161.22	52%
41	Department of Revenue						
	Gross	1178.59	332.49	28%	13356.90	1169.38	9%
	Less : Receipts	366.73	171.20	47%	312.00	191.26	61%
	Recoveries	42.22	0.00	0%	53.97	0.00	0%
	Net	769.64	161.29	21%	12990.93	978.12	8%
42	Direct Taxes						
	Gross	3880.46	1699.44	44%	3881.55	1645.36	42%
	Less :Recoveries	2.00	0.64	32%	2.00	5.52	276%
	Net	3878.46	1698.80	44%	3879.55	1639.84	42%
43	Indirect Taxes						
	Gross	3601.08	1851.54	51%	3378.89	1671.73	49%
	Less : Recoveries	0.50	0.26	52%	0.50	0.22	44%
	Net	3600.58	1851.28	51%	3378.39	1671.51	49%
44	Department of Disinvestment	63.24	10.19	16%	62.63	13.09	21%
	MINISTRY OF FOOD PROCESSING INDUSTRIES	**10.54**	**5.01**	**48%**	**10.09**	**4.39**	**44%**
45	Ministry of Food Processing Industries	10.54	5.01	48%	10.09	4.39	44%
	MINISTRY OF HEALTH AND FAMILY WELFARE	**4011.00**	**2687.32**	**67%**	**3696.00**	**2294.68**	**62%**
46	Department of Health and Family Welfare						
	Gross	5853.29	3003.48	51%	5341.33	2622.17	49%
	Less :Recoveries	2278.29	521.91	23%	2004.33	550.76	27%
	Net	3575.00	2481.57	69%	3337.00	2071.41	62%
47	Department of Ayurveda, Yoga & Naturopathy,Unani, Siddha and Homoeopathy (Ayush)	188.00	117.90	63%	188.00	95.06	51%
48	Department of Health Research	248.00	87.85	35%	171.00	128.21	75%
	MINISTRY OF HEAVY INDUSTRIES AND PUBLIC ENTERPRISES	**465.60**	**200.08**	**43%**	**464.34**	**54.82**	**12%**
50	Department of Heavy Industry	456.67	195.92	43%	456.65	50.41	11%
51	Department of Public Enterprises	8.93	4.16	47%	7.69	4.41	57%
	MINISTRY OF HOME AFFAIRS	**42308.10**	**23016.83**	**54%**	**37357.85**	**21644.89**	**58%**
52	Ministry of Home Affairs	835.69	461.49	55%	1713.39	1257.91	73%
53	Cabinet	741.87	465.22	63%	434.61	353.79	81%
54	Police						
	Gross	38816.26	21189.63	55%	33584.99	19155.66	57%
	Less :Recoveries	230.00	24.57	11%	360.00	77.49	22%
	Net	38586.26	21165.06	55%	33224.99	19078.17	57%
55	Other Expenditure of the Ministry of Home Affairs	1558.28	632.56	41%	1416.86	672.51	47%
56	Transfers to UT Govts.	586.00	292.50	50%	568.00	282.51	50%
	MINISTRY OF HOUSING AND URBAN POVERTY ALLEVIATION	**8.00**	**3.63**	**45%**	**7.60**	**4.06**	**53%**
57	Ministry of Housing and Urban Poverty Alleviation	8.00	3.63	45%	7.60	4.06	53%
	MINSTRY OF HUMAN RESOURCE DEVELOPMENT	**12649.00**	**5024.18**	**40%**	**11306.00**	**4935.46**	**44%**
58	Department of School Education and Literacy	2812.00	1339.93	48%	2494.00	1728.16	69%
59	Department of Higher Education	9837.00	3684.25	37%	8812.00	3207.30	36%

Annex continued

(1) (2)	(3)	(4)	(5)	(6)	(7)	(8)
MINISTRY OF INFORMATION AND BROADCASTING	**1832.32**	**919.65**	**50%**	**1782.64**	**1242.33**	**70%**
60 Ministry of Information and Broadcasting						
Gross	1832.39	919.67	50%	1782.71	1242.41	70%
Less : Recoveries	0.07	0.02	29%	0.07	0.08	114%
Net	1832.32	919.65	50%	1782.64	1242.33	70%
MINISTRY OF LABOUR AND EMPLOYMENT	**1929.80**	**1735.02**	**90%**	**1861.00**	**1643.00**	**88%**
61 Ministry of Labour and Employment						
Gross	2120.19	1735.02	82%	2041.39	1643.00	80%
Less : Recoveries	190.39	0.00	0%	180.39	0.00	0%
Net	1929.80	1735.02	90%	1861.00	1643.00	88%
MINISTRY OF LAW AND JUSTICE	**669.54**	**252.54**	**38%**	**553.45**	**298.96**	**54%**
62 Election Commission	72.17	20.73	29%	25.93	15.26	59%
63 Law and Justice	485.62	167.67	35%	432.30	223.04	52%
64 Supreme Court of India	111.75	64.14	57%	95.22	60.66	64%
MINISTRY OF MICRO, SMALL AND MEDIUM ENTERPRISES	**320.66**	**152.30**	**47%**	**301.29**	**138.32**	**46%**
65 Ministry of Micro, Small and Medium Enterprises	320.66	152.30	47%	301.29	138.32	46%
MINISTRY OF MINES	**466.44**	**276.08**	**59%**	**440.28**	**242.92**	**55%**
66 Ministry of Mines	466.44	276.08	59%	440.28	242.92	55%
MINISTRY OF MINORITY AFFAIRS	**19.70**	**7.03**	**36%**	**16.00**	**6.66**	**42%**
67 Ministry of Minority Affairs	19.70	7.03	36%	16.00	6.66	42%
MINISTRY OF NEW AND RENEWABLE ENERGY	**14.79**	**7.52**	**51%**	**14.38**	**6.05**	**42%**
68 Ministry of New and Renewable Energy	14.79	7.52	51%	14.38	6.05	42%
MINISTRY OF OVERSEAS INDIANS AFFAIRS	**114.77**	**25.81**	**22%**	**81.00**	**28.70**	**35%**
69 Ministry of Overseas Indians Affairs	114.77	25.81	22%	81.00	28.70	35%
MINISTRY OF PANCHAYATI RAJ	**0.74**	**0.28**	**38%**	**0.65**	**0.18**	**28%**
70 Ministry of Panchayati Raj	0.74	0.28	38%	0.65	0.18	28%
MINISTRY OF PARLIAMENTARY AFFAIRS	**11.72**	**5.16**	**44%**	**10.48**	**4.88**	**47%**
71 Ministry of Parliamentary Affairs	11.72	5.16	44%	10.48	4.88	47%
MINISTRY OF PERSONNEL, PUBLIC GRIEVANCES & PENSIONS	**615.67**	**339.35**	**55%**	**506.78**	**279.76**	**55%**
72 Ministry of Personnel, Public Grievances and Pensions	615.67	339.35	55%	506.78	279.76	55%
MINISTRY OF PETROLEUM AND NATURAL GAS	**43716.85**	**39935.74**	**91%**	**23676.20**	**22720.93**	**96%**
73 Ministry of Petroleum and Natural Gas	43716.85	39935.74	91%	23676.20	22720.93	96%
MINISTRY OF PLANNING	**77.03**	**40.76**	**53%**	**76.00**	**37.51**	**49%**
74 Ministry of Planning	77.03	40.76	53%	76.00	37.51	49%
MINISTRY OF POWER	**-122.89**	**56.71**	**-46%**	**-135.01**	**-91.61**	**68%**
75 Ministry of Power						
Gross	168.56	67.57	40%	137.68	50.74	37%
Less : Receipts	256.66	0.00	0%	272.69	142.35	52%
Recoveries	34.79	10.86	31%	0.00	0.00	
Net	-122.89	56.71	-46%	-135.01	-91.61	68%

Annex continued

(1) (2)	(3)	(4)	(5)	(6)	(7)	(8)
THE PRESIDENT, PARLIAMENT, UNION PUBLIC SERVICE COMMISSION AND THE SECRETARIAT OF THE VICE-PRESIDENT	**902.98**	**453.38**	**50%**	**801.59**	**386.52**	**48%**
76 President	30.24	15.51	51%	27.67	15.34	55%
77 Lok Sabha	435.00	230.75	53%	400.00	195.52	49%
78 Rajya Sabha	284.05	135.33	48%	224.35	100.81	45%
79 Union Public Service Commission	150.57	70.12	47%	146.58	73.46	50%
80 Secretariat of the Vice-President	3.12	1.67	54%	2.99	1.39	46%
MINISTRY OF ROAD TRANSPORT AND HIGHWAYS	**5438.21**	**1272.57**	**23%**	**4190.00**	**673.95**	**16%**
81 Ministry of Road Transport and Highways						
Gross	5578.22	1294.36	23%	4340.50	704.62	16%
Less : Recoveries	140.01	21.79	16%	150.50	30.67	20%
Net	5438.21	1272.57	23%	4190.00	673.95	16%
MINISTRY OF RURAL DEVELOPMENT	**59.26**	**32.90**	**56%**	**55.16**	**29.34**	**53%**
82 Department of Rural Development	46.82	25.91	55%	43.72	23.16	53%
83 Department of Land Resources	7.20	4.05	56%	6.20	3.52	57%
84 Department of Drinking Water and Sanitation	5.24	2.94	56%	5.24	2.66	51%
MINISTRY OF SCIENCE AND TECHNOLOGY	**1882.61**	**955.82**	**51%**	**1865.92**	**923.21**	**49%**
85 Department of Science and Technology						
Gross	405.86	224.15	55%	393.64	181.77	46%
Less : Recoveries	9.64	11.92	124%	9.64	3.60	37%
Net	396.22	212.23	54%	384.00	178.17	46%
86 Research	1471.00	734.76	50%	1455.00	726.34	50%
87 Department of Biotechnology	15.39	8.83	57%	26.92	18.70	69%
MINISTRY OF SHIPPING	**867.49**	**188.06**	**22%**	**1063.00**	**30.88**	**3%**
88 Ministry of Shipping						
Gross	1164.49	300.48	26%	1328.60	130.22	10%
Less : Receipts	190.00	105.92	56%	170.00	96.82	57%
Recoveries	107.00	6.50	6%	95.60	2.52	3%
Net	867.49	188.06	22%	1063.00	30.88	3%
MINISTRY OF SOCIAL JUSTICE & EMPOWERMENT	**93.30**	**48.91**	**52%**	**78.00**	**49.02**	**63%**
89 Ministry of Social Justice & Empowerment	93.30	48.91	52%	78.00	49.02	63%
DEPARTMENT OF SPACE	**1100.00**	**603.76**	**55%**	**926.00**	**488.00**	**53%**
90 Department of Space	1100.00	603.76	55%	926.00	488.00	53%
MINISTRY OF STATISTICS AND PROGRAMME IMPLEMENTATION	**357.54**	**190.61**	**53%**	**347.36**	**183.18**	**53%**
91 Ministry of Statistics and Programme Implementation	357.54	190.61	53%	347.36	183.18	53%
MINISTRY OF STEEL	**69.29**	**32.35**	**47%**	**70.76**	**33.75**	48%
92 Ministry of Steel						
Gross	75.89	37.53	49%	77.71	40.70	52%
Less: Receipts	6.60	5.18	78%	6.95	6.95	100%
Net	69.29	32.35	47%	70.76	33.75	48%
MINISTRY OF TEXTILES	**836.41**	**412.51**	**49%**	**855.75**	**340.56**	**40%**
93 Ministry of Textiles	836.41	412.51	49%	855.75	340.56	40%
MINISTRY OF TOURISM	**72.98**	**32.70**	**45%**	**70.76**	**27.85**	**39%**
94 Ministry of Tourism	72.98	32.70	45%	70.76	27.85	39%

Annex continued

(1) (2)	(3)	(4)	(5)	(6)	(7)	(8)
MINISTRY OF TRIBAL AFFAIRS	**18.00**	**8.93**	**50%**	**17.00**	**7.86**	**46%**
95 Ministry of Tribal Affairs	18.00	8.93	50%	17.00	7.86	46%
U.Ts WITHOUT LEGISLATURE	**3706.92**	**2340.56**	**63%**	**3408.89**	**2182.25**	**64%**
96 Andaman & Nicobar Islands						
Gross	1390.74	688.18	49%	1285.31	746.57	58%
Less : Recoveries	114.13	44.56	39%	111.41	41.25	37%
Net	1276.61	643.62	50%	1173.90	705.32	60%
97 Chandigarh						
Gross	2178.78	1302.23	60%	2068.31	1159.75	56%
Less : Recoveries	374.00	78.84	21%	421.78	76.18	18%
Net	1804.78	1223.39	68%	1646.53	1083.57	66%
98 Dadra & Nagar Haveli						
Gross	1780.32	679.96	38%	1527.02	774.51	51%
Less : Recoveries	1673.76	625.91	37%	1429.72	712.95	50%
Net	106.56	54.05	51%	97.30	61.56	63%
99 Daman & Diu						
Gross	835.80	469.72	56%	708.00	397.89	56%
Less : Recoveries	722.60	360.94	50%	602.60	333.77	55%
Net	113.20	108.78	96%	105.40	64.12	61%
100 Lakshadweep						
Gross	503.06	317.44	63%	483.05	275.29	57%
Less : Recoveries	97.29	6.72	7%	97.29	7.61	8%
Net	405.77	310.72	77%	385.76	267.68	69%
MINISTRY OF URBAN DEVELOPMENT	**2673.87**	**1419.49**	**53%**	**2261.71**	**1229.30**	**54%**
101 Department of Urban Development						
Gross	946.17	475.27	50%	786.51	395.05	50%
Less : Recoveries	0.04	0.00	0%	0.04	0.00	0%
Net	946.13	475.27	50%	786.47	395.05	50%
102 Public Works						
Gross	1686.55	915.83	54%	1443.45	789.37	55%
Less : Recoveries	61.15	11.14	18%	65.44	5.51	8%
Net	1625.40	904.69	56%	1378.01	783.86	57%
103 Stationery and Printing						
Gross	264.42	116.09	44%	253.24	113.78	45%
Less : Recoveries	162.08	76.56	47%	156.01	63.39	41%
Net	102.34	39.53	39%	97.23	50.39	52%
MINISTRY OF WATER RESOURCES	**541.00**	**291.22**	**54%**	**502.73**	**255.77**	**51%**
104 Ministry of Water Resources						
Gross	555.60	296.85	53%	517.33	261.41	51%
Less : Recoveries	14.60	5.63	39%	14.60	5.64	39%
Net	541.00	291.22	54%	502.73	255.77	51%
MINISTRY OF WOMEN AND CHILD DEVELOPMENT	**84.00**	**40.66**	**48%**	**83.00**	**36.31**	**44%**
105 Ministry of Women and Child Development	84.00	40.66	48%	83.00	36.31	44%
MINISTRY OF YOUTH AFFAIRS & SPORTS	**111.00**	**80.17**	**72%**	**121.00**	**57.63**	**48%**
106 Ministry of Youth Affairs and Sports	111.00	80.17	72%	121.00	57.63	48%
MINISTRY OF RAILWAYS						
Ministry of Railways						
Gross	109393.25	60592.26	55%	109393.25	52577.55	48%
Less : Receipts	109393.25	57882.19	53%	109393.25	47846.52	44%
: Reserve fund	0.00	2710.07		0.00	4731.03	
Net	0.00	0.00		0.00	0.00	
Exp. From Contingency Fund		0.00			240.84	
GRAND TOTAL	**969900.29**	**491278.97**	**51%**	**816182.08**	**421269.86**	**52%**

Annex continued

10. RESOURCES TRANSFERRED TO STATE & UT GOVERNMENTS

(₹ in crore)

	DESCRIPTION	2012-2013			2011-2012		
		BE	ACTUALS upto 09/2012	%	BE	ACTUALS upto 09/2011	%
	(1)	(2)	(3)	(4)	(5)	(6)	(7)
1	**States' share of Taxes & Duties**	**301921**	**129395**	**43%**	**263458**	**113174**	**43%**
2	**Non-plan Grants & Loans**	**64296**	**20138**	**31%**	**66396**	**20236**	**30%**
	Grants	64211	20102	31%	66311	20200	30%
	Loans	85	36	42%	85	36	42%
	Ways and Means Advances (Net)		0			0	
3	**Central Assistance for State & UT**	**122014**	**38561**	**32%**	**101292**	**36070**	**36%**
	Grants	111014	34735	31%	92292	31756	34%
	Loans	11000	3826	35%	9000	4314	48%
4	**Assistance for Central & Centrally sponsored Schemes**	**41592**	**26041**	**63%**	**34045**	**22139**	**65%**
	Grants	41592	26041	63%	34025	22139	65%
	Loans				20		
5	**Total Grants & Loans (2+3+4)**	**227902**	**84740**	**37%**	**201733**	**78445**	**39%**
	Grants	216817	80878	37%	192628	74095	38%
	Loans	11085	3862	35%	9105	4350	48%
6	***Less* : *Recovery of Loans & Advances***	**8529**	**3817**	**45%**	**8416**	**3421**	**41%**
7	**Net Resources transferred to State & UT Governments (1+5-6)**	**521294**	**210318**	**40%**	**456775**	**188198**	**41%**
	(i) Of Which State Govts.	518182	209121	40%	453882	187350	41%
	(ii) Of Which UT. Govts.	3112	1197	38%	2893	848	29%